The American Baron

A Novel

James De Mille

Alpha Editions

This edition published in 2024

ISBN : 9789366388175

Design and Setting By
Alpha Editions
www.alphaedis.com
Email - info@alphaedis.com

As per information held with us this book is in Public Domain.
This book is a reproduction of an important historical work. Alpha Editions uses the best technology to reproduce historical work in the same manner it was first published to preserve its original nature. Any marks or number seen are left intentionally to preserve its true form.

CHAPTER I.

THE AVALANCHE.

SOMEWHAT less than a hundred years ago a party of travelers might have been seen crossing over the Simplon Road, *en route* for Italy. They had been detained at Brieg by reports that the road was impassable; and, as it was the month of March, the prospect of snow and storms and avalanches was sufficient to make them hesitate. At length the road had been reopened, and they were informed that the journey might be made on sleds.

Unwilling to wait at Brieg, and equally unwilling to make a detour so as to take the railroad, the party decided to go on. They were informed that they could go on wheels as far as the line of snow, but that afterward their accommodations would not be so comfortable as they might desire. The road had been cleared for only a few feet; the snow was deep; the sleds were rude; and progress would be slow. 7b These statements, however, did not shake the resolution of the party; and the end of it was that they determined to go on, and cross the mountain if it were possible.

On leaving Brieg the road began to ascend with a very slight incline, winding around in an intricate sort of way, sometimes crossing deep gullies, at other times piercing the hillside in long dark tunnels; but amidst all these windings ever ascending, so that every step took them higher and higher above the little valley where Brieg lay. The party saw also that every step brought them steadily nearer to the line of snow; and at length they found the road covered with a thin white layer. Over this they rolled, and though the snow became deeper with every furlong of their progress, yet they encountered but little actual difficulty until they approached the first station where the horses were to be changed. Here they came to a deep drift. Through this a pathway had been cleared, so that there was no difficulty about going through; but the sight of this served to show them what might be expected further on, and to fill them all with grave doubts as to the practicability of a journey which was thus interrupted so early.

On reaching the station these doubts were confirmed. They were informed that the road had been cleared for sleds on the preceding day, but that on the previous night fresh snow had fallen, and in such quantities that the road would have to be cleared afresh. The worst of it was that there was every probability of new snow-storms, which would cover the road still deeper, and once more obliterate the track. This led to a fresh debate about the journey; but they were all unwilling to turn back. Only a few miles separated them from Domo d'Ossola, and they were assured that, if no fresh snow should fall, they would be able to start on the following morning. This last assurance once more confirmed their wavering resolution, and they concluded to wait at the station.

For the remainder of that day they waited at the little way-side inn, amusing themselves with looking out upon their surroundings. They were environed by a scene of universal white. Above them towered vast Alpine summits, where the wild wind blew, sweeping the snow-wreaths into the air. In front was a deep ravine, at the bottom of which there ran a torrent that foamed and tossed over rocks and boulders. It was not possible to take a walk to any distance. Their boots were made for lighter purposes than plunging through snow-drifts; and so they were forced to remain indoors, and pass the time as best they could.

On the following morning they found every thing in readiness for a start. In front of the inn they saw five sleds of that kind which is universally used in the northern part of America. Each sled was of the rudest possible construction, and was drawn by one horse; straw was spread over the sled, upon which fur robes and blankets were flung. The party was distributed among these sleds, so that each one should have as light a load as possible, while one of the rude vehicles carried the luggage.

Thus arranged, they all started off. And now, since they are all fairly under way, I propose to introduce them, individually and collectively, to my very good friend the reader.

First of all I must mention the fact that the party consisted chiefly of ladies and their attendants.

Of these the most prominent was a slim, tall, elderly lady, with large, dark, soft eyes, that spoke of a vanished youth and beauty from her heavily wrinkled face. She was the Dowager Lady Dalrymple, and acted toward the rest of the party in the multifarious capacity of chaperon, general, courier, guide, philosopher, friend, and Mentor.

Next came Mrs. Willoughby, a widow of great beauty and fascination, a brunette, good-natured, clever, and shrewd. I might here pause, and go into no end of raptures on the various qualities of this lady's character; but, on the whole, I think I'd better not, as they will be sufficiently apparent before the end of this story is reached.

Then there was Miss Minnie Fay, sister to Mrs. Willoughby, and utterly unlike her in every respect. Minnie was a blonde, with blue eyes, golden hair cut short and clustering about her little head, little bit of a mouth, with very red, plump lips, and very white teeth. Minnie was very small, and very elegant in shape, in gesture, in dress, in every attitude and every movement. The most striking thing about her, however, was the expression of her eyes and her face. There was about her brow the glory of perfect innocence. Her eyes had a glance of unfathomable melancholy, mingled with childlike trust in the particular person upon whom her gaze was fastened. Minnie was considered by all her friends as a child—was treated as a child—humored, petted, coaxed, indulged, and talked to as a child. Minnie, on her part, thought, spoke, lived, moved, and acted as a child. She fretted, she teased, she pouted, she cried, she did every thing as a child does; and thus carried up to the age of eighteen the bloom and charm of eight.

The two sisters were nieces of the Dowager 8b Lady Dalrymple. Another niece also accompanied them, who was a cousin of the two sisters. This was Miss Ethel Orne, a young lady who had flourished through a London season, and had refused any number of brilliant offers. She was a brunette, with most wonderful dark eyes, figure of perfect grace, and an expression of grave self-poise that awed the butterflies of fashion, but offered an irresistible attraction to people of sense, intellect, intelligence, esprit, and all that sort of thing—like you and me, my boy.

I am taking up too much time and anticipating somewhat, I fear, by these descriptions; so let us drop Miss Ethel.

These ladies being thus all related formed a family party, and had made the journey thus far on the best of terms, without any other escort than that which was afforded by their chaperon, general, courier, guide, philosopher, friend, and Mentor—the Dowager Lady Dalrymple.

The party was enlarged by the presence of four maids and a foreign gentleman. This last-mentioned personage was small in stature, with a very handsome face and very brilliant eyes. His frame, though slight, was sinewy and well knit, and he looked like an Italian. He had come on alone, and had passed the night at the station-house.

A track about six feet wide had been cut out through the snow, and over this they passed. The snow was soft, and the horses sank deep, so that progress was slow. Nor was the journey without the excitement of apparent danger. At times before them and behind them there would come a low, rumbling sound, and they would see a mass of snow and ice rushing down some neighboring slope. Some of these fell on the road, and more than once they had to quit their sleds and wait for the drivers to get them over the heaps that had been formed across their path. Fortunately, however, none of these came near them; and Minnie Fay, who at first had screamed at intervals of about five minutes, gradually gained confidence, and at length changed her mood so completely that she laughed and clapped her little hands whenever she saw the rush of snow and ice. Thus slowly, yet in safety, they pushed onward, and at length reached the little village of Simplon. Here they waited an hour to warm themselves, lunch, and change horses. At the end of that time they set out afresh, and once more they were on their winding way.

They had now the gratification of finding that they were descending the slope, and of knowing that this descent took them every minute further from the regions of snow, and nearer to the sunny plains of Italy. Minnie in particular gave utterance to her delight: and now, having lost every particle of fear, she begged to be allowed to drive in the foremost sled. Ethel had been in it thus far, but she willingly changed places with Minnie, and thus the descent was made.

The sleds and their occupants were now arranged in the following order:

First, Minnie Fay alone with the driver.

Second, Mrs. Willoughby and Ethel.

Third, the Dowager and her maid.

Fourth, the three other maids.

Fifth, the luggage.

After these five sleds, containing our party, came another with the foreign gentleman.

Each of these sleds had a driver to itself.

In this order the party went, until at length they came to the Gorge of Gondo. This is a narrow valley, the sides of which rise up very abruptly, and in some places precipitously, to a great height. At the bottom flows a furious torrent, which boils and foams and roars as it forces its impetuous way onward over fallen masses of rock and trees and boulders, at one time gathering into still pools, at other times roaring into cataracts. Their road had been cut out on the side of the mountain, and the path had been cleared away here many feet above the buried road; and as they wound along the slope they could look up at the stupendous heights above them, and down at the abyss beneath them, whose white snow-covering was marked at the bottom by the black line of the roaring torrent. The smooth slope of snow ran down as far as the eye could reach at a steep angle, filling up all crevices, with here and there a projecting rock or a dark clump of trees to break its surface.

The road was far beneath them. The drivers had informed them that it was forty feet deep at the top of the pass, and that its depth here was over thirty. Long poles which were inserted in the snow projected above its surface, and served to mark where the road ran.

Here, then, they drove along, feeling wearied with the length of the way, impatient at the slowness of their progress, and eager to reach their journey's end. But little was said. All had talked till all were tired out. Even Minnie Fay, who at first had evinced great enthusiasm on finding herself leading the way, and had kept turning back constantly to address remarks to her friends, had at length subsided, and had rolled herself up more closely in her furs, and heaped the straw higher about her little feet.

Suddenly, before them, and above them, and behind them, and all around them, there arose a deep, low, dull, rushing sound, which seemed as if all the snow on the slope was moving. Their ears had by this time become sufficiently well acquainted with the peculiar sound of the rushing snow-masses to know that this was the noise that heralded their progress, and to feel sure that this was an avalanche of no common size. Yes, this was an avalanche, and every one heard it; but no one could tell where it was moving, or whether it was near or far, or whether it was before or behind. They only knew that it was somewhere along the slope which they were traversing.

A warning cry came from the foremost driver. 9b He looked back, and his face was as pale as death. He waved his hands above him, and then shouting for the others to follow, he whipped up his horse furiously. The animal plunged into the snow, and tossed and floundered and made a rush onward.

But the other drivers held back, and, instead of following, shouted to the first driver to stop, and cried to the passengers to hold on. Not a cry of fear escaped from any one of the ladies. All did as they were directed, and grasped the stakes of their sleds, looking up at the slope with white lips, and expectation of horror in their eyes, watching for the avalanche.

And down it came, a vast mass of snow and ice—down it came, irresistibly, tremendously, with a force that nothing could withstand. All eyes watched its progress in the silence of utter and helpless terror. It came. It struck. All the sleds in the rear escaped, but Minnie's sled lay in the course of the falling mass. The driver had madly rushed into the very midst of the danger which he sought to avoid. A scream from Minnie and a cry of despair from the driver burst upon the ears of the horrified listeners, and the sled that bore them, buried in the snow, went over the edge of the slope, and downward to the abyss.

CHAPTER II.

THE PERILOUS DESCENT.

THE shriek of Minnie and the driver's cry of despair were both stopped abruptly by the rush of snow, and were smothered in the heap under which they were buried. The whole party stood paralyzed, gazing stupidly downward where the avalanche was hurrying on to the abyss, bearing with it the ill-fated Minnie. The descent was a slope of smooth snow, which went down at an angle of forty-five degrees for at least a thousand feet. At that point there seemed to be a precipice. As their aching eyes watched the falling mass they saw it approach this place, and then as it came near the whole avalanche seemed to divide as though it had been severed by some projecting rock. It divided thus, and went to ruin; while in the midst of the ruin they saw the sled, looking like a helpless boat in the midst of foaming breakers. So, like such a helpless boat, it was dashed forward, and shot out of sight over the precipice.

Whither had it gone? Into what abyss had it fallen? What lay beneath that point over which it had been thrown? Was it the fierce torrent that rolled there, or were there black rocks and sharp crags lying at the foot of the awful precipice? Such were the questions which flashed through every mind, and deepened the universal horror into universal despair.

In the midst of this general dismay Ethel was the first to speak and to act. She started to her feet, and looking back, called in a loud voice:

"Go down after her! A thousand pounds to the man who saves her! Quick!"

At this the drivers came forward. None of them could understand English, and so had not comprehended her offer; but they saw by her gestures what she wanted. They, however, did not seem inclined to act. They pointed down, and pointed up, and shook their heads, and jabbered some strange, unintelligible patois.

"Cowards!" cried Ethel, "to leave a young girl to die. I will go down myself."

And then, just as she was, she stepped from the sled, and paused for a moment, looking down the slope as though selecting a place. Lady Dalrymple and Mrs. Willoughby screamed to her to come back, and the drivers surrounded her with wild gesticulations. To all this she paid no attention whatever, and would certainly have gone down in another moment had not a hand been laid on her arm, and a voice close by her said, with a strong foreign accent,

"Mees!"

She turned at once.

It was the foreign gentleman who had been driving behind the party. He had come up and had just reached the place. He now stood before her with his hat in one hand and the other hand on his heart.

"Pardon, mees," he said, with a bow. "Eet is too periloss. I sall go down eef you 'low me to mak ze attemp."

"Oh, monsieur," cried Ethel, "save her if you can!"

"Do not fear. Be calm. I sall go down. Nevare mine."

The stranger now turned to the drivers, and spoke to them in their own language. They all obeyed at once. He was giving them explicit directions in a way that showed a perfect command of the situation. It now appeared that each sled had a coil of rope, which was evidently supplied from an apprehension of some such accident as this. Hastily yet dextrously the foreign gentleman took one of these coils, and then binding a blanket around his waist, he passed the rope around this, so that it would press against the blanket without cutting him. Having secured this tightly, he gave some further directions to the drivers, and then prepared to go down.

Hitherto the drivers had acted in sullen submission rather than with ready acquiescence. They were evidently afraid of another avalanche; and the frequent glances which they threw at the slope above them plainly showed that they expected this snow to follow the example of the other. In spite of themselves an expression of this fear escaped them, and came to the ears of the foreign gentleman. He turned at once on the brink of the descent, and burst into a torrent of invective against them. The ladies could not understand him, but they could perceive that he was uttering threats, and that the men quailed before him. He did not waste any time, however. After reducing the men to a state of sulky submission, he turned once more and began the descent.

As he went down the rope was held by the men, who allowed it to pass through their hands so as to steady his descent. The task before the adventurer was one of no common difficulty. The snow was soft, and at every step he sank in at least to his knees. Frequently he came to treacherous places, where he sank down above his waist, and was only able to scramble out with difficulty. But the rope sustained him; and as his progress was downward, he succeeded in moving with some rapidity toward his destination. The ladies on the height above sat in perfect silence, watching the progress of the man who was thus descending with his life in his hand to seek and to save their lost companion, and in the intensity of their anxiety forgot utterly about any danger to themselves, though from time to time there arose the well-known sound of sliding masses, not so far away but that under other circumstances of less anxiety it might have filled them with alarm. But now there was no alarm for themselves.

And now the stranger was far down, and the coil of rope was well-nigh exhausted. But this had been prepared for, and the drivers fastened this rope to another coil, and after a time began to let out that one also.

Farther and farther down the descent went on. They saw the stranger pursuing his way still with unfaltering resolution; and they sent after him all their hearts and all their prayers. At last he plunged down almost out of sight, but the next moment he emerged, and then, after a few leaps, they saw that he had gained the place where lay the ruins of the shattered avalanche. Over this he walked, sometimes sinking, at other times running and leaping, until at length he came to the precipice over which the sled had been flung.

And now the suspense of the ladies became terrible. This was the critical moment. Already his eyes could look down upon the mystery that lay beneath that precipice. And what lay revealed there? Did his eyes encounter a spectacle of horror? Did they gaze down into the inaccessible depths of some hideous abyss? Did they see those jagged rocks, those sharp crags, those giant boulders, those roaring billows, which, in their imaginations, had drawn down their lost companion to destruction? Such conjectures were too terrible. Their breath failed them, and their hearts for a time almost ceased to beat as they sat there, overcome by such dread thoughts as these.

Suddenly a cry of delight escaped Ethel. She was kneeling down beside Lady Dalrymple and Mrs. Willoughby, with her eyes staring from her pallid face, when she saw the stranger turn and look up. He took off his hat, and waved it two or three times. Then he beckoned to the drivers. Then he sat down and prepared to let himself over the precipice. This incident inspired hope. It did more. It gave a moment's confidence, and the certainty that all was not lost. They looked at each other, and wept tears of joy. But soon that momentary hope vanished, and uncertainty returned. After all, what did the stranger's gesture mean? He might have seen her—but how? He might reach her, but would she be safe from harm? Could such a thing be hoped for? Would she not, rather, be all marred and mutilated? Dared they hope for any thing better? They dared not. And now they sat once more, as sad as before, and their short-lived gleam of hope faded away.

They saw the stranger go over the precipice.

Then he disappeared.

The rope was let out for a little distance, and then stopped. Then more went out. Then it stopped again.

The rope now lay quite loose. There was no tension.

What was the meaning of this? Was he clinging to the side of the precipice? Impossible. It looked rather as though he had reached some place where he was free to move, and had no further need of descent. And it seemed as though the precipice might not be so deep or so fearful as they had supposed.

In a short time their eyes were greeted by the appearance of the stranger above the precipice. He waved his hat again. Then he made some gestures, and detached the rope from his person. The drivers understood him as if this had been preconcerted. Two of them instantly unharnessed the horse from one of the sleds, while the others pulled up the rope which the stranger had cast off. Then the latter disappeared once more behind the precipice. The ladies watched now in deep suspense; inclining to hope, yet dreading the worst. They saw the drivers fasten the rope to the sled, and let it down the slope. It was light, and the runners were wide. It did not sink much, but slid down quite rapidly. Once or twice it stuck, but by jerking it back it was detached, and went on as before. At last it reached the precipice at a point not more than a hundred feet from where the stranger had last appeared.

And now as they sat there, reduced once more to the uttermost extremity of suspense, they saw a sight which sent a thrill of rapture through their aching hearts. They saw the stranger come slowly above the precipice, and then stop, and stoop, and look back. Then they saw—oh, Heavens! who was that? Was not that her red hood—and that figure who thus slowly emerged from behind the edge of the precipice which had so long concealed her—that figure! Was it possible? Not dead—not mangled, but living, moving, and, yes—wonder of wonders—scaling a precipice! Could it be! Oh joy! Oh bliss! Oh revulsion from despair! The ladies trembled and shivered, and laughed and sobbed convulsively, and wept in one another's arms by turns.

As far as they could see through the tears that dimmed their eyes, Minnie could not be much injured. She moved quite lightly over the snow, as the stranger led her toward the sled; only sinking once or twice, and then extricating herself even more readily than her companion. At last she reached the sled, and the stranger, taking off the blanket that he had worn under the rope, threw it over her shoulders.

Then he signaled to the men above, and they began to pull up the sled. The stranger climbed up after it through the deep snow, walking behind it for some distance. At last he made a despairing gesture to the men, and sank down.

The men looked bewildered, and stopped pulling.

The stranger started up, and waved his hands impatiently, pointing to Minnie.

The drivers began to pull once more at the sled, and the stranger once more sank exhausted in the snow.

At this Ethel started up.

"That noble soul!" she cried; "that generous heart! See! he is saving Minnie, and sitting down to die in the snow!"

She sprang toward the men, and endeavored to make them do something. By her gestures she tried to get two of the men to pull at the sled, and the third man to let the fourth man down with a rope to the stranger. The men refused; but at the offer of her purse, which was well filled with gold, they consented. Two of them then pulled at the sled, and number four bound the rope about him, and went down, while number three held the rope. He went down without difficulty, and reached the stranger. By this time Minnie had been drawn to the top, and was clasped in the arms of her friends.

But now the strength and the sense which had been so wonderfully maintained gave way utterly; and no sooner did she find herself safe than she fell down unconscious.

They drew her to a sled, and tenderly laid her on the straw, and lovingly and gently they tried to restore her, and call her back to consciousness. But for a long time their efforts were of no avail.

She lay there a picture of perfect loveliness, as beautiful as a dream—like some child-angel. Her hair, frosted with snow dust, clustered in golden curls over her fair white brow; her little hands were folded meekly over her breast; her sweet lips were parted, and disclosed the pearly teeth; the gentle eyes no longer looked forth with their piteous expression of mute appeal; and her hearing was deaf to the words of love and pity that were lavished upon her.

CHAPTER III.

THE CHILD-ANGEL AND HER WOES.

MRS. WILLOUGHBY was in her room at the hotel in Milan, when the door opened, and Minnie came in. She looked around the room, drew a long breath, then locked the door, and flinging herself upon a sofa, she reclined there in silence for some time, looking hard at the ceiling. Mrs. Willoughby looked a little surprised at first; but after waiting a few moments for Minnie to say something, resumed her reading, which had been interrupted.

"Kitty," said Minnie at last.

"What?" said her sister, looking up.

"I think you're horrid."

"Why, what's the matter?"

"Why, because when you see and know that I'm dying to speak to you, you go on reading that wretched book."

"Why, Minnie darling," said Mrs. Willoughby, "how in the world was I to know that you wanted to speak to me?"

"You *might* have known," said Minnie, with a pout—"you saw me look all round, and lock the door; and you saw how worried I looked, and I think it a shame, and I've a great mind not to tell you any thing about it."

"About it—what *it?*" and Mrs. Willoughby put down her book, and regarded her sister with some curiosity.

"I've a great mind not to tell you, but I can't help it. Besides, I'm dying to ask your advice. I don't know what to do; and I wish I was dead—there!"

"My poor Minnie! what *is* the matter? You're *so* incoherent."

"Well, Kitty, it's all my accident."

"Your accident!"

"Yes; on the Alps, you know."

"What! You haven't received any serious injury, have you?" asked Mrs. Willoughby, with some alarm.

"Oh! I don't mean that, but I'll tell you what I mean;" and here Minnie got up from her reclining position, and allowed her little feet to touch the carpet, while she fastened her great, fond, pleading, piteous eyes upon her sister.

"It's the Count, you know," said she.

"The Count!" repeated Mrs. Willoughby, somewhat dryly. "Well?"

"Well—don't you know what I mean? Oh, how stupid you are!"

"I really can not imagine."

"Well—he—he—he pro—proposed, you know."

"Proposed!" cried the other, in a voice of dismay.

"Now, Kitty, if you speak in that horrid way I won't say another word. I'm worried too much already, and I don't want you to scold me. And I won't have it."

"Minnie darling, I wish you would tell me something. I'm not scolding. I merely wish to know what you mean. Do you really mean that the Count has proposed to you?"

"Of course that's what I mean."

"What puzzles me is, how he could have got the chance. It's more than a week since he saved you, and we all felt deeply grateful to him. But saving a girl's life doesn't give a man any claim over her; and we don't altogether like him; and so we all have tried, in a quiet way, without hurting his feelings, you know, to prevent him from having any acquaintance with you."

"Oh, I know, I know," said Minnie, briskly. "He told me all that. He understands that; but he doesn't care, he says, if *I* only consent. He will forgive *you*, he says."

Minnie's volubility was suddenly checked by catching her sister's eye fixed on her in new amazement.

"Now you're beginning to be horrid," she cried. "Don't, don't—"

"Will you have the kindness to tell me," said Mrs. Willoughby, very quietly, "how in the world the Count contrived to tell you all this?"

"Why—why—several times."

"Several times!"

"Yes."

"Tell me where?"

"Why, once at the amphitheatre. You were walking ahead, and I sat down to rest, and he came and joined me. He left before you came back."

"He must have been following us, then."

"Yes. And another time in the picture-gallery; and yesterday in a shop; and this morning at the Cathedral."

"The Cathedral!"

"Yes, Kitty. You know we all went, and Lady Dalrymple would not go up. So Ethel and I went up. And when we got up to the top I walked about, and Ethel sat down to admire the view. And, you know, I found myself off at a little distance, when suddenly I saw Count Girasole. And then, you know, he—he—proposed."

Mrs. Willoughby sat silent for some time.

"And what did you say to him?" she asked at length.

"Why, what else could I say?"

"What else than *what*?"

"I don't see why you should act *so* like a grand inquisitor, Kitty. You really make me feel quite nervous," said Minnie, who put her little rosy-tipped fingers to one of her eyes, and attempted a sob, which turned out a failure.

"Oh, I only asked you what you told him, you know."

"Well," said Minnie, gravely, "I told him, you know, that I was awfully grateful to him, and that I'd give any thing if I could to express my gratitude. And then, you know—oh, he speaks such darling broken English—he called me his 'mees,' and tried to make a pretty speech, which was so mixed with Italian that I didn't understand one single word. By-the-way, Kitty, isn't it odd how every body here speaks Italian, even the children?"

"Yes, very odd; but, Minnie dear, I want to know what you told him."

"Why, I told him that I didn't know, you know."

"And then?"

"And then he took my hand. Now, Kitty, you're unkind. I really *can not* tell you all this."

"Yes, but I only ask so as to advise you. I want to know how the case stands."

"Well, you know, he was so urgent—"

"Yes?"

"And so handsome—"

"Well?"

"And then, you know, he saved my life—didn't he, now? You must acknowledge that much, mustn't you?"

"Oh yes."

"Well—"

"Well?"

Minnie sighed.

"So what could I say?"

Minnie paused.

Mrs. Willoughby looked troubled.

"Kitty, I *wish* you wouldn't look at me with that dreadful expression. You really make me feel quite frightened."

"Minnie," said the other, in a serious voice, "do you really *love* this man?"

"Love this man! why no, not particularly; but I *like* him; that is, I think I do, or rather I thought I did; but really I'm so worried about all my troubles that I wish he had never come down after me. I don't see why he did, either. I didn't ask him to. I remember, now, I really felt quite embarrassed when I saw him. I knew there would be trouble about it. And I wish you would take me back home. I hate Italy. Do, Kitty darling. But then—"

Minnie paused again.

"Well, Minnie dear, we certainly must contrive some plan to shake him off without hurting his feelings. It can't be thought of. There are a hundred objections. If the worst comes to the worst we can go back, as you say, to England."

"I know; but then," said Minnie, "that's the very thing that I can't do—"

"Can't do what?"

"Go back to England."

"Back to England! Why not? I don't know what you mean."

"Well, you see, Kitty, that's the very thing I came to see you about. This dreadful man—the Count, you know—has some wonderful way of finding out where I go; and he keeps all the time appearing and disappearing in the very strangest manner; and when I saw him on the roof of the Cathedral it really made me feel quite giddy. He is *so* determined to win me that I'm afraid to look round. He takes the commonest civility as encouragement. And then, you know—there it is—I really can't go back to England."

"What do you mean by that?"

"Why there's—a—a dreadful person there," said Minnie, with an awful look in her eyes.

"A what?"

"A—person," said Minnie.

"A man?"

Minnie nodded. "Oh yes—of course. Really when one thinks of one's troubles it's enough to drive one distracted. This person is a man. I don't know why it is that I should be *so* worried and *so* distracted by men. I do *not* like them, and I wish there were no such persons."

"Another man!" said Mrs. Willoughby, in some surprise. "Well, Minnie, you certainly—"

"Now don't, don't—not a word; I know all you're going to say, and I won't stand it;" and Minnie ran over to her sister and held her hand over her mouth.

"I won't say a word," said Mrs. Willoughby, as soon as she had removed Minnie's hand; "so begin."

Minnie resumed her place on the sofa, and gave a long sigh.

"Well, you know, Kitty darling, it happened at Brighton last September. You were in Scotland then. I was with old Lady Shrewsbury, who is as blind as a bat—and where's the use of having a person to look after you when they're blind! You see, my horse ran away, and I think he must have gone ever so many miles, over railroad bridges and hedges and stone walls. I'm certain he jumped over a small cottage. Well, you know, when all seemed lost, suddenly there was a strong hand laid on the reins, and my horse was stopped. I tumbled into some strange gentleman's arms, and was carried into a house, where I was resuscitated. I returned home in the gentleman's carriage.

"Now the worst of it is," said Minnie, with a piteous look, "that the person who stopped the horse called to inquire after me the next day. Lady Shrewsbury, like an old goose, was awfully civil to him; and so there I was! His name is Captain Kirby, and I wish there were no captains in the world. The life he led me! He used to call, and I had to go out riding with him, and old Lady Shrewsbury utterly neglected me; and so, you know, Kitty darling, he at last, you know, of course, proposed. That's what they all do, you know, when they save your life. Always! It's awful!"

Minnie heaved a sigh, and sat apparently meditating on the enormous baseness of the man who saved a lady's life and then proposed; and it was not until Mrs. Willoughby had spoken twice that she was recalled to herself.

"What did you tell him?" was her sister's question.

"Why, what could I tell him?"

"What!" cried Mrs. Willoughby; "you don't—"

"Now, Kitty, I think it's very unkind in you, when I want all your sympathy, to be *so* horrid."

"Well, tell it your own way, Minnie dearest."

Minnie sat for a time regarding vacancy with a soft, sad, and piteous expression in her large blue eyes; with her head also a little on one side, and her delicate hands gently clasped in front of her.

"ANOTHER MAN!"

"You see, Kitty darling, he took me out riding, and—he took me to the place where I had met him, and then he proposed. Well, you know, I didn't know what to say. He was *so* earnest, and *so* despairing. And then, you know, Kitty dearest, he had saved my life, and so—"

"And so?"

"Well, I told him I didn't know, and was shockingly confused, and then we got up quite a scene. He swore that he would go to Mexico, though why I can't imagine; and I really wish he had; but I was frightened at the time, and I cried; and then he got worse, and I told him not to; whereupon he went into raptures, and began to call me no end of names—spooney names, you know; and I—oh, I did *so* want him to stop!—I think I must have promised him all that he wanted; and when I got home I was frightened out of my poor little wits, and cried all night."

"Poor dear child!" exclaimed Mrs. Willoughby, with tender sympathy. "What a wretch!"

"No, he wasn't a wretch at all; he was awfully handsome, only, you know, he—was—so—*aw*fully persevering, and kept *so* at my heels; but I hurried home from Brighton, and thought I had got rid of him."

"And hadn't you?"

"Oh dear, no," said Minnie, mournfully. "On the day after my arrival there came a letter; and, you know, I had to answer it; and then another; and so it went on—"

"Oh, Minnie! why didn't you tell me before?"

"How could I when you were off in that horrid Scotland? I *always* hated Scotland."

"You might have told papa."

"I couldn't. I think papa's cruel *too*. He doesn't care for me at all. Why didn't he find out our correspondence and intercept it, the way papas always do in novels? If I were *his* papa I'd not let *him* be so worried."

"And did he never call on you?"

"Yes; he got leave of absence once, and I had a dreadful time with him. He was in a desperate state of mind. He was ordered off to Gibraltar. But I managed to comfort him; and, oh dear, Kitty dear, did you *ever* try to comfort a man, and the man a total stranger?"

At this innocent question Mrs. Willoughby's gravity gave way a little.

Minnie frowned, and then sighed.

"Well, you needn't be so unkind," said she; and then her little hand tried to wipe away a tear, but failed.

"Did he go to Gibraltar?" asked Mrs. Willoughby at length.

"Yes, he did," said Minnie, with a little asperity.

"Did he write?"

"Of course he wrote," in the same tone.

"Well, how did it end?"

"End! It didn't end at all. And it never will end. It'll go on getting worse and worse every day. You see he wrote, and said a lot of rubbish about his getting leave of absence and coming to see me. And then I determined to run away; and you know I begged you to take me to Italy, and this is the first time I've told you the real reason."

"So that was the real reason?"

"Yes."

"Well, Minnie, my poor child," said Mrs. Willoughby, after a pause, "you're safe from your officer, at any rate; and as to Count Girasole, we must save you from him. Don't give way."

"But you can't save me. They'll come after me, I know. Captain Kirby, the moment he finds out that I am here, will come flying after me; and then, oh dear! the other one will come, and the American, too, of course."

"The what? who?" cried Mrs. Willoughby, starting up with new excitement. "Who's that? What did you say, Minnie? The American? What American?"

Minnie threw a look of reproach at her sister, and her eyes fell.

"You can't possibly mean that there are any more—"

"There—is—*one*—more," said Minnie, in a low, faint voice, stealing a glance at her sister, and looking a little frightened.

"One more!" repeated her sister, breathless.

"Well, I didn't come here to be scolded," said Minnie, rising, "and I'll go. But I hoped that you'd help me; and I think you're very unkind; and I wouldn't treat you so."

"No, no, Minnie," said Mrs. Willoughby, rising, and putting her arm round her sister, and drawing her back. "I had no idea of scolding. I never scolded any one in my life, and wouldn't speak a cross word to you for the world. Sit down now, Minnie darling, and tell me all. What about the American? I won't express any more astonishment, no matter what I may feel."

"But you mustn't *feel* any astonishment," insisted Minnie.

"Well, darling, I won't," said her sister.

Minnie gave a sigh.

"It was last year, you know, in the spring. Papa and I were going out to Montreal, to bring you home. You remember?"

Mrs. Willoughby nodded, while a sad expression came over her face.

"And, you remember, the steamer was wrecked."

"Yes."

"But I never told you how my life was saved."

"Why, yes, you did. Didn't papa tell all about the heroic sailor who swam ashore with you? how he was frantic about you, having been swept away by a wave from you? and how he fainted away with joy when you were brought to him? How can you suppose I would forget that? And then how papa tried to find the noble sailor to reward him."

"Oh yes," said Minnie, in a despondent tone. "That's all very true; but he wasn't a noble sailor at all."

"What!"

"You see, he wasn't going to have a scene with papa, and so he kept out of his way. Oh dear, how I wish he'd been as considerate with me! But that's the way always; yes, always."

"Well, who was he?"

"Why, he was an American gentleman, returning home from a tour in Europe. He saved me, as you have heard. I really don't remember much about it, only there was a terrible rush of water, and a strong arm seized me, and I thought it was papa all the time. And I found myself carried, I don't know how, through the waves, and then I fainted; and I really don't know any thing about it except papa's story."

Mrs. Willoughby looked at Minnie in silence, but said nothing.

"And then, you know, he traveled with us, and papa thought he was one of the passengers, and was civil; and so he used to talk to me, and at last, at Montreal, he used to call on me."

"Where?"

"At your house, dearest."

"Why, how was that?"

"You could not leave your room, darling, so I used to go down."

"Oh, Minnie!"

"And he proposed to me there."

"Where? in my parlor?"

"Yes; in your parlor, dearest."

"I suppose it's not necessary for me to ask what you said."

"I suppose not," said Minnie, in a sweet voice. "He was so grand and so strong, and he never made any allusions to the wreck; and it was—the—the—*very first* time that any body ever—proposed; and so, you know, I didn't know how to take it, and I didn't want to hurt his feelings, and I couldn't deny that he had saved my life; and I don't know when I *ever* was so confused. It's awful, Kitty darling.

"And then, you know, darling," continued Minnie, "he went away, and used to write regularly every month. He came to see me once, and I was frightened to death almost. He is going to marry me next year. He used an awful expression, dearest. He told me he was a struggling man. Isn't that horrid? What is it, Kitty? Isn't it something very, very dreadful?"

"He writes still, I suppose?"

"Oh dear, yes."

Mrs. Willoughby was silent for some time.

"Oh, Minnie," said she at last, "what a trouble all this is! How I wish you had been with me all this time!"

"Well, what made you go and get married?" said Minnie.

"Hush," said Mrs. Willoughby, sadly, "never mind. I've made up my mind to one thing, and that is, I will never leave you alone with a gentleman, unless—"

"Well, I'm sure I don't want the horrid creatures," said Minnie. "And you needn't be so unkind. I'm sure I don't see why people will come always and save my life wherever I go. I don't want them to. I don't want to have my life saved any more. I think it's dreadful to have men chasing me all over the world. I'm afraid to stop in Italy, and I'm afraid to go back to England. Then I'm always afraid of that dreadful American. I suppose it's no use for me to go to the Holy Land, or Egypt, or Australia; for then my life would be saved by an Arab, or a New Zealander. And oh, Kitty, wouldn't it be dreadful to have some Arab proposing to me, or a Hindu! Oh, what *am* I to do?"

"Trust to me, darling. I'll get rid of Girasole. We will go to Naples. He has to stop at Rome; I know that. We will thus pass quietly away from him, without giving him any pain, and he'll soon forget all about it. As for the others, I'll stop this correspondence first, and then deal with them as they come."

"You'll never do it, never!" cried Minnie; "I know you won't. You don't know them."

CHAPTER IV.

IN THE CRATER OF VESUVIUS.

"HE BENT HIS HEAD DOWN, AND RAN HIS HAND THROUGH HIS BUSHY HAIR."

LORD Harry Hawbury had been wandering for three months on the Continent, and had finally found himself in Naples. It was always a favorite place of his, and he had established himself in comfortable quarters on the Strada Nuova, from the windows of which there was a magnificent view of the whole bay, with Vesuvius, Capri, Baiæ, and all the regions round about. Here an old friend had unexpectedly turned up in the person of Scone Dacres. Their friendship had been formed some five or six years before in South America, where they had made a hazardous journey in company across the continent, and had thus acquired a familiarity with one another which years of ordinary association would have failed to give. Scone Dacres was several years older than Lord Hawbury.

One evening Lord Hawbury had just finished his dinner, and was dawdling about in a listless way, when Dacres entered, quite unceremoniously, and flung himself into a chair by one of the windows.

"Any Bass, Hawbury?" was his only greeting, as he bent his head down, and ran his hand through his bushy hair.

"Lachryma Christi?" asked Hawbury, in an interrogative tone.

"No, thanks. That wine is a humbug. I'm beastly thirsty, and as dry as a cinder."

Hawbury ordered the Bass, and Dacres soon was refreshing himself with copious draughts.

The two friends presented a singular contrast. Lord Hawbury was tall and slim, with straight flaxen hair and flaxen whiskers, whose long, pendent points hung down to his shoulders. His thin face, somewhat pale, had an air of high refinement; and an ineradicable habit of lounging, together with a drawling intonation, gave him the appearance of being the laziest mortal alive. Dacres, on the other hand, was the very opposite of all this. He was as tall as Lord Hawbury, but was broad-shouldered and massive. He had a big head, a big mustache, and a thick beard. His hair was dark, and covered his head in dense, bushy curls. His voice was loud, his manner abrupt, and he always sat bolt upright.

"Any thing up, Sconey?" asked Lord Hawbury, after a pause, during which he had been languidly gazing at his friend.

"Well, no, nothing, except that I've been up Vesuvius."

Lord Hawbury gave a long whistle.

"And how did you find the mountain?" he asked; "lively?"

"Rather so. In fact, infernally so," added Dacres, thoughtfully. "Look here, Hawbury, do you detect any smell of sulphur about me?"

"Sulphur! What in the name of—sulphur! Why, now that you mention it, I *do* notice something of a brimstone smell. Sulphur! Why, man, you're as strong as a lighted match. What have you been doing with yourself? Down inside, eh?"

Dacres made no answer for some time, but sat stroking his beard with his left hand, while his right held a cigar which he had just taken out of a box at his elbow. His eyes were fixed upon a point in the sky exactly half-way between Capri and Baiæ, and about ten degrees above the horizon.

"Hawbury," said he, solemnly, after about two minutes of portentous silence.

"Well, old man?"

"I've had an adventure."

"An adventure! Well, don't be bashful. Breathe forth the tale in this confiding ear."

"You see," said Dacres, "I started off this morning for a ride, and had no more intention of going to Vesuvius than to Jericho."

"I should hope not. What business has a fellow like you with Vesuvius—a fellow that has scaled Cotopaxi, and all that sort of thing? Not you."

Dacres put the cigar thoughtfully in his mouth, struck a light, and tried to light it, but couldn't. Then he bit the end off, which he had forgotten to do before. Then he gave three long, solemn, and portentous puffs. Then he took the cigar between his first and second fingers, and stretched his hand out toward Hawbury.

"Hawbury, my boy," said he again.

"All right."

"You remember the time when I got that bullet in Uruguay?"

"Yes."

"Well, I had a shot to-day."

"A shot! The deuce you had. Cool, too. Any of those confounded bandits about? I thought that was all rot."

"It wasn't a real shot; only figurative."

"Figurative!"

"Yes; it was a—a girl."

"By Jove!" cried Hawbury, starting up from an easy posture which he had secured for himself after fifteen minutes shifting and changing. "A girl! You, Dacres, spooney! A fellow like you, and a girl! By Jove!"

Hawbury fell back again, and appeared to be vainly trying to grapple with the thought. Dacres put his cigar between his lips again, and gave one or two puffs at it, but it had gone out. He pitched it out of the window, and struck his hand heavily on the arm of his chair.

"Yes, Hawbury, a girl; and spooney, too—as spooney as blazes; but I'll swear there isn't such another girl upon the whole face of the earth; and when you bear in mind the fact that my observation, with extended view, has surveyed mankind from China to Peru, you'll be able to appreciate the value of my statement."

"All right, old man; and now for the adventure."

"The adventure? Well, you see, I started for a ride. Had a misty idea of going to Sorrento, and was jogging along among a million pigs or so at Portici, when I overtook a carriage that was going slowly along. There were three ladies in it. The backs of two of them were turned toward me, and I afterward saw that one was old—no doubt the chaperon—and the other was young. But the third lady, Hawbury—Well, it's enough to say that I, who have seen all women in all lands, have never seen any thing like her. She was on the front seat, with her face turned toward me. She was small, a perfect blonde; hair short and curling; a round, girlish face; dimpled cheeks, and little mouth. Her eyes were large and blue; and, as she looked at me, I saw such a bewitching innocence, such plaintive entreaty, such pathetic trust, such helpless, childlike—I'll be hanged if I can find words to express what I want to say. The English language doesn't contain them."

"Do it in Latin, then, or else skip the whole description. All the same. I know the whole story by heart. Love's young dream, and all that sort of thing, you know."

"Well," continued Dacres, "there was something so confoundedly bewitching in the little girl's face that I found myself keeping on at a slow pace in the rear of the carriage, and feasting on her looks. Of course I wasn't rude about it or demonstrative."

"Oh, of course. No demonstration. It's nothing to ride behind a carriage for several hours, and 'feast' one's self on a pretty girl's looks! But go on, old man."

"Oh, I managed it without giving offense. You see, there was such a beastly lot of pigs, peasants, cows, dirty children, lazaroni, and all that sort of thing, that it was simply impossible to go any faster; so you see I was compelled to ride behind. Sometimes, indeed, I fell a good distance back."

"And then caught up again to resume the 'feast?'"

"Well—yes."

"But I don't see what this has to do with your going to Vesuvius."

"It has every thing to do. You see, I started without any fixed purpose, and after I saw this carriage, I kept on insensibly after it."

"Oh, I see—yes. By Jove!"

"And they drove up as far as they could."

"Yes?"

"And I followed. You see, I had nothing else to do—and that little girl! Besides, it was the most natural thing in the world for me to be going up; and the fact that I was bent on the same errand as themselves was sufficient to account for my being near the carriage, and would prevent them from supposing that I was following them. So, you see, I followed, and at length they stopped at the Hermitage. I left my horse there, and strolled forward, without going very far away; my only idea was to keep the girl in sight. I had no idea that they would go any further. To ascend the cone seemed quite out of the question. I thought they would rest at the Hermitage, drink some Lachryma Christi, and go back. But to my surprise, as I was walking about, I saw the two young ladies come out and go toward the cone.

"I kept out of the way, as you may suppose, and watched them, wondering what idea they had. As they passed I heard the younger one—the child-angel, you know, *my* girl—teasing the other to make the ascent of the cone, and the other seemed to be quite ready to agree to the proposal.

"Now, as far as the mere ascent is concerned, of course you know *that* is not much. The guides were there with straps and chairs, and that sort of thing, all ready, so that there was no difficulty about that. The real difficulty was in these girls going off unattended; and I could only account for it by supposing that the chaperon knew nothing whatever about their proposal. No doubt the old lady was tired, and the young ones went out, as *she* supposed, for a stroll; and now, as *they* proposed, this stroll meant nothing less than an ascent of the cone. After all, there is nothing surprising in the fact that a couple of active and spirited girls should attempt this. From the Hermitage it does not seem to be at all difficult, and they had no idea of the actual nature of the task.

"What made it worse, however, was the state of the mountain at this particular time. I don't know whether you have taken the trouble to raise your eyes so high as the top of Vesuvius—"

Hawbury languidly shook his head.

"Well, I supposed not; but if you had taken the trouble, you would have noticed an ugly cloud which is generally regarded here as ominous. This morning, you know, there was an unusually large canopy of very dirty smoke overhead. I knew by the look of things that it was not a very pleasant place to go to. But of course they could not be supposed to know any thing of the kind, and their very ignorance made them rash.

"Well, I walked along after them, not knowing what might turn up, but determined to keep them in sight. Those beggars with chairs were not to be trusted, and the ladies had gold enough about them to tempt violence. What a reckless old devil of a chaperon she was, to let those young girls go! So I walked on, cursing all the time the conventionalities of civilization that prevented me from giving them warning. They were rushing straight on into danger, and I had to keep silent.

"On reaching the foot of the cone a lot of fellows came up to them, with chairs and straps, and that sort of thing. They employed some of them, and, mounting the chairs, they were carried up, while I walked up by myself at a distance from which I could observe all that was going on. The girls were quite merry, appeared to be enchanted with their ride up the cone, enjoyed the novelty of the sensation, and I heard their lively chatter and their loud peals of ringing laughter, and longed more than ever to be able to speak to them.

"Now the little girl that I had first seen—the child-angel, you know—seemed, to my amazement, to be more adventurous than the other. By her face you would suppose her to be as timid as a dove, and yet on this occasion she was the one who proposed the ascent, urged on her companion, and answered all her objections. Of course she could not have really been so plucky as she seemed. For my part, I believe the other one had more real pluck of the two, but it was the child-angel's ignorance that made her so bold. She went up the cone as she would have gone up stairs, and looked at the smoke as she would have looked at a rolling cloud.

"At length the bearers stopped, and signified to the girls that they could not go any further. The girls could not speak Italian, or any other language apparently than English, and therefore could not very well make out what the bearers were trying to say, but by their gestures they might have known that they were warning them against going any further. One might have supposed that no warning would have been needed, and that one look upward would have been enough. The top of the cone rose for upward of a hundred feet above them, its soil composed of lava blocks and ashes intermingled with sulphur. In this soil there were a million cracks and crevices, from which sulphurous smoke was issuing; and the smoke, which was but faint and thin near where they stood, grew denser farther up, till it intermingled with the larger volumes that rolled up from the crater.

"Now, as I stood there, I suddenly heard a wild proposal from the child-angel.

"'Oh, Ethel,' she said, 'I've a great mind to go up—'"

Here Hawbury interrupted his friend:

"What's that? Was that her friend's name?" he asked, with some animation. "Ethel?—odd, too. Ethel? H'm. Ethel? Brunette, was she?"

"Yes."

"Odd, too; infernally odd. But, pooh! what rot! Just as though there weren't a thousand Ethels!"

"What's that you're saying about Ethel?" asked Dacres.

"Oh, nothing, old man. Excuse my interrupting you. Go ahead. How did it end?"

"I SAW HER TURN AND WAVE HER HAND IN TRIUMPH."

"Well, the child-angel said, 'Ethel, I've a great mind to go up.'

"This proposal Ethel scouted in horror and consternation.

"'You must not—you shall not!' she cried.

"'Oh, it's nothing, it's nothing,' said the child-angel. 'I'm dying to take a peep into the crater. It must be awfully funny. Do come; do, do come, Ethel darling.'

"'Oh, Minnie, don't,' cried the other, in great alarm. And I now learned that the child-angel's name was Minnie. 'Minnie,' she cried, clinging to the child-angel, 'you must not go. I would not have come up if I had thought you would be so unreasonable.'

"'Ethel,' said the other, 'you are really getting to be quite a scold. How ridiculous it is in you to set yourself up in this place as a duenna! How can I help going up? and only one peep. And I never saw a crater in my life, and I'm dying to know what it looks like. I know it's awfully funny; and it's horrid in you to be so unkind about it. And I really must go. Won't you come? Do, do, dear—dearest darling, do—do—do!'

"Ethel was firm, however, and tried to dissuade the other, but to no purpose; for at length, with a laugh, the child-angel burst away, and skipped lightly up the slope toward the crater.

"'Just one peep,' she said. 'Come, Ethel, I must, I really must, you know.'

"She turned for an instant as she said this, and I saw the glory of her child-face as it was irradiated by a smile of exquisite sweetness. The play of feature, the light of her eyes, and the expression of innocence and ignorance unconscious of danger, filled me with profound sadness. And there was I, standing alone, seeing that sweet child flinging herself to ruin, and yet unable to prevent her, simply because I was bound hand and foot by the infernal restrictions of a miserable and a senseless conventionality. Dash it, I say!"

As Dacres growled out this Hawbury elevated his eyebrows, and stroked his long, pendent whiskers lazily with his left hand, while with his right he drummed on the table near him.

"Well," resumed Dacres, "the child-angel ran up for some distance, leaving Ethel behind. Ethel called after her for some time, and then began to follow her up. Meanwhile the guides, who had thus far stood apart, suddenly caught sight of the child-angel's figure, and, with a loud warning cry, they ran after her. They seemed to me, however, to be a lazy lot, for they scarce got up as far as the place where Ethel was. Now, you know, all this time I was doomed to inaction. But at this juncture I strolled carelessly along, pretending not to see any thing in particular; and so, taking up an easy attitude, I waited for the dénouement. It was a terrible position too. That child-angel! I would have laid down my life for her, but I had to stand idle, and see her rush to fling her life away. And all because I had not happened to have the mere formality of an introduction."

"Well, you know, I stood there waiting for the dénouement. Now it happened that, as the child-angel went up, a brisk breeze had started, which blew away all the smoke, so that she went along for some distance without any apparent inconvenience. I saw her reach the top; I saw her turn and wave her hand in triumph. Then I saw her rush forward quickly and nimbly straight toward the crater. She seemed to go down into it. And then the wind changed or died away, or both, for there came a vast cloud of rolling smoke, black, cruel, suffocating; and the mountain crest and the child-angel were snatched from my sight.

"I was roused by a shriek from Ethel. I saw her rush up the slope, and struggle in a vain endeavor to save her friend. But before she had taken a dozen steps down came the rolling smoke, black, wrathful, and sulphurous; and I saw her crouch down and stagger back, and finally emerge pale as death, and gasping for breath. She saw me as I stood there; in fact, I had moved a little nearer.

"'Oh, Sir,' she cried, 'save her! Oh, my God, she's lost!'

"This was very informal, you know, and all that sort of thing; but *she* had broken the ice, and had accosted *me*; so I waived all ceremony, and considered the introduction sufficient. I took off my hat, and told her to calm herself.

"But she only wrung her hands, and implored me to save her friend.

"And now, my boy, lucky was it for me that my experience at Cotopaxi and Popocatepetl had been so thorough and so peculiar. My knowledge came into play at this time. I took my felt hat and put it over my mouth, and then tied it around my neck so that the felt rim came over my cheeks and throat. Thus I secured a plentiful supply of air, and the felt acted as a kind of ventilator to prevent the access to my lungs of too much of the sulphurous vapor. Of course such a contrivance would not be good for more than five minutes; but then, you know, five minutes were all that I wanted.

"So up I rushed, and, as the slope was only about a hundred feet, I soon reached the top. Here I could see nothing whatever. The tremendous smoke-clouds rolled all about on every side, enveloping me in their dense folds, and shutting every thing from view. I heard the cry of the asses of guides, who were howling where I left them below, and were crying to me to come back—the infernal idiots! The smoke was impenetrable; so I got down on my hands and knees and groped about. I was on her track, and knew she could not be far away. I could not spend more than five minutes there, for my felt hat would not assist me any longer. About two minutes had already passed. Another minute was taken up in creeping about on my hands and knees. A half minute more followed. I was in despair. The child-angel I saw must have run in much further than I had supposed, and perhaps I could not find her at all. A sickening fear came to me that she had grown dizzy, or had slid down over the loose sand into the terrific abyss of the crater itself. So another half minute passed; and now only one minute was left."

"I don't see how you managed to be so confoundedly accurate in your reckoning. How was it? You didn't carry your watch in one hand, and feel about with the other, I suppose?"

"No; but I looked at my watch at intervals. But never mind that. Four minutes, as I said, were up, and only one minute remained, and that was not enough to take me back. I was at the last gasp already, and on the verge of despair, when suddenly, as I crawled on, there lay the child-angel full before me, within my reach.

"Yes," continued Dacres, after a pause, "there she lay, just in my grasp, just at my own last gasp. One second more and it must have been all up. She was senseless, of course. I caught her up; I rose and ran back as quick as I could, bearing my precious burden. She was as light as a feather—no weight at all. I carried her as tenderly as if she was a little baby. As I emerged from the smoke Ethel rushed up to me and set up a cry, but I told her to keep quiet and it would be all right. Then I directed the guides to carry her down, and I myself then carried down the child-angel.

"You see I wasn't going to give her up. I had had hard work enough getting her. Besides, the atmosphere up there was horrible. It was necessary, first of all, to get her down to the foot of the cone, where she could have pure air, and then resuscitate her. Therefore I directed the guides to take down Ethel in a chair, while I carried down the child-angel. They had to carry her down over the lava blocks, but I went to a part of the cone where it was all loose sand, and went down flying. I was at the bottom a full half hour before the others.

"Then I laid her upon the loose sand; and I swear to you, Hawbury, never in all my life have I seen such a sight. She lay there before my eyes a picture of loveliness beyond imagination—as beautiful as a dream—more like a child-angel than ever. Her hair clustered in golden curls over her white brow, her little hands were folded meekly over her breast, her lips were parted into a sweet smile, the gentle eyes no longer looked at me with the piteous, pleading, trustful, innocent expression which I had noticed in them before, and her hearing was deaf to the words of love and tenderness that I lavished upon her."

"Good!" muttered Hawbury; "you talk like a novel. Drive on, old man. I'm really beginning to feel excited."

"'The fact is," said Dacres, "I have a certain set of expressions about the child-angel that will come whenever I begin to describe her."

"It strikes me, though, that you are getting on pretty well. You were speaking of 'love and tenderness.' Well?"

"I BENT DOWN CLOSE."

"Well, she lay there senseless, you know, and I gently unclasped her hands and began to rub them. I think the motion of carrying her, and the fresh air, had both produced a favorable effect; for I had not rubbed her hands ten minutes when she gave a low sigh. Then I rubbed on, and her lips moved. I bent down close so as to listen, and I heard her say, in a low voice,

"'Am I at home?'

"'Yes,' said I, gently, for I thought it was best to humor her delirious fancy.

"Then she spoke again:

"'Is that you, papa dear?'

"'Yes, darling,' said I, in a low voice; and I kissed her in a kind of paternal way, so as to reassure her, and comfort her, and soothe her, and all that sort of thing, you know."

At this Hawbury burst into a shout of laughter.

"What the mischief are you making that beastly row about?" growled Dacres.

"Excuse me, old boy. I couldn't help it. It was at the idea of your doing the father so gravely."

"Well, am I not old enough to be her father? What else could I do? She had such a pleading, piteous way. By Jove! Besides, how did she know any thing about it? It wasn't as if she was in her senses. She really thought I *was* her father, you know. And I'm sure I almost felt as if I was, too."

"All right, old man, don't get huffy. Drive on."

"Well, you know, she kept her eyes closed, and didn't say another word till she heard the voice of Ethel at a distance. Then she opened her eyes, and got up on her feet. Then there was no end of a row—kissing, crying, congratulating, reproaching, and all that sort of thing. I withdrew to a respectful distance and waited. After a time they both came to me, and the child-angel gave me a look that made me long to be a father to her again. She held out her little hand, and I took it and pressed it, with my heart beating awfully. I was horribly embarrassed.

"'I'm awfully grateful to you,' she said; 'I'm sure I'd do any thing in the world to repay you. I'm sure I don't know what would have become of me if it hadn't been for you. And I hope you'll excuse me for putting you to so much trouble. And, oh!' she concluded, half to herself, 'what *will* Kitty say now?'"

"Kitty! Who's Kitty?"

"I don't know."

"All right. Never mind. Drive on, old chap."

"Well, I mumbled something or other, and then offered to go and get their carriage. But they would not hear of it. The child-angel said she could walk. This I strongly dissuaded her from doing, and Ethel insisted that the men should carry her. This was done, and in a short time we got back to the Hermitage, where the old lady was in no end of a worry. In the midst of the row I slipped away, and waited till the carriage drove off. Then I followed at a sufficient distance not to be observed, and saw where their house was."

THE MEETING.

CHAPTER V.

THE BEGINNING OF BLUNDERS.

DACRES paused now, and lighting a fresh cigar, smoked away at it in silence, with long and solemn and regular puffs. Hawbury watched him for some time, with a look of dreamy curiosity and lazy interest. Then he rose, and dawdled about the room for a few minutes. Then he lighted a cigar, and finally, resuming his seat, he said:

"By Jove!"

Dacres puffed on.

"I'm beginning to think," said Hawbury, "that your first statement is correct. You are shot, my boy—hit hard—and all that; and now I should like to ask you one question."

"Ask away."

"What are you going to do about it? Do you intend to pursue the acquaintance?"

"Of course. Why not?"

"What do you intend to do next?"

"Next? Why, call on her, and inquire after her health."

"Very good."

"Well, have you any thing to say against that?"

"Certainly not. Only it surprises me a little."

"Why?"

"Because I never thought of Scone Dacres as a marrying man, and can't altogether grapple with the idea."

"I don't see why a fellow shouldn't marry if he wants to," said Dacres. "What's the matter with me that I shouldn't get married as well as lots of fellows?"

"No reason in the world, my dear boy. Marry as many wives as you choose. My remark referred merely to my own idea of you, and not to any thing actually innate in your character. So don't get huffy at a fellow."

Some further conversation followed, and Dacres finally took his departure, full of thoughts about his new acquaintance, and racking his brains to devise some way of securing access to her.

On the following evening he made his appearance once more at Hawbury's rooms.

"Well, old man, what's up? Any thing more about the child-angel?"

"Well, a little. I've found out her name."

"Ah! What is it?"

"Fay. Her name is Minnie Fay."

"Minnie Fay. I never heard of the name before. Who are her people?"

"She is traveling with Lady Dalrymple."

"The Dowager, I suppose?"

"Yes."

"Who are the other ladies?"

"Well, I don't exactly remember."

"Didn't you find out?"

"Yes; I heard all their names, but I've forgotten. I know one of them is the child-angel's sister, and the other is her cousin. The one I saw with her was probably the sister."

"What, the one named Ethel?"

"Yes."

"Ethel—Ethel Fay. H'm," said Hawbury, in a tone of disappointment. "I knew it would be so. There are so many Ethels about."

"What's that?"

"Oh, nothing. I once knew a girl named Ethel, and—Well, I had a faint idea that it would be odd if this should be the one. But there's no such chance."

"Oh, the name Ethel is common enough."

"Well, and didn't you find out any thing about her people?"

"Whose—Ethel's?"

"Your child-angel's people."

"No. What do I care about her people? They might be Jews or Patagonians for all I care."

"Still I should think your interest in her would make you ask."

"Oh no; my interest refers to herself, not to her relatives. Her sister Ethel is certainly a deuced pretty girl, though."

"Sconey, my boy, I'm afraid you're getting demoralized. Why, I remember the time when you regarded the whole female race with a lofty scorn and a profound indifference that was a perpetual rebuke to more inflammable natures. But now what a change! Here you are, with a finely developed eye for female beauty, actually reveling in dreams of child-angels and their sisters. By Jove!"

"Nonsense," said Dacres.

"Well, drive on, and tell all about it. You've seen her, of course?"

"Oh yes."

"Did you call?"

"Yes; she was not at home. I went away with a snubbed and subdued feeling, and rode along near the Villa Reale, when suddenly I met the carriage with Lady Dalrymple and the child-angel. She knew me at once, and gave a little start. Then she looked awfully embarrassed. Then she turned to Lady Dalrymple; and by the time I had got up the carriage had stopped, and the ladies both looked at me and bowed. I went up, and they both held out their hands. Lady Dalrymple then made some remarks expressive of gratitude, while the child-angel sat and fastened her wonderful eyes on me, and threw at me such a pleading, touching, entreating, piteous, grateful, beseeching look, that I fairly collapsed.

"When Lady Dalrymple stopped, she turned to her and said:

"'And oh, aunty darling, did you *ever* hear of any thing like it? It was *so* brave. Wasn't it an awfully plucky thing to do, now? And I was really inside the crater! I'm sure *I* never could have done such a thing—no, not even for my *own papa*! Oh, how I do *wish* I could do something to show how *awfully* grateful I am! And, aunty darling, I do *wish* you'd tell me what to do.'

"All this quite turned my head, and I couldn't say any thing; but sat on my saddle, devouring the little thing with my eyes, and drinking in the wonderful look which she threw at me. At last the carriage started, and the ladies, with a pleasant smile, drove on. I think I stood still there for about five minutes, until I was nearly run down by one of those beastly Neapolitan calèches loaded with twenty or thirty natives."

"See here, old man, what a confoundedly good memory you have! You remember no end of a lot of things, and give all her speeches verbatim. What a capital newspaper reporter you'd make!"

"Oh, it's only *her* words, you know. She quickens my memory, and makes a different man of me."

"By Jove!"

"Yes, old chap, a different man altogether."

"So I say, by Jove! Head turned, eyes distorted, heart generally upset, circulation brought up to fever point, peace of mind gone, and a general mania in the place of the old self-reliance and content."

"Not content, old boy; I never had much of that."

"Well, we won't argue, will we? But as to the child-angel—what next? You'll call again?"

"Of course."

"When?"

"To-morrow."

"Strike while the iron is hot, hey? Well, old man, I'll stand by you. Still I wish you could find out who her people are, just to satisfy a legitimate curiosity."

"Well, I don't know the Fays, but Lady Dalrymple is her aunt; and I know, too, that she is a niece of Sir Gilbert Biggs."

"What!" cried Hawbury, starting. "Who? Sir what?"

"Sir Gilbert Biggs."

"Sir Gilbert Biggs?"

"Yes."

"Sir Gilbert Biggs! By Jove! Are you sure you are right? Come, now. Isn't there some mistake?"

"Not a bit of a mistake; she's a niece of Sir Gilbert. I remember that, because the name is a familiar one."

"Familiar!" repeated Hawbury; "I should think so. By Jove!"

Hawbury here relapsed into silence, and sat with a frown on his face, and a puzzled expression. At times he would mutter such words as, "Deuced odd!" "Confounded queer!" "What a lot!" "By Jove!" while Dacres looked at him in some surprise.

"Look here, old fellow!" said he at last. "Will you have the kindness to inform me what there is in the little fact I just mentioned to upset a man of your size, age, fighting weight, and general coolness of blood?"

"Well, there is a deuced odd coincidence about it, that's all."

"Coincidence with what?"

"Well, I'll tell some other time. It's a sore subject, old fellow. Another time, my boy. I'll only mention now that it's the cause of my present absence from England. There's a bother that I don't care to encounter, and Sir Gilbert Biggs's nieces are at the bottom of it."

"You don't mean this one, I hope?" cried Dacres, in some alarm.

"Heaven forbid! By Jove! No. I hope not."

"No, I hope not, by Jove!" echoed the other.

"Well, old man," said Hawbury, after a fit of silence, "I suppose you'll push matters on now, hard and fast, and launch yourself into matrimony?"

"Well—I—suppose—so," said Dacres, hesitatingly.

"You *suppose* so. Of course you will. Don't I know you, old chap? Impetuous, tenacious of purpose, iron will, one idea, and all that sort of thing. Of course you will; and you'll be married in a month."

"Well," said Dacres, in the same hesitating way, "not so soon as that, I'm afraid."

"Why not?"

"Why, I have to get the lady first."

"The lady; oh, she seems to be willing enough, judging from your description. Her pleading look at you. Why, man, there was love at first sight. Then tumbling down the crater of a volcano, and getting fished out. Why, man, what woman could resist a claim like that, especially when it is enforced by a man like Scone Dacres? And, by Jove! Sconey, allow me to inform you that I've always considered you a most infernally handsome man; and what's more, my opinion is worth something, by Jove!"

Hereupon Hawbury stretched his head and shoulders back, and pulled away with each hand at his long yellow pendent whiskers. Then he yawned. And then he slowly ejaculated,

"By Jove!"

"Well," said Dacres, thoughtfully, "there is something in what you say; and, to tell the truth, I think there's not a bad chance for me, so far as the lady herself is concerned; but the difficulty is not in that quarter."

"Not in that quarter! Why, where the mischief else could there be any difficulty, man?"

Dacres was silent.

"You're eager enough?"

Dacres nodded his head sadly.

"Eager! why, eager isn't the word. You're mad, man—mad as a March hare! So go in and win."

Dacres said nothing.

"You're rich, not over old, handsome, well born, well bred, and have saved the lady's life by extricating her from the crater of a volcano. She seems too young and childlike to have had any other affairs. She's probably just out of school; not been into society; not come out; just the girl. Confound these girls, I say, that have gone through engagements with other fellows!"

"Oh, as to that," said Dacres, "this little thing is just like a child, and in her very simplicity does not know what love is. Engagement! By Jove, I don't believe she knows the meaning of the word! She's perfectly fresh, artless, simple, and guileless. I don't believe she ever heard a word of sentiment or tenderness from any man in her life."

"Very likely; so where's the difficulty?"

"Well, to tell the truth, the difficulty is in my own affairs."

"Your affairs! Odd, too. What's up? I didn't know any thing had happened. That's too infernal bad, too."

"Oh, it's nothing of that sort; money's all right; no swindle. It's an affair of another character altogether."

"Oh!"

"And one, too, that makes me think that—"

He hesitated.

"That what?"

"That I'd better start for Australia."

"Australia!"

"Yes."

"What's the meaning of that?"

"Why," said Dacres, gloomily, "it means giving up the child-angel, and trying to forget her—if I ever can."

"Forget her! What's the meaning of all this? Why, man, five minutes ago you were all on fire about her, and now you talk quietly about giving her up! I'm all adrift."

"Well, it's a mixed up matter."

"What is?"

"My affair."

"Your affair; something that has happened?"

"Yes. It's a sore matter, and I don't care to speak about it just now."

"Oh!"

"And it's the real cause why I don't go back to England."

"The mischief it is! Why, Dacres, I'll be hanged if you're not using the very words I myself used a few minutes ago."

"Am I?" said Dacres, gloomily.

"You certainly are; and that makes me think that our affairs are in a similar complication."

"Oh no; mine is very peculiar."

"Well, there's one thing I should like to ask, and you needn't answer unless you like."

"Well?"

"Doesn't your difficulty arise from some confounded woman or other?"

"Well—yes."

"By Jove, I knew it! And, old fellow, I'm in the same situation."

"Oh ho! So you're driven away from England by a woman?"

"Exactly."

Dacres sighed heavily.

"Yours can't be as bad as mine," said he, with a dismal look. "Mine is the worst scrape that ever you heard of. And look at me now, with the child-angel all ready to take me, and me not able to be taken. Confound the abominable complications of an accursed civilization, I say!"

"And I say, Amen!" said Hawbury.

"BY JOVE, I KNEW IT!"

CHAPTER VI.

THE FIERY TRIAL.

"SEE here, old chap," said Hawbury, "I'm going to make a clean breast of it."

"Of what?"

"Of my affair."

"That's right," said Dacres, dolefully. "I should like of all things to hear it."

"You see I wouldn't tell you, only you yourself turn out to be in a similar situation, and so what I have to say may prove of use to you. At any rate, you may give me some useful suggestion.

"Very well, then," continued Hawbury—"to begin. You may remember that I told you when we met here where I had been passing the time since I saw you last."

Dacres nodded assent.

"Well, about two years ago I was in Canada. I went there for sport, and plunged at once into the wilderness. And let me tell you it's a very pretty country for hunting. Lots of game—fish, flesh, and fowl—from the cariboo down to the smallest trout that you would care to hook. Glorious country; magnificent forests waiting for the lumberman; air that acts on you like wine, or even better; rivers and lakes in all directions; no end of sport and all that sort of thing, you know. Have you ever been in Canada?"

"Only traveled through."

"Well, the next time you feel inclined for high art sport we'll go together, and have no end of fun—that is, if you're not married and done for, which, of course, you will be. No matter. I was saying that I was in a fine country. I spent a couple of months there with two or three Indians, and at length started for Ottawa on my way home. The Indians put me on the right path, after which I dismissed them, and set out alone with my gun and fishing-rod.

"The first day was all very well, and I slept well enough the first night; but on the morning of the second day I found the air full of smoke. However, I did not give much thought to that, for there had been a smoky look about the sky for a week, and the woods are always burning there, I believe, in one place or another. I kept on, and shot enough for food, and thus the second day passed. That evening the air was quite suffocating, and it was as hot as an oven. I struggled through the night, I don't know how; and then on the third day made another start. This third day was abominable. The atmosphere was beastly hot; the sky was a dull yellow, and the birds seemed to have all disappeared. As I went on it grew worse, but I found it was not because the fires were in front of me. On the contrary, they were behind me, and were driving on so that they were gradually approaching nearer. I could do my thirty miles a day even in that rough country, but the fires could do more. At last I came into a track that was a little wider than the first one. As I went on I met cattle which appeared stupefied. Showers of dust were in the air; the atmosphere was worse than ever, and I never had such difficulty in my life in walking along. I had to throw away my rifle and fishing-rod, and was just thinking of pitching my clothes after them, when suddenly I turned a bend in the path, and met a young girl full in the face.

"By Jove! I swear I never was so astounded in my life. I hurried up to her, and just began to ask where I was, when she interrupted me with a question of the same kind. By-the-way, I forgot to say that she was on horseback. The poor devil of a horse seemed to have had a deuced hard time of it too, for he was trembling from head to foot, though whether that arose from fatigue or fright I don't know. Perhaps it was both.

"Well, the girl was evidently very much alarmed. She was awfully pale; she was a monstrous pretty girl too—the prettiest by all odds I ever saw, and that's saying a good deal. By Jove! Well, it turned out that she had been stopping in the back country for a month, at a house somewhere up the river, with her father. Her father had gone down to Ottawa a week before, and was expected back on this day. She had come out to meet him, and had lost her way. She had been out for hours, and was completely bewildered. She was also frightened at the fires, which now seemed to be all around us. This she told me in a few words, and asked if I knew where the river was.

"Of course I knew no more than she did, and it needed only a few words from me to show her that I was as much in the dark as she was. I began to question her, however, as to this river, for it struck me that in the present state of affairs a river would not be a bad thing to have near one. In answer to my question she said that she had come upon this road from the woods on the left, and therefore it was evident that the river lay in that direction.

"I assured her that I would do whatever lay in my power; and with that I walked on in the direction in which I had been going, while she rode by my side. Some further questions as to the situation of the house where she had been staying showed me that it was on the banks of the river about fifty miles above Ottawa. By my own calculations I was about that distance away. It seemed to me, then, that she had got lost in the woods, and had wandered thus over some trail to the path where she had met me. Every thing served to show me that the river lay to the left, and so I resolved to turn in at the first path which I reached.

"At length, after about two miles, we came to a path which went into the woods. My companion was sure that this was the very one by which she had come out, and this confirmed the impression which the sight of it had given me. I thought it certainly must lead toward the river. So we turned into this path. I went first, and she followed, and so we went for about a couple of miles further.

"All this time the heat had been getting worse and worse. The air was more smoky than ever; my mouth was parched and dry. I breathed with difficulty, and could scarcely drag one leg after another. The lady was almost as much exhausted as I was, and suffered acutely, as I could easily see, though she uttered not a word of complaint. Her horse also suffered terribly, and did not seem able to bear her weight much longer. The poor brute trembled and staggered, and once or twice stopped, so that it was difficult to start him again. The road had gone in a winding way, but was not so crooked as I expected. I afterward found that she had gone by other paths until she had found herself in thick woods, and then on trying to retrace her way she had strayed into this path. If she had turned to the left on first reaching it, instead of to the right, the fate of each of us would have been different. Our meeting was no doubt the salvation of both.

"There was a wooded eminence in front, which we had been steadily approaching for some time. At last we reached the top, and here a scene burst upon us which was rather startling. The hill was high enough to command an extensive view, and the first thing that we saw was a vast extent of woods and water and smoke. By-and-by we were able to distinguish each. The water was the river, which could be seen for miles. Up the river toward the left the smoke arose in great volumes, covering every thing; while in front of us, and immediately between us and the river, there was a line of smoke which showed that the fires had penetrated there and had intercepted us.

"We stood still in bewilderment. I looked all around. To go back was as bad as to go forward, for there, also, a line of smoke arose which showed the progress of the flames. To the right there was less smoke; but in that direction there was only a wilderness, through which we could not hope to pass for any distance. The only hope was the river. If we could traverse the flames in that direction, so as to reach the water, we would be safe. In a few words I communicated my decision to my companion. She said nothing, but bowed her head in acquiescence.

"Without delaying any longer we resumed our walk. After about a mile we found ourselves compelled once more to halt. The view here was worse than ever. The path was now as wide as an ordinary road, and grew wider still as it went on. It was evidently used to haul logs down to the river, and as it approached the bank it grew steadily wider; but between us and the river the woods were all burning. The first rush of the fire was over, and now we looked forward and saw a vast array of columns—the trunks of burned trees—some blackened and charred, others glowing red. The ground below was also glowing red, with blackened spaces here and there.

"Still the burned tract was but a strip, and there lay our hope. The fire, by some strange means, had passed on a track not wider than a hundred yards, and this was what had to be traversed by us. The question was, whether we could pass through that or not. The same question came to both of us, and neither of us said a word. But before I could ask the lady about it, her horse became frightened at the flames. I advised her to dismount, for I knew that the poor brute could never be forced through those fires. She did so, and the horse, with a horrible snort, turned and galloped wildly away.

"I now looked around once more, and saw that there was no escape except in front. The flames were encircling us, and a vast cloud of smoke surrounded us every where, rising far up and rolling overhead. Cinders fell in immense showers, and the fine ashes, with which the air was filled, choked us and got into our eyes.

"'There is only one chance,' said I; 'and that is to make a dash for the river. Can you do it?'

"'I'll try,' she said.

"'We'll have to go through the fires.'

"She nodded.

"'Well, then,' I said, 'do as I say. Take off your sacque and wrap it around your head and shoulders.'

"She took off her sacque at this. It was a loose robe of merino or alpaca, or something of that sort, and very well suited for what I wanted. I wrapped it round her so as to protect her face, head, and shoulders; and taking off my coat I did the same.

"'Now,' said I, 'hold your breath as well as you can. You may keep your eyes shut. Give me your hand—I'll lead you.'

"Taking her hand I led her forward at a rapid pace. Once she fell, but she quickly recovered herself, and soon we reached the edge of the flames.

"I tell you what it is, my boy, the heat was terrific, and the sight was more so. The river was not more than a hundred yards away, but between us and it there lay what seemed as bad as the burning fiery furnace of Messrs. Shadrach, Meshach, and Abednego. If I were now standing there, I don't think I could face it. But then I was with the girl; I had to save her. Fire was behind us, racing after us; water lay in front. Once there and we were safe. It was not a time to dawdle or hesitate, I can assure you.

"'Now,' said I, 'run for your life!'

"Grasping her hand more firmly, I started off with her at the full run. The place was terrible, and grew worse at every step. The road here was about fifty feet wide. On each side was the burning forest, with a row of burned trees like fiery columns, and the moss and underbrush still glowing beneath. To pass through that was a thing that it don't do to look back upon. The air was intolerable. I wrapped my coat tighter over my head; my arms were thus exposed, and I felt the heat on my hands. But that was nothing to the torments that I endured from trying to breathe. Besides this, the enormous effort of keeping up a run made breathing all the more difficult. A feeling of despair came over me. Already we had gone half the distance, but at that moment the space seemed lengthened out interminably, and I looked in horror at the rest of the way, with a feeling of the utter impossibility of traversing it.

THE FIERY TRIAL.

"Suddenly the lady fell headlong. I stopped and raised her up. My coat fell off; I felt the fiery air all round my face and head. I called and screamed to the lady as I tried to raise her up; but she said nothing. She was as lifeless as a stone.

"Well, my boy, I thought it was all up with me; but I, at least, could stand, though I did not think that I could take another breath. As for the lady, there was no help for it; so I grasped her with all my strength, still keeping her head covered as well as I could, and slung her over my shoulders. Then away I ran. I don't remember much after that. I must have lost my senses then, and, what is more, I must have accomplished the rest of the journey in that semi-unconscious state.

"What I do remember is this—a wild plunge into the water; and the delicious coolness that I felt all around restored me, and I at once comprehended all. The lady was by my side; the shock and the cool water had restored her also. She was standing up to her shoulders just where she had fallen, and was panting and sobbing. I spoke a few words of good cheer, and then looked around for some place of refuge. Just where we stood there was nothing but fire and desolation, and it was necessary to go further away. Well, some distance out, about half-way across the river, I saw a little island, with rocky sides, and trees on the top. It looked safe and cool and inviting. I determined to try to get there. Some deals were in the water by the bank, which had probably floated down from some saw-mill. I took half a dozen of these, flung two or three more on top of them, and then told the lady my plan. It was to float out to the island by means of this raft. I offered to put her on it and let her float; but she refused, preferring to be in the water.

"The river was pretty wide here, and the water was shallow, so that we were able to wade for a long distance, pushing the raft before us. At length it became deep, and then the lady held on while I floated and tried to direct the raft toward the island. I had managed while wading to guide the raft up the stream, so that when we got into deep water the current carried us toward the island. At length we reached it without much difficulty, and then, utterly worn out, I fell down on the grass, and either fainted away or fell asleep.

"When I revived I had several very queer sensations. The first thing that I noticed was that I hadn't any whiskers."

"What! no whiskers?"

"No—all gone; and my eyebrows and mustache, and every wisp of hair from my head."

"See here, old fellow, do you mean to say that you've only taken one year to grow those infernally long whiskers that you have now?"

"It's a fact, my boy!"

"I wouldn't have believed it; but some fellows can do such extraordinary things. But drive on."

"Well, the next thing I noticed was that it was as smoky as ever. Then I jumped up and looked around. I felt quite dry, though it seemed as if I had just come from the river. As I jumped up and turned I saw my friend. She looked much better than she had. Her clothes also were quite dry. She greeted me with a mournful smile, and rose up from the trunk of a tree where she had been sitting, and made inquiries after my health with the most earnest and tender sympathy.

"I told her I was all right, laughed about my hair, and inquired very anxiously how she was. She assured me that she was as well as ever. Some conversation followed; and then, to my amazement, I found that I had slept for an immense time, or had been unconscious, whichever it was, and that the adventure had taken place on the preceding day. It was now about the middle of the next day. You may imagine how confounded I was at that.

"ALL GONE; MY EYEBROWS, AND MUSTACHE, AND EVERY WISP OF HAIR FROM MY HEAD."

"The air was still abominably close and smoky; so I looked about the island, and found a huge crevice in the rocks, which was almost a cave. It was close by the water, and was far cooler than outside. In fact, it was rather comfortable than otherwise. Here we took refuge, and talked over our situation. As far as we could see, the whole country was burned up. A vast cloud of smoke hung over all. One comfort was that the glow had ceased on the river-bank, and only a blackened forest now remained, with giant trees arising, all blasted. We found that our stay would be a protracted one.

"The first thing that I thought of was food. Fortunately I had my hooks and lines; so I cut a pole, and fastening my line to it, I succeeded in catching a few fish.

"We lived there for two days on fish in that manner. The lady was sad and anxious. I tried to cheer her up. Her chief trouble was the fear that her father was lost. In the course of our conversations I found out that her name was Ethel Orne."

"Ethel Orne?"

"Yes."

"Don't think I ever heard the name before. Orne? No, I'm sure I haven't. It isn't Horn?"

"No; Orne—O R N E. Oh, there's no trouble about that.

"Well, I rather enjoyed this island life, but she was awfully melancholy; so I hit upon a plan for getting away. I went to the shore and collected a lot of the deals that I mentioned, and made a very decent sort of raft. I found a pole to guide it with, cut a lot of brush for Ethel, and then we started, and floated down the river. We didn't have any accidents. The only bother was that she was too confoundedly anxious about me, and wouldn't let me work. We went ashore every evening. We caught fish enough to eat. We were afloat three days, and, naturally enough, became very well acquainted."

Hawbury stopped, and sighed.

"I tell you what it is, Dacres," said he, "there never lived a nobler, more generous, and at the same time a braver soul than Ethel Orne. She never said a word about gratitude and all that, but there was a certain quiet look of devotion about her that gives me a deuced queer feeling now when I think of it all."

"And I dare say—But no matter."

"What?"

"Well, I was only going to remark that, under the circumstances, there might have been a good deal of quiet devotion about you."

Hawbury made no reply, but sat silent for a time.

"Well, go on, man; don't keep me in suspense."

"Let me see—where was I? Oh! floating on the raft. Well, we floated that way, as I said, for three days, and at the end of that time we reached a settlement. Here we found a steamer, and went on further, and finally reached Ottawa. Here she went to the house of a friend. I called on her as soon as possible, and found her in fearful anxiety. She had learned that her father had gone up with a Mr. Willoughby, and neither had been heard from.

"Startled at this intelligence, I instituted a search myself. I could not find out any thing, but only that there was good reason to believe that both of the unhappy gentlemen had perished. On returning to the house to call on Ethel, about a week after, I found that she had received full confirmation of this dreadful intelligence, and had gone to Montreal. It seems that Willoughby's wife was a relative of Ethel's, and she had gone to stay with her. I longed to see her, but of course I could not intrude upon her in her grief; and so I wrote to her, expressing all the condolence I could. I told her that I was going to Europe, but would return in the following year. I couldn't say any more than that, you know. It wasn't a time for sentiment, of course.

"Well, I received a short note in reply. She said she would look forward to seeing me again with pleasure, and all that; and that she could never forget the days we had spent together.

"So off I went, and in the following year I returned. But on reaching Montreal, what was my disgust, on calling at Mrs. Willoughby's, to find that she had given up her house, sold her furniture, and left the city. No one knew any thing about her, and they said that she had only come to the city a few months before her bereavement, and after that had never made any acquaintances. Some said she had gone to the United States; others thought she had gone to Quebec; others to England; but no one knew any thing more."

CHAPTER VII.

A STARTLING REVELATION.

"It seems to me, Hawbury," said Dacres, after a period of thoughtful silence—"it seems to me that when you talk of people having their heads turned, you yourself comprehend the full meaning of that sensation?"

"Somewhat."

"You knocked under at once, of course, to your Ethel?"

"Yes."

"And feel the same way toward her yet?"

"Yes."

"Hit hard?"

"Yes; and that's what I'm coming to. The fact is, my whole business in life for the last year has been to find her out."

"You haven't dawdled so much, then, as people suppose?"

"No; that's all very well to throw people off a fellow's scent; but you know me well enough, Dacres; and we didn't dawdle much in South America, did we?"

"That's true, my boy; but as to this lady, what is it that makes it so hard for you to find her? In the first place, is she an American?"

"Oh no."

"Why not?"

"Oh, accent, manner, tone, idiom, and a hundred other things. Why, of course, you know as well as I that an American lady is as different from an English as a French or a German lady is. They may be all equally ladies, but each nation has its own peculiarities."

"Is she Canadian?"

"Possibly. It is not always easy to tell a Canadian lady from an English. They imitate us out there a good deal. I could tell in the majority of cases, but there are many who can not be distinguished from us very easily. And Ethel may be one."

"Why mayn't she be English?"

"She may be. It's impossible to perceive any difference."

"Have you ever made any inquiries about her in England?"

"No; I've not been in England much, and from the way she talked to me I concluded that her home was in Canada."

"Was her father an Englishman?"

"I really don't know."

"Couldn't you find out?"

"No. You see he had but recently moved to Montreal, like Willoughby; and I could not find any people who were acquainted with him."

"He may have been English all the time."

"Yes."

"And she too."

"By Jove!"

"And she may be in England now."

Hawbury started to his feet, and stared in silence at his friend for several minutes.

"By Jove!" he cried; "if I thought that, I swear I'd start for home this evening, and hunt about every where for the representatives of the Orne family. But no—surely it can't be possible."

"Were you in London last season?"

"No."

"Well, how do you know but that she was there?"

"By Jove!"

"And the belle of the season, too?"

"She would be if she were there, by Jove!"

"Yes, if there wasn't another present that I wot of."

"Well, we won't argue about that; besides, I haven't come to the point yet."

"The point?"

"Yes, the real reason why I'm here, when I'm wanted home."

"The real reason? Why, haven't you been telling it to me all along?"

"Well, no; I haven't got to the point yet."

"Drive on, then, old man."

"Well, you know," continued Hawbury, "after hunting all through Canada I gave up in despair, and concluded that Ethel was lost to me, at least for the present. That was only about six or seven months ago. So I went home, and spent a month in a shooting-box on the Highlands; then I went to Ireland to visit a friend; and then to London. While there I got a long letter from my mother. The good soul was convinced that I was wasting my life; she urged me to settle down, and finally informed me that she had selected a wife for me. Now I want you to understand, old boy, that I fully appreciated my mother's motives. She was quite right, I dare say, about my wasting my life; quite right, too, about the benefit of settling down; and she was also very kind to take all the trouble of selecting a wife off my hands. Under other circumstances I dare say I should have thought the matter over, and perhaps I should have been induced even to go so far as to survey the lady from a distance, and argue the point with my mother pro and con. But the fact is, the thing was distasteful, and wouldn't bear thinking about, much less arguing. I was too lazy to go and explain the matter, and writing was not my forte. Besides, I didn't want to thwart my mother in her plans, or hurt her feelings; and so the long and the short of it is, I solved the difficulty and cut the knot by crossing quietly over to Norway. I wrote a short note to my mother, making no allusion to her project, and since then I've been gradually working my way down to the bottom of the map of Europe, and here I am."

"You didn't see the lady, then?"

"No."

"Who was she?"

"I don't know."

"Don't know the lady?"

"No."

"Odd, too! Haven't you any idea? Surely her name was mentioned?"

"No; my mother wrote in a roundabout style, so as to feel her way. She knew me, and feared that I might take a prejudice against the lady. No doubt I should have done so. She only alluded to her in a general way."

"A general way?"

"Yes; that is, you know, she mentioned the fact that the lady was a niece of Sir Gilbert Biggs."

"What!" cried Dacres, with a start.

"A niece of Sir Gilbert Biggs," repeated Hawbury.

"A niece—of—Sir Gilbert Biggs?" said Dacres, slowly. "Good Lord!"

"Yes; and what of that?"

"Very much. Don't you know that Minnie Fay is a niece of Sir Gilbert Biggs?"

"By Jove! So she is. I remember being startled when you told me that, and for a moment an odd fancy came to me. I wondered whether your child-angel might not be the identical being about whom my poor dear mother went into such raptures. Good Lord! what a joke! By Jove!"

"A joke!" growled Dacres. "I don't see any joke in it. I remember when you said that Biggs's nieces were at the bottom of your troubles, I asked whether it might be this one."

"So you did, old chap; and I replied that I hoped not. So you need not shake your gory locks at me, my boy."

"But I don't like the looks of it."

"Neither do I."

"Yes, but you see it looks as though she had been already set apart for you especially."

"And pray, old man, what difference can that make, when I don't set myself apart for any thing of the kind?"

Dacres sat in silence with a gloomy frown over his brow.

"Besides, are you aware, my boy, of the solemn fact that Biggs's nieces are legion?" said Hawbury. "The man himself is an infernal old bloke; and as to his nieces—heavens and earth!—old! old as Methuselah; and as to this one, she must be a grandniece—a second generation. She's not a true, full-blooded niece. Now the lady I refer to was one of the original Biggs's nieces. There's no mistake whatever about that, for I have it in black and white, under my mother's own hand."

"Oh, she would select the best of them for you."

"No, she wouldn't. How do you know that?"

"There's no doubt about that."

"It depends upon what you mean by the best. The one *you* call the best might not seem so to *her*, and so on. Now I dare say she's picked out for me a great, raw-boned, redheaded niece, with a nose like a horse. And she expects me to marry a woman like that! with a pace like a horse! Good Lord!"

And Hawbury leaned back, lost in the immensity of that one overwhelming idea.

"Besides," said he, standing up, "I don't care if she was the angel Gabriel. I don't want any of Biggs's nieces. I won't have them. By Jove! And am I to be entrapped into a plan like that? I want Ethel. And what's more, I will have her, or go without. The child-angel may be the very identical one that my mother selected, and if you assert that she is, I'll be hanged if I'll argue the point. I only say this, that it doesn't alter my position in the slightest degree. I don't want her. I won't have her. I don't want to see her. I don't care if the whole of Biggs's nieces, in solemn conclave, with old Biggs at their head, had formally discussed the whole matter, and finally resolved unanimously that she should be mine. Good Lord, man! don't you understand how it is? What the mischief do I care about any body? Do you think I went through that fiery furnace for nothing? And what do you suppose that life on the island meant? Is all that nothing? Did you ever live on an island with the child-angel? Did you ever make a raft for her and fly? Did you ever float down a river current between banks burned black by raging fires, feeding her, soothing her, comforting her, and all the while feeling in a general fever about her? You hauled her out of a crater, did you? By Jove! And what of that? Why, that furnace that I pulled Ethel out of was worse than a hundred of your craters. And yet, after all that, you think that I could be swayed by the miserable schemes of a lot of Biggs's nieces! And you scowl at a fellow, and get huffy and jealous. By Jove!"

After this speech, which was delivered with unusual animation, Hawbury lighted a cigar, which he puffed at most energetically.

"All right, old boy," said Dacres. "A fellow's apt to judge others by himself, you know. Don't make any more set speeches, though. I begin to understand your position. Besides, after all—"

Dacres paused, and the dark frown that was on his brow grew still darker.

"After all what?" asked Hawbury, who now began to perceive that another feeling besides jealousy was the cause of his friend's gloomy melancholy.

"Well, after all, you know, old fellow, I fear I'll have to give her up."

"Give her up?"

"Yes."

"That's what you said before, and you mentioned Australia, and that rot."

"The more I think of it," said Dacres, dismally, and regarding the opposite wall with a steady yet mournful stare—"the more I think of it, the more I see that there's no such happiness in store for me."

"Pooh, man! what is it all about? This is the secret that you spoke about, I suppose?"

"Yes; and it's enough to put a barrier between me and her. Was I jealous? Did I seem huffy? What an idiot I must have been! Why, old man, I can't do any thing or say any thing."

"The man's mad," said Hawbury, addressing himself to a carved tobacco-box on the table.

"Mad? Yes, I was mad enough in ever letting myself be overpowered by this bright dream. Here have I been giving myself up to a phantom—an empty illusion—and now it's all over. My eyes are open."

"You may as well open my eyes too; for I'll be hanged if I can see my way through this!"

"Strange! strange! strange!" continued Dacres, in a kind of soliloquy, not noticing Hawbury's words. "How a man will sometimes forget realities, and give himself up to dreams! It was my dream of the child-angel that so turned my brain. I must see her no more."

"Very well, old boy," said Hawbury. "Now speak Chinese a little for variety. I'll understand you quite as well. I will, by Jove!"

"And then, for a fellow that's had an experience like mine—before and since," continued Dacres, still speaking in the tone of one who was meditating aloud—"to allow such an idea even for a moment to take shape in his brain! What an utter, unmitigated, unmanageable, and unimprovable idiot, ass, dolt, and blockhead! Confound such a man! I say; confound him!"

"CONFOUND SUCH A MAN! I SAY."

And as Dacres said this he brought his fist down upon the table near him with such an energetic crash that a wine-flask was sent spinning on the floor, where its ruby contents splashed out in a pool, intermingled with fragments of glass.

Dacres was startled by the crash, and looked at it for a while in silence. Then he raised his head and looked at his friend. Hawbury encountered his glance without any expression. He merely sat and smoked and passed his fingers through his pendent whiskers.

"Excuse me," said Dacres, abruptly.

"Certainly, my dear boy, a thousand times; only I hope you will allow me to remark that your style is altogether a new one, and during the whole course of our acquaintance I do not remember seeing it before. You have a melodramatic way that is overpowering. Still I don't see why you should swear at yourself in a place like Naples, where there are so many other things to swear at. It's a waste of human energy, and I don't understand it. We usedn't to indulge in soliloquies in South America, used we?"

"No, by Jove! And look here, old chap, you'll overlook this little outburst, won't you? In South America I was always cool, and you did the hard swearing, my boy. I'll be cool again; and what's more, I'll get back to South America again as soon as I can. Once on the pampas, and I'll be a man again. I tell you what it is, I'll start to-morrow. What do you say? Come."

"Oh no," said Hawbury, coolly; "I can't do that. I have business, you know."

"Business?"

"Oh yes, you know—Ethel, you know."

"By Jove! so you have. That alters the matter."

"But in any case I wouldn't go, nor would you. I still am quite unable to understand you. Why you should grow desperate, and swear at yourself, and then propose South America, is quite beyond me. Above all, I don't yet see any reason why you should give up your child-angel. You were all raptures but a short time since. Why are you so cold now?"

"I'll tell you," said Dacres.

"So you said ever so long ago."

"It's a sore subject, and difficult to speak about."

"Well, old man, I'm sorry for you; and don't speak about it at all if it gives you pain."

"Oh, I'll make a clean breast of it. You've told your affair, and I'll tell mine. I dare say I'll feel all the better for it."

"Drive on, then, old man."

"HAWBURY SANK BACK IN HIS SEAT, OVERWHELMED."

Dacres rose, took a couple of glasses of beer in quick succession, then resumed his seat, then picked out a cigar from the box with unusual fastidiousness, then drew a match, then lighted the cigar, then sent out a dozen heavy volumes of smoke, which encircled him so completely that he became quite concealed from Hawbury's view. But even this cloud did not seem sufficient to correspond with the gloom of his soul. Other clouds rolled forth, and still others, until all their congregated folds encircled him, and in the midst there was a dim vision of a big head, whose stiff, high, curling, crisp hair, and massive brow, and dense beard, seemed like some living manifestation of cloud-compelling Jove.

For some time there was silence, and Hawbury said nothing, but waited for his friend to speak.

At last a voice was heard—deep, solemn, awful, portentous, ominous, sorrow-laden, weird, mysterious, prophetic, obscure, gloomy, doleful, dismal, and apocalyptic.

"*Hawbury!*"

"Well, old man?"

"HAWBURY!"

"All right."

"Are you listening?"

"Certainly."

"*Well—I'm—married!*"

Hawbury sprang to his feet as though he had been shot.

"What!" he cried.

"*I'm married!*"

"You're what? Married? *You! married!* Scone Dacres! not you—not *married?*"

"*I'm married!*"

"Good Lord!"

"*I'm married!*"

Hawbury sank back in his seat, overwhelmed by the force of this sudden and tremendous revelation. For some time there was a deep silence. Both were smoking. The clouds rolled forth from the lips of each, and curled over their heads, and twined in voluminous folds, and gathered over them in dark, impenetrable masses. Even so rested the clouds of doubt, of darkness, and of gloom over the soul of each, and those which were visible to the eye seemed to typify, symbolize, characterize, and body forth the darker clouds that overshadowed the mind.

"*I'm married!*" repeated Dacres, who now seemed to have become like Poe's raven, and all his words one melancholy burden bore.

"You were not married when I was last with you?" said Hawbury at last, in the tone of one who was recovering from a fainting fit.

"Yes, I was."

"Not in South America?"

"Yes, in South America."

"Married?"

"Yes, married."

"By Jove!"

"Yes; and what's more, I've been married for ten years."

"Ten years! Good Lord!"

"It's true."

"Why, how old could you have been when you got married?"

"A miserable, ignorant, inexperienced dolt, idiot, and brat of a boy."

"By Jove!"

"Well, the secret's out; and now, if you care to hear, I will tell you all about it."

"I'm dying to hear, dear boy; so go on."

And at this Scone Dacres began his story.

CHAPTER VIII.

A MAD WIFE.

"I'LL tell you all about it," said Scone Dacres; "but don't laugh, for matters like these are not to be trifled with, and I may take offense."

"Oh, bother, as if I ever laugh at any thing serious! By Jove! no. You don't know me, old chap."

"All right, then. Well, to begin. This wife that I speak of happened to me very suddenly. I was only a boy, just out of Oxford, and just into my fortune. I was on my way to Paris—my first visit—and was full of no end of projects for enjoyment. I went from Dover, and in the steamer there was the most infernally pretty girl. Black, mischievous eyes, with the devil's light in them; hair curly, crispy, frisky, luxuriant, all tossing over her head and shoulders, and an awfully enticing manner. A portly old bloke was with her—her father, I afterward learned. Somehow my hat blew off. She laughed. I laughed. Our eyes met. I made a merry remark. She laughed again; and there we were, introduced. She gave me a little felt hat of her own. I fastened it on in triumph with a bit of string, and wore it all the rest of the way.

"Well, you understand it all. Of course, by the time we got to Calais, I was head over heels in love, and so was she, for that matter. The old man was a jolly old John Bull of a man. I don't believe he had the slightest approach to any designs on me. He didn't know any thing about me, so how could he? He was jolly, and when we got to Calais he was convivial. I attached myself to the two, and had a glorious time. Before three days I had exchanged vows of eternal fidelity with the lady, and all that, and had gained her consent to marry me on reaching England. As to the old man there was no trouble at all. He made no inquiries about my means, but wrung my hand heartily, and said God bless me. Besides, there were no friends of my own to consider. My parents were dead, and I had no relations nearer than cousins, for whom I didn't care a pin.

"My wife lived at Exeter, and belonged to rather common people; but, of course, I didn't care for that. Her own manners and style were refined enough. She had been sent by her father to a very fashionable boarding-school, where she had been run through the same mould as that in which her superiors had been formed, and so she might have passed muster any where. Her father was awfully fond of her, and proud of her. She tyrannized over him completely. I soon found out that she had been utterly spoiled by his excessive indulgence, and that she was the most whimsical, nonsensical, headstrong, little spoiled beauty that ever lived. But, of course, all that, instead of deterring me, only increased the fascination which she exercised, and made me more madly in love than ever.

"Her name was not a particularly attractive one; but what are names! It was Arethusa Wiggins. Now the old man always called her "Arry," which sounded like the vulgar pronunciation of "Harry." Of course I couldn't call her that, and Arethusa was too infernally long, for a fellow doesn't want to be all day in pronouncing his wife's name. Besides, it isn't a bad name in itself, of course; it's poetic, classic, and does to name a ship of war, but isn't quite the thing for one's home and hearth.

"After our marriage we spent the honeymoon in Switzerland, and then came home. I had a very nice estate, and have it yet. You've never heard of Dacres Grange, perhaps—well, there's where we began life, and a devil of a life she began to lead me. It was all very well at first. During the honey-moon there were only a few outbursts, and after we came to the Grange she repressed herself for about a fortnight; but finally she broke out in the most furious fashion; and I began to find that she had a devil of a temper, and in her fits she was but a small remove from a mad woman. You see she had been humored and indulged and petted and coddled by her old fool of a father, until at last she had grown to be the most whimsical, conceited, tetchy, suspicious, imperious, domineering, selfish, cruel, hard-hearted, and malignant young vixen that ever lived; yet this evil nature dwelt in a form as beautiful as ever lived. She was a beautiful demon, and I soon found it out.

"It began out of nothing at all. I had been her adoring slave for three weeks, until I began to be conscious of the most abominable tyranny on her part. I began to resist this, and we were on the verge of an outbreak when we arrived at the Grange. The sight of the old hall appeased her for a time, but finally the novelty wore off, and her evil passions burst out. Naturally enough, my first blind adoration passed away, and I began to take my proper position toward her; that is to say, I undertook to give her some advice, which she very sorely needed. This was the signal for a most furious outbreak. What was worse, her outbreak took place before the servants. Of course I could do nothing under such circumstances, so I left the room. When I saw her again she was sullen and vicious. I attempted a reconciliation, and kneeling down I passed my arms caressingly around her. 'Look here,' said I, 'my own poor little darling, if I've done wrong, I'm sorry, and—'

"Well, what do you think my lady did?"

"I don't know."

"She *kicked me*! that's all; she kicked me, just as I was apologizing to her—just as I was trying to make it up. She kicked me! when I had done nothing, and she alone had been to blame. What's more, her boots were rather heavy, and that kick made itself felt unmistakably.

"I at once arose, and left her without a word. I did not speak to her then for some time. I used to pass her in the house without looking at her. This galled her terribly. She made the house too hot for the servants, and I used to hear her all day long scolding them in a loud shrill voice, till the sound of that voice became horrible to me.

"You must not suppose, however, that I became alienated all at once. That was impossible. I loved her very dearly. After she had kicked me away my love still lasted. It was a galling thought to a man like me that she, a common girl, the daughter of a small tradesman, should have kicked me; me, the descendant of Crusaders, by Jove! and of the best blood in England; but after a while pride gave way to love, and I tried to open the way for a reconciliation once or twice. I attempted to address her in her calmer moods, but it was without any success. She would not answer me at all. If servants were in the room she would at once proceed to give orders to them, just as though I had not spoken. She showed a horrible malignancy in trying to dismiss the older servants, whom she knew to be favorites of mine. Of course I would not let her do it.

"Well, one day I found that this sort of life was intolerable, and I made an effort to put an end to it all. My love was not all gone yet, and I began to think that I had been to blame. She had always been indulged, and I ought to have kept up the system a little longer, and let her down more gradually. I thought of her as I first saw her in the glory of her youthful beauty on the Calais boat, and softened my heart till I began to long for a reconciliation. Really I could not see where I had done any thing out of the way. I was awfully fond of her at first, and would have remained so if she had let me; but, you perceive, her style was not exactly the kind which is best adapted to keep a man at a woman's feet. If she had shown the slightest particle of tenderness, I would have gladly forgiven her all—yes, even the kick, by Jove!

"We had been married about six months or so, and had not spoken for over four months; so on the day I refer to I went to her room. She received me with a sulky expression, and a hard stare full of insult.

"'My dear,' said I, 'I have come to talk seriously with you.'

"'Kate,' said she, 'show this gentleman out.'

"It was her maid to whom she spoke. The maid colored. I turned to her and pointed to the door, and she went out herself. My wife stood trembling with rage—a beautiful fury.

"'I have determined,' said I, quietly, 'to make one last effort for reconciliation, and I want to be heard. Hear me now, dear, dear wife. I want your love again; I can not live this way. Can nothing be done? Must I, must you, always live this way? Have I done any wrong? If I have, I repent. But come, let us forget our quarrel; let us remember the first days of our acquaintance. We loved one another, darling. And how beautiful you were! You are still as beautiful; won't you be as loving? Don't be hard on a fellow, dear. If I've done any wrong, tell me, and I'll make it right. See, we are joined together for life. Can't we make life sweeter for one another than it is now? Come, my wife, be mine again.'

"I went on in this strain for some time, and my own words actually softened me more as I spoke. I felt sorry, too, for my wife, she seemed so wretched. Besides, it was a last chance, and I determined to humble myself. Any thing was better than perpetual hate and misery. So at last I got so affected by my own eloquence that I became quite spooney. Her back was turned to me; I could not see her face. I thought by her silence that she was affected, and, in a gush of tenderness, I put my arm around her.

"In an instant she flung it off, and stepped back, confronting me with a face as hard and an eye as malevolent as a demon.

"She reached out her hand toward the bell.

"'What are you going to do?' I asked.

"'Ring for my maid,' said she.

"VERY WELL. HERE IT IS."

"'Don't,' said I, getting between her and the bell. 'Think; stop, I implore you. This is our last chance for a reconciliation.'

"She stepped back with a cruel smile. She had a small penknife in her hand. Her eyes glittered venomously.

"'Reconciliation,' she said, with a sneer. '*I* don't want it; *I* don't want *you*. *You* came and forced yourself here. Ring for my maid, and I will let her show you the door.'

"'You can't mean it?' I said.

"'I do mean it,' she replied. 'Ring the bell,' she added, imperiously.

"I stood looking at her.

"'Leave the room, then,' she said.

"'I must have a satisfactory answer,' said I.

"'Very well,' said she. 'Here it is.'

"And saying this she took the penknife by the blade, between her thumb and finger, and slung it at me. It struck me on the arm, and buried itself deep in the flesh till it touched the bone. I drew it out, and without another word left the room. As I went out I heard her summoning the maid in a loud, stern voice.

"Well, after that I went to the Continent, and spent about six months. Then I returned.

"On my return I found every thing changed. She had sent off all the servants, and brought there a lot of ruffians whom she was unable to manage, and who threw every thing into confusion. All the gentry talked of her, and avoided the place. My friends greeted me with strange, pitying looks. She had cut down most of the woods, and sold the timber; she had sent off a number of valuable pictures and sold them. This was to get money, for I afterward found out that avarice was one of her strongest vices.

"The sight of all this filled me with indignation, and I at once turned out the whole lot of servants, leaving only two or three maids. I obtained some of the old servants, and reinstated them. All this made my wife quite wild. She came up to me once and began to storm, but I said something to her which shut her up at once.

"One day I came home and found her on the portico, in her riding-habit. She was whipping one of the maids with the butt end of her riding-whip. I rushed up and released the poor creature, whose cries were really heart-rending, when my wife turned on me, like a fury, and struck two blows over my head. One of the scars is on my forehead still. See."

And Dacres put aside his hair on the top of his head, just over his right eye, and showed a long red mark, which seemed like the scar of a dangerous wound.

"It was an ugly blow," he continued. "I at once tore the whip from her, and, grasping her hand, led her into the drawing-room. There I confronted her, holding her tight. I dare say I was rather a queer sight, for the blood was rushing down over my face, and dripping from my beard.

"'Look here, now,' I said; 'do you know any reason why I shouldn't lay this whip over your shoulders? The English law allows it. Don't you feel that you deserve it?'

"She shrank down, pale and trembling. She was a coward, evidently, and accessible to physical terror.

"'If I belonged to your class,' said I, 'I would do it. But I am of a different order. I am a gentleman. Go. After all, I'm not sorry that you gave me this blow.'

"I stalked out of the room, had a doctor, who bound up the wound, and then meditated over my situation. I made up my mind at once to a separation. Thus far she had done nothing to warrant a divorce, and separation was the only thing. I was laid up and feverish for about a month, but at the end of that time I had an interview with my wife. I proposed a separation, and suggested that she should go home to her father. This she refused. She declared herself quite willing to have a separation, but insisted on living at Dacres Grange.

"'And what am I to do?' I asked.

"'Whatever you please,' she replied, calmly.

"'Do you really propose,' said I, 'to drive me out of the home of my ancestors, and live here yourself? Do you think I will allow this place to be under your control after the frightful havoc that you have made?'

"'I shall remain here,' said she, firmly.

"I said nothing more. I saw that she was immovable. At the same time I could not consent. I could not live with her, and I could not go away leaving her there. I could not give up the ancestral home to her, to mar and mangle and destroy. Well, I waited for about two months, and then—"

"Well?" asked Hawbury, as Dacres hesitated.

"Dacres Grange was burned down," said the other, in a low voice.

"Burned down!"

"Yes."

"Good Lord!"

"It caught fire in the daytime. There were but few servants. No fire-engines were near, for the Grange was in a remote place, and so the fire soon gained headway and swept over all. My wife was frantic. She came to me as I stood looking at the spectacle, and charged me with setting fire to it. I smiled at her, but made no reply.

"So you see she was burned out, and that question was settled. It was a terrible thing, but desperate diseases require desperate remedies; and I felt it more tolerable to have the house in ruins than to have her living there while I had to be a wanderer.

"She was now at my mercy. We went to Exeter. She went to her father, and I finally succeeded in effecting an arrangement which was satisfactory on all sides.

"First of all, the separation should be absolute, and neither of us should ever hold communication with the other in any shape or way.

"Secondly, she should take another name, so as to conceal the fact that she was my wife, and not do any further dishonor to the name.

"In return for this I was to give her outright twenty thousand pounds as her own absolutely, to invest or spend just as she chose. She insisted on this, so that she need not be dependent on any annual allowance. In consideration of this she forfeited every other claim, all dower right in the event of my death, and every thing else. This was all drawn up in a formal document, and worded as carefully as possible. I don't believe that the document would be of much use in a court of law in case she wished to claim any of her rights, but it served to satisfy her, and she thought it was legally sound and actually inviolable.

"Here we separated. I left England, and have never been there since."

Dacres stopped, and sat silent for a long time.

"Could she have been mad?" asked Hawbury.

"I used to think so, but I believe not. She showed too much sense in every thing relating to herself. She sold pictures and timber, and kept every penny. She was acute enough in grasping all she could. During our last interviews while making these arrangements she was perfectly cool and lady-like."

"Have you ever heard about her since?"

"Never."

"Is she alive yet?"

"That's the bother."

"What! don't you know?"

"No."

"Haven't you ever tried to find out?"

"Yes. Two years ago I went and had inquiries made at Exeter. Nothing could be found out. She and her father had left the place immediately after my departure, and nothing was known about them."

"I wonder that you didn't go yourself?"

"What for? I didn't care about seeing her or finding her."

"Do you think she's alive yet?"

"I'm afraid she is. You see she always had excellent health, and there's no reason why she should not live to be an octogenarian."

"Yet she may be dead."

"*May* be! And what sort of comfort is that to me in my present position, I should like to know? *May* be? Is that a sufficient foundation for me to build on? No. In a moment of thoughtlessness I have allowed myself to forget the horrible position in which I am. But now I recall it. I'll crush down my feelings, and be a man again. I'll see the child-angel once more; once more feast my soul over her sweet and exquisite loveliness; once more get a glance from her tender, innocent, and guileless eyes, and then away to South America."

"You said your wife took another name."

"Yes."

"What was it? Do you know it?"

"Oh yes; it was *Willoughby*"

"*Willoughby*!" cried Hawbury, with a start; "why, that's the name of my Ethel's friend, at Montreal. Could it have been the same?"

"Pooh, man! How is that possible? Willoughby is not an uncommon name. It's not more likely that your Willoughby and mine are the same than it is that your Ethel is the one I met at Vesuvius. It's only a coincidence, and not a very wonderful one, either."

"It seems con-foundedly odd, too," said Hawbury, thoughtfully. "Willoughby? Ethel? Good Lord! But pooh! What rot? As though they *could* be the same. Preposterous! By Jove!"

And Hawbury stroked away the preposterous idea through his long, pendent whiskers.

"SHE CAUGHT MINNIE IN HER ARMS."

CHAPTER IX.

NEW EMBARRASSMENTS.

MRS. WILLOUGHBY had been spending a few days with a friend whom she had found in Naples, and on her return was greatly shocked to hear of Minnie's adventure on Vesuvius. Lady Dalrymple and Ethel had a story to tell which needed no exaggerations and amplifications to agitate her strongly. Minnie was not present during the recital; so, after hearing it, Mrs. Willoughby went to her room.

Here she caught Minnie in her arms, and kissed her in a very effusive manner.

"Oh, Minnie, my poor darling, what is all this about Vesuvius? Is it true? It is terrible. And now I will never dare to leave you again. How could I think that you would be in any danger with Lady Dalrymple and Ethel? As to Ethel, I am astonished. She is always so grave and so sad that she is the very last person I would have supposed capable of leading you into danger."

"Now, Kitty dearest, that's not true," said Minnie; "she didn't lead me at all. I led her. And how did I know there was any danger? I remember now that dear, darling Ethel said there was, and I didn't believe her. But it's always the way." And Minnie threw her little head on one side, and gave a resigned sigh.

"And did you really get into the crater?" asked Mrs. Willoughby, with a shudder.

"Oh, I suppose so. They all said so," said Minnie, folding her little hands in front of her. "I only remember some smoke, and then jolting about dreadfully on the shoulder of some great—big—awful—man."

"Oh dear!" sighed Mrs. Willoughby.

"What's the matter, Kitty dearest?"

"Another man!" groaned her sister.

"Well, and how *could* I help it?" said Minnie. "I'm *sure* I didn't want him. I'm *sure* I think he might have let me alone. I don't see *why* they all act so. I *wish* they wouldn't be all the time coming and saving my life. If people *will* go and save my life, I can't help it. I think it's very, very horrid of them."

"Oh dear! oh dear!" sighed her sister again.

"Now, Kitty, stop."

"Another man!" sighed Mrs. Willoughby.

"Now, Kitty, if you are so unkind, I'll cry. You're *always* teasing me. You *never* do any thing to comfort me. You *know* I want comfort, and I'm not strong, and people all come and save my life and worry me; and I really sometimes think I'd rather not live at all if my life *has* to be saved so often. I'm sure *I* don't know why they go and do it. I'm sure *I* never heard of any person who is always going and getting her life saved, and bothered, and proposed to, and written to, and chased, and frightened to death. And I've a *great* mind to go and get married, just to stop it all. And I'd *just* as soon marry this last man as not, and make him drive all the others away from me. He's big enough."

Minnie ended all this with a little sob; and her sister, as usual, did her best to soothe and quiet her.

"Well, but, darling, how did it all happen?"

"Oh, don't, don't."

"But you might tell *me*"

"Oh, I can't bear to think of it. It's too horrible."

"Poor darling—the crater?"

"No, the great, big man. I didn't see any crater."

"Weren't you in the crater?"

"No, I wasn't."

"They said you were."

"I wasn't. I was on the back of a big, horrid man, who gave great jumps down the side of an awful mountain, all sand and things, and threw me down at the bottom of it, and—and—disarranged all my hair. And I was so frightened that I couldn't even cur—cur—cry."

Here Minnie sobbed afresh, and Mrs. Willoughby petted her again.

"And you shouldn't tease me so; and it's very unkind in you; and you know I'm not well; and I can't bear to think about it all; and I know you're going to scold me; and you're *always* scolding me; and you *never* do what I want you to. And then people are *always* coming and saving my life, and I can't bear it any more."

"No-o-o-o-o-o, n-n-no-o-o-o, darling!" said Mrs. Willoughby, soothingly, in the tone of a nurse appeasing a fretful child. "You sha'n't bear it any more."

"I don't *want* them to save me any more."

"Well, they sha'n't *do* it, then," said Mrs. Willoughby, affectionately, in a somewhat maudlin tone.

"And the next time I lose my life, I don't want to be saved. I want them to let me alone, and I'll come home myself."

"And so you shall, darling; you shall do just as you please. So, now, cheer up; don't cry;" and Mrs. Willoughby tried to wipe Minnie's eyes.

"But you're treating me just like a baby, and I don't want to be talked to so," said Minnie, fretfully.

Mrs. Willoughby retreated with a look of despair.

"Well, then, dear, I'll do just whatever you want me to do."

"Well, then, I want you to tell me what I am to do."

"About what?"

"Why, about this great, big, horrid man."

"I thought you didn't want me to talk about this any more."

"But I *do* want you to talk about it. You're the only person that I've got to talk to about it; nobody else knows how peculiarly I'm situated; and I didn't think that you'd give me up because I had fresh troubles."

"Give you up, darling!" echoed her sister, in surprise.

"You said you wouldn't talk about it any more."

"But I thought you didn't want me to talk about it."

"But I *do* want you to."

"Very well, then; and now I want you first of all, darling, to tell me how you happened to get into such danger."

"Well, you know," began Minnie, who now seemed calmer—"you know we all went out for a drive. And we drove along for miles. Such a drive! There were lazaroni, and donkeys, and calèches with as many as twenty in each, all pulled by one poor horse, and it's a great shame; and pigs—oh, *such* pigs! Not a particle of hair on them, you know, and looking like young elephants, you know; and we saw great droves of oxen, and long lines of booths, no end; and people selling macaroni, and other people eating it right in the open street, you know—such fun!—and fishermen and fish-wives. Oh, how they *were* screaming, and oh, *such* a hubbub as there was! and we couldn't go on fast, and Dowdy seemed really frightened."

"Dowdy?" repeated Mrs. Willoughby, in an interrogative tone.

"Oh, that's a name I've just invented for Lady Dalrymple. It's better than Rymple. She said so. It's Dowager shortened. She's a dowager, you know. And so, you know, I was on the front seat all the time, when all at once I saw a gentleman on horseback. He was a great big man—oh, *so* handsome!—and he was looking at poor little me as though he would eat me up. And the moment I saw him I was frightened out of my poor little wits, for I knew he was coming to save my life."

"You poor little puss! what put such an idea as that into your ridiculous little head?"

"Oh, I knew it—second-sight, you know. We've got Scotch blood, Kitty darling, you know. So, you know, I sat, and I saw that he was pretending not to see me, and not to be following us; but all the time he was taking good care to keep behind us, when he could easily have passed us, and all to get a good look at poor me, you know.

"Well," continued Minnie, drawing a long breath, "you know I was awfully frightened; and so I sat looking at him, and I whispered all the time to myself: 'Oh, please don't!—ple-e-e-e-ease don't! Don't come and save my life! Ple-e-e-e-ease let me alone! I don't want to be saved at all.' I said this, you know, all to myself, and the more I said it the more he seemed to fix his eyes on me."

"It was very, very rude in him, *I* think," said Mrs. Willoughby, with some indignation.

"No, it wasn't," said Minnie, sharply. "He wasn't rude at all. He tried not to look at me. He pretended to be looking at the sea, and at the pigs, and all that sort of thing, you know; but all the time, you know, I knew very well that he saw me out of the corner of his eye—this way."

And Minnie half turned her head, and threw upon her sister, out of the corner of her eyes, a glance so languishing that the other laughed.

"He didn't look at you that way. I hope?"

"There was nothing to laugh at in it at all," said Minnie. "He had an awfully solemn look—it was so earnest, so sad, and so dreadful, that I really began to feel quite frightened. And so would *you*; wouldn't *you*, now, Kitty darling; now *wouldn't* you? Please say so."

"Oh yes!"

"Of course you would. Well, this person followed us. I could see him very easily, though he tried to avoid notice; and so at last we got to the Hermitage, and he came too. Well, you know, I think I was very much excited, and I asked Dowdy to let us go and see the cone; so she let us go. She gave no end of warnings, and we promised to do all that she said. So Ethel and I went out, and there was the stranger. Well, I felt more excited than ever, and a little bit frightened—just a very, very, tiny, little bit, you know, and I teased Ethel to go to the cone. Well, the stranger kept in sight all the time, you know, and I *felt* his eyes on me—I really *felt* them. So, you know, when we got at the foot of the cone, I was so excited that I was really quite beside myself, and I teased and teased, till at last Ethel consented to go up. So the men took us up on chairs, and all the time the stranger was in sight. He walked up by himself with great, big, long, strong strides. So we went on till we got at the top, and then I was wilder than ever. I didn't know that there was a particle of danger. I was dying with curiosity to look down, and see where the smoke came from. The stranger was standing there too, and that's what made me so excited. I wanted to show him—I don't know what. I think my idea was to show him that I could take care of myself. So then I teased and teased, and Ethel begged and prayed, and she cried, and I laughed; and there stood the stranger, seeing it all, until at last I started off, and ran up to the top, you know."

Mrs. Willoughby shuddered, and took her sister's hand.

"There was no end of smoke, you know, and it was awfully unpleasant, and I got to the top I don't know how, when suddenly I fainted."

Minnie paused for a moment, and looked at her sister with a rueful face.

"Well, now, dear, darling, the very—next—thing—that I remember is this, and it's horrid: I felt awful jolts, and found myself in the arms of a great, big, horrid man, who was running down the side of the mountain with dreadfully long jumps, and I felt as though he was some horrid ogre carrying poor me away to his den to eat me up. But I didn't say one word. I wasn't much frightened. I felt provoked. I knew it was that horrid man. And then I wondered what you'd say; and I thought, oh, how you *would* scold! And then I knew that this horrid man would chase me away from Italy; and then I would have to go to Turkey, and have my life saved by a Mohammedan. And that was horrid.

"Well, at last he stopped and laid me down. He was very gentle, though he was so big. I kept my eyes shut, and lay as still as a mouse, hoping that Ethel would come. But Ethel didn't. She was coming down with the chair, you know, and her men couldn't run like mine. And oh, Kitty darling, you have no *idea* what I suffered. This horrid man was rubbing and pounding at my hands, and sighing and groaning. I stole a little bit of a look at him—just a little bit of a bit—and saw tears in his eyes, and a wild look of fear in his face. Then I knew that he was going to propose to me on the spot, and kept my eyes shut tighter than ever.

"Well, at last he hurt my hands so that I thought I'd try to make him stop. So I spoke as low as I could, and asked if I was home, and he said yes."

Minnie paused.

"Well?" asked her sister.

"Well," said Minnie, in a doleful tone, "I then asked, 'Is that you, papa dear?'" Minnie stopped again.

"Well?" asked Mrs. Willoughby once more.

"Well—"

"Well, go on."

"Well, he said—he said, 'Yes, darling'—and—"

"And what?"

"And he kissed me," said Minnie, in a doleful voice.

"Kissed you!" exclaimed her sister, with flashing eyes.

"Ye-yes," stammered Minnie, with a sob; "and I think it's a shame; and none of them ever did so before; and I don't want you ever to go away again, Kitty darling."

"The miserable wretch!" cried Mrs. Willoughby, indignantly.

"No, he isn't—he isn't that," said Minnie. "He isn't a miserable wretch at all."

"How could any one be so base who pretends to the name of gentleman!" cried Mrs. Willoughby.

"He wasn't base—and it's very wicked of you, Kitty. He only pretended, you know."

"Pretended!"

"Yes."

"Pretended what?"

"Why, that he was my—my father, you know."

"Does Ethel know this?" asked Mrs. Willoughby, after a curious look at Minnie.

"No, of course not, nor Dowdy either; and you mustn't go and make any disturbance."

"Disturbance? no; but if I ever see him, I'll let him know what I think of him," said Mrs. Willoughby, severely.

"But he saved my life, and so you know you can't be *very* harsh with him. Please don't—ple-e-e-ease now, Kitty darling."

"Oh, you little goose, what whimsical idea have you got now?"

"Please don't, ple-e-e-ease don't," repeated Minnie.

"Oh, never mind; go on now, darling, and tell me about the rest of it."

"Well, there isn't any more. I lay still, you know, and at last Ethel came; and then we went back to Dowdy, and then we came home, you know."

"Well, I hope you've lost him."

"Lost him? Oh no; I never do. They always *will* come. Besides, this one will, I know."

"Why?"

"Because he said so."

"Said so? when?"

"Yesterday."

"Yesterday?"

"Yes; we met him."

"Who?"

"Dowdy and I. We were out driving. We stopped and spoke to him. He was dreadfully earnest and awfully embarrassed; and I knew he was going to propose; so I kept whispering to myself all the time, 'Oh, please don't—please don't;' but I know he will; and he'll be here soon too."

"He sha'n't. I won't let him. I'll never give him the chance."

"I think you needn't be so cruel."

"Cruel!"

"Yes; to the poor man."

"Why, you don't want another man, I hope?"

"N-no; but then I don't want to hurt his feelings. It was awfully good of him, you know, and *aw*fully plucky."

"IF I EVER SEE HIM, I'LL LET HIM KNOW WHAT I THINK OF HIM."

"Well, I should think that you would prefer avoiding him, in your peculiar situation."

"Yes, but he may feel hurt."

"Oh, he may see you once or twice with me."

"But he may want to see me alone, and what *can* I do?"

"Really now, Minnie, you must remember that you are in a serious position. There is that wretched Captain Kirby."

"I know," said Minnie, with a sigh.

"And that dreadful American. By-the-way, darling, you have never told me his name. It isn't of any consequence, but I should like to know the American's name."

"It's—Rufus K. Gunn."

"Rufus K. Gunn; what a funny name! and what in the world is 'K' for?"

"Oh, nothing. He says it is the fashion in his country to have some letter of the alphabet between one's names, and he chose 'K,' because it was so awfully uncommon. Isn't it funny, Kitty darling?"

"Oh dear!" sighed her sister; "and then there is that pertinacious Count Girasole. Think what trouble we had in getting quietly rid of him. I'm afraid all the time that he will not stay at Florence, as he said, for he seems to have no fixed abode. First he was going to Rome, and then Venice, and at last he committed himself to a statement that he had to remain at Florence, and so enabled us to get rid of him. But I know he'll come upon us again somewhere, and then we'll have all the trouble over again. Oh dear! Well, Minnie darling, do you know the name of this last one?"

"Oh yes."

"What is it?"

"It's a funny name," said Minnie; "a very funny name."

"Tell it to me."

"It's Scone Dacres; and isn't that a funny name?"

Mrs. Willoughby started at the mention of that name. Then she turned away her head, and did not say a word for a long time.

"Kitty!"

No answer.

"Kitty darling, what's the matter?"

Mrs. Willoughby turned her head once more. Her face was quite calm, and her voice had its usual tone, as she asked,

"Say that name again."

"Scone Dacres," said Minnie.

"Scone Dacres!" repeated Mrs. Willoughby; "and what sort of a man is he?"

"Big—very big—awfully big!" said Minnie. "Great, big head and broad shoulders. Great, big arms, that carried me as if I were a feather; big beard too; and it tickled me so when he—he pretended that he was my father; and very sad. And, oh! I know I should be so *aw*fully fond of him. And, oh! Kitty darling, what do you think?"

"What, dearest?"

"Why, I'm—I'm afraid—I'm really beginning to—to—like him—just a little tiny bit, you know."

"Scone Dacres!" repeated Mrs. Willoughby, who didn't seem to have heard this last effusion. "Scone Dacres! Well, darling, don't trouble yourself; he sha'n't trouble you."

"But I *want* him to," said Minnie.

"Oh, nonsense, child!"

"HALLO, OLD MAN, WHAT'S UP NOW?"

CHAPTER X.

A FEARFUL DISCOVERY.

A FEW days after this Hawbury was in his room, when Dacres entered.

"Hallo, old man, what's up now? How goes the war?" said Hawbury. "But what the mischief's the matter? You look cut up. Your brow is sad; your eyes beneath flash like a falchion from its sheath. What's happened? You look half snubbed, and half desperate."

Dacres said not a word, but flung himself into a chair with a look that suited Hawbury's description of him quite accurately. His brows lowered into a heavy frown, his lips were compressed, and his breath came quick and hard through his inflated nostrils. He sat thus for some time without taking any notice whatever of his friend, and at length lighted a cigar, which he smoked, as he often did when excited, in great voluminous puffs. Hawbury said nothing, but after one or two quick glances at his friend, rang a bell and ordered some "Bass."

"Here, old fellow," said he, drawing the attention of Dacres to the refreshing draught. "Take some—'Quaff, oh, quaff this kind nepenthe, and forget thy lost Lenore.'"

Dacres at this gave a heavy sigh that sounded like a groan, and swallowed several tumblers in quick succession.

"Hawbury!" said he at length, in a half-stifled voice.

"Well, old man?"

"I've had a blow to-day full on the breast that fairly staggered me."

"By Jove!"

"Fact. I've just come from a mad ride along the shore. I've been mad, I think, for two or three hours. Of all the monstrous, abominable, infernal, and unheard-of catastrophes this is the worst."

He stopped, and puffed away desperately at his cigar.

"Don't keep a fellow in suspense this way," said Hawbury at last. "What's up? Out with it, man."

"Well, you know, yesterday I called there."

Hawbury nodded.

"She was not at home."

"So you said."

"You know she really wasn't, for I told you that I met their carriage. The whole party were in it, and on the front seat beside Minnie there was another lady. This is the one that I had not seen before. She makes the fourth in that party. She and Minnie had their backs turned as they came up. The other ladies bowed as they passed, and as I held off my hat I half turned to catch Minnie's eyes, when I caught sight of the face of the lady. It startled me so much that I was thunder-struck, and stood there with my hat off after they had passed me for some time."

"You said nothing about that, old chap. Who the deuce could she have been?"

"No, I said nothing about it. As I cantered off I began to think that it was only a fancy of mine, and finally I was sure of it, and laughed it off. For, you must know, the lady's face looked astonishingly like a certain face that I don't particularly care to see—certainly not in such close connection with Minnie. But, you see, I thought it might have been my fancy, so that I finally shook off the feeling, and said nothing to you about it."

Dacres paused here, rubbed his hand violently over his hair at the place where the scar was, and then, frowning heavily, resumed:

"Well, this afternoon I called again. They were at home. On entering I found three ladies there. One was Lady Dalrymple, and the others were Minnie and her friend Ethel—either her friend or her sister. I think she's her sister. Well, I sat for about five minutes, and was just beginning to feel the full sense of my happiness, when the door opened and another lady entered. Hawbury"—and Dacres's tones deepened into an awful solemnity—"Hawbury, it was the lady that I saw in the carriage yesterday. One look at her was enough. I was assured then that my impressions yesterday were not dreams, but the damnable and abhorrent truth!"

"What impressions—you haven't told me yet, you know?"

"Wait a minute. I rose as she entered, and confronted her. She looked at me calmly, and then stood as though expecting to be introduced. There was no emotion visible whatever. She was prepared for it: I was not: and so she was as cool as when I saw her last, and, what is more, just as young and beautiful."

"The devil!" cried Hawbury.

"I STOOD TRANSFIXED."

Dacres poured out another glass of ale and drank it. His hand trembled slightly as he put down the glass, and he sat for some time in thought before he went on.

"Well, Lady Dalrymple introduced us. It was Mrs. Willoughby!"

"By Jove!" cried Hawbury. "I saw you were coming to that."

"Well, you know, the whole thing was so sudden, so unexpected, and so perfectly overwhelming, that I stood transfixed. I said nothing. I believe I bowed, and then somehow or other, I really don't know how, I got away, and, mounting my horse, rode off like a madman. Then I came home, and here you see me."

There was a silence now for some time.

"Are you sure that it was your wife?"

"Of course I am. How could I be mistaken?"

"Are you sure the name was Willoughby?"

"Perfectly sure."

"And that is the name your wife took?"

"Yes; I told you so before, didn't I?"

"Yes. But think now. Mightn't there be some mistake?"

"Pooh! how could there be any mistake?"

"Didn't you see any change in her?"

"No, only that she looked much more quiet than she used to. Not so active, you know. In her best days she was always excitable, and a little demonstrative; but now she seems to have sobered down, and is as quiet and well-bred as any of the others."

"Was there not any change in her at all?"

"Not so much as I would have supposed; certainly not so much as there is in me. But then I've been knocking about all over the world, and she's been living a life of peace and calm, with the sweet consciousness of having triumphed over a hated husband, and possessing a handsome competency. Now she mingles in the best society. She associates with lords and ladies. She enjoys life in England, while I am an exile. No doubt she passes for a fine young widow. No doubt, too, she has lots of admirers. They aspire to her hand. They write poetry to her. They make love to her. Confound her!"

Dacres's voice grew more and more agitated and excited as he spoke, and at length his tirade against his wife ended in something that was almost a roar.

Hawbury said nothing, but listened, with his face full of sympathy. At last his pent-up feeling found expression in his favorite exclamation, "By Jove!"

"Wouldn't I be justified in wringing her neck?" asked Dacres, after a pause. "And what's worse," he continued, without waiting for an answer to his question—"what's worse, her presence here in this unexpected way has given me, *me*, mind you, a sense of guilt, while she is, of course, immaculate. *I*, mind you—*I*, the injured husband, with the scar on my head from a wound made by *her* hand, and all the ghosts of my ancestors howling curses over me at night for my desolated and ruined home—*I* am to be conscience-stricken in her presence, as if I were a felon, while *she*, the really guilty one—the blight and bitter destruction of my life—*she* is to appear before me now as injured, and must make her appearance here, standing by the side of that sweet child-angel, and warning me away. Confound it all, man! Do you mean to say that such a thing is to be borne?"

Dacres was now quite frantic; so Hawbury, with a sigh of perplexity, lighted a fresh cigar, and thus took refuge from the helplessness of his position. It was clearly a state of things in which advice was utterly useless, and consolation impossible. What could he advise, or what consolation could he offer? The child-angel was now out of his friend's reach, and the worst fears of the lover were more than realized.

"I told you I was afraid of this," continued Dacres. "I had a suspicion that she was alive, and I firmly believe she'll outlive me forty years; but I must say I never expected to see her in this way, under such circumstances. And then to find her so infernally beautiful! Confound her! she don't look over twenty-five. How the mischief does she manage it? Oh, she's a deep one! But perhaps she's changed. She seems so calm, and came into the room so gently, and looked at me so steadily. Not a tremor, not a shake, as I live. Calm, Sir; cool as steel, and hard too. She looked away, and then looked back. They were searching glances, too, as though they read me through and through. Well, there was no occasion for that. She ought to know Scone Dacres well enough, I swear. Cool! And there stood I, with the blood flashing to my head, and throbbing fire underneath the scar of her wound—hers—her own property, for she made it! That was the woman that kicked me, that struck at me, that caused the destruction of my ancestral house, that drove me to exile, and that now drives me back from my love. But, by Heaven! it'll take more than her to do it; and I'll show her again, as I showed her once before, that Scone Dacres is her master. And, by Jove! she'll find that it'll take more than herself to keep me away from Minnie Fay."

"See here, old boy," said Hawbury, "you may as well throw up the sponge."

"I won't," said Dacres, gruffly.

"You see it isn't your wife that you have to consider, but the girl; and do you think the girl or her friends would have a married man paying his attentions in that quarter? Would you have the face to do it under your own wife's eye? By Jove!"

The undeniable truth of this assertion was felt by Dacres even in his rage. But the very fact that it was unanswerable, and that he was helpless, only served to deepen and intensify his rage. Yet he said nothing; it was only in his face and manner that his rage was manifested. He appeared almost to suffocate under the rush of fierce, contending passions; big distended veins swelled out in his forehead, which was also drawn far down in a gloomy frown; his breath came thick and fast, and his hands were clenched tight together. Hawbury watched him in silence as before, feeling all the time the impossibility of saying any thing that could be of any use whatever.

"Well, old fellow," said Dacres at last, giving a long breath, in which he seemed to throw off some of his excitement, "you're right, of course, and I am helpless. There's no chance for me. Paying attentions is out of the question, and the only thing for me to do is to give up the whole thing. But that isn't to be done at once. It's been long since I've seen any one for whom

I felt any tenderness, and this little thing, I know, is fond of me. I can't quit her at once. I must stay on for a time, at least, and have occasional glimpses at her. It gives me a fresh sense of almost heavenly sweetness to look at her fair young face. Besides, I feel that I am far more to her than any other man. No other man has stood to her in the relation in which I have stood. Recollect how I saved her from death. That is no light thing. She must feel toward me as she has never felt to any other. She is not one who can forget how I snatched her from a fearful death, and brought her back to life. Every time she looks at me she seems to convey all that to me in her glance."

"Oh, well, my dear fellow, really now," said Hawbury, "just think. You can't do any thing."

"But I don't want to do any thing."

"It never can end in any thing, you know."

"But I don't want it to end in any thing."

"You'll only bother her by entangling her affections."

"But I don't want to entangle her affections."

"Then what the mischief *do* you want to do?"

"Why, very little. I'll start off soon for the uttermost ends of the earth, but I wish to stay a little longer and see her sweet face. It's not much, is it? It won't compromise her, will it? She need not run any risk, need she? And I'm a man of honor, am I not? You don't suppose me to be capable of any baseness, do you?"

"My dear fellow, how absurd! Of course not. Only I was afraid by giving way to this you might drift on into a worse state of mind. She's all safe, I fancy, surrounded as she is by so many guardians. It is you that I'm anxious about."

"Don't be alarmed, old chap, about me. I feel calmer already. I can face my situation firmly, and prepare for the worst. While I have been sitting here I have thought out the future. I will stay here four or five weeks. I will only seek solace for myself by riding about where I may meet her. I do not intend to go to the house at all. My demon of a wife may have the whole house to herself. I won't even give her the pleasure of supposing that she has thwarted me. She shall never even suspect the state of my heart. That would be bliss indeed to one like her, for then she would find herself able to put me on the rack. No, my boy; I've thought it all over. Scone Dacres is himself again. No more nonsense now. Do you understand now what I mean?"

"Yes," said Hawbury, slowly, and in his worst drawl; "but ah, really, don't you think it's all nonsense?"

"What?"

"Why, this ducking and diving about to get a glimpse of her face."

"I don't intend to duck and dive about. I merely intend to ride like any other gentleman. What put that into your head, man?"

"Well, I don't know; I gathered it from the way you expressed yourself."

"Well, I don't intend any thing of the kind. I simply wish to have occasional looks at her—to get a bow and a smile of recognition when I meet her, and have a few additional recollections to turn over in my thoughts after I have left her forever. Perhaps this seems odd."

"Oh no, it doesn't. I quite understand it. A passing smile or a parting sigh is sometimes more precious than any other memory. I know all about it, you know—looks, glances, smiles, sighs, and all that sort of thing, you know."

"Well, now, old chap, there's one thing I want you to do for me."

"Well, what is it?"

"It isn't much, old fellow. It isn't much. I simply wish you to visit there."

"*Me?*—visit *there?* What! me—and visit? Why, my dear fellow, don't you know how I hate such bother?"

"I know all about that; but, old boy, it's only for a few weeks I ask it, and for my sake, as a particular favor. I put it in that light."

"Oh, well, really, dear boy, if you put it in that light, you know, of course, that I'll do any thing, even if it comes to letting myself be bored to death."

"Just a visit a day or so."

"A visit a day!" Hawbury looked aghast.

"It isn't much to ask, you know," continued Dacres. "You see my reason is this: I can't go there myself, as you see, but I hunger to hear about her. I should like to hear how she looks, and what she says, and whether she thinks of me."

"Oh, come now! look here, my dear fellow, you're putting it a little too strong. You don't expect me to go there and talk to her about you, you know. Why, man alive, that's quite out of my way. I'm not much of a talker at any time; and besides, you know, there's something distasteful in acting as—as—By Jove! I don't know what to call it."

"My dear boy, you don't understand me. Do you think I'm a sneak? Do you suppose I'd ask you to act as a go-between? Nonsense! I merely ask you to go as a cursory visitor. I don't want you to breathe my name, or even think of me while you are there."

"But suppose I make myself too agreeable to the young lady. By Jove! she might think I was paying her attentions, you know."

"Oh no, no! believe me, you don't know her. She's too earnest; she has too much soul to shift and change. Oh no! I feel that she is mine, and that the image of my own miserable self is indelibly impressed upon her heart. Oh no! you don't know her. If you had heard her thrilling expressions of gratitude, if you had seen the beseeching and pleading looks which she gave me, you would know that she is one of those natures who love once, and once only."

"Oh, by Jove, now! Come! If that's the 'state of the case, why, I'll go."

"Thanks, old boy."

"As a simple visitor."

"Yes—that's all."

"To talk about the weather, and that rot."

"Yes."

"And no more."

"No."

"Not a word about you."

"Not a word."

"No leading questions, and that sort of thing."

"Nothing of the kind."

"No hints, no watching, but just as if I went there of my own accord."

"That's exactly the thing."

"Very well; and now, pray, what good is all this going to do to you, my boy?"

"Well, just this; I can talk to you about her every evening, and you can tell me how she looks, and what she says, and all that sort of thing, you know."

"By Jove!"

"And you'll cheer my heart, old fellow."

"Heavens and earth! old boy, you don't seem to think that this is going to be no end of a bore."

"I know it, old man; but then, you know, I'm desperate just now."

"By Jove!"

And Hawbury, uttering this exclamation, relapsed into silence, and wondered over his friend's infatuation.

On the following day when Dacres came in he found that Hawbury had kept his word.

"Great bore, old fellow," said he; "but I did it. The old lady is an old acquaintance, you know. I'm going there to-morrow again. Didn't see any thing to-day of the child-angel. But it's no end of a bore, you know."

"'IT'S HE!' SHE MURMURED."

CHAPTER XI.

FALSE AND FORGETFUL.

THE day when Lord Hawbury called on Lady Dalrymple was a very eventful one in his life, and had it not been for a slight peculiarity of his, the immediate result of that visit would have been of a highly important character. This slight peculiarity consisted in the fact that he was short-sighted, and, therefore, on a very critical occasion turned away from that which would have been his greatest joy, although it was full before his gaze.

It happened in this wise:

On the day when Hawbury called, Ethel happened to be sitting by the window, and saw him as he rode up. Now the last time that she had seen him he had a very different appearance—all his hair being burned off, from head and cheeks and chin; and the whiskers which he had when she first met him had been of a different cut from the present appendages. In spite of this she recognized him almost in a moment; and her heart beat fast, and her color came and went, and her hands clutched the window ledge convulsively.

"It's *he*!" she murmured.

Of course there was only one idea in her mind, and that was that he had heard of her presence in Naples, and had come to call on her.

She sat there without motion, with her head eagerly bent forward, and her eyes fixed upon him. He looked up carelessly as he came along, and with his chin in the air, in a fashion peculiar to him, which, by-the-way, gave a quite unintentional superciliousness to his expression. For an instant his eyes rested upon her, then they moved away, without the slightest recognition, and wandered elsewhere.

Ethel's heart seemed turned to stone. He had seen her. He had not noticed her. He had fixed his eyes on her and then looked away. Bitter, indeed, was all this to her. To think that after so long a period of waiting—after such hope and watching as hers had been—that this should be the end. She turned away from the window, with a choking sensation in her throat. No one was in the room. She was alone with her thoughts and her tears.

Suddenly her mood changed. A thought came to her which dispelled her gloom. The glance that he had given was too hasty; perhaps he really had not fairly looked at her. No doubt he had come for her, and she would shortly be summoned down.

And now this prospect brought new hope. Light returned to her eyes, and joy to her heart. Yes, she would be summoned. She must prepare herself to encounter his eager gaze. Quickly she stepped to the mirror, hastily she arranged those little details in which consists the charm of a lady's dress, and severely she scrutinized the face and figure reflected there. The scrutiny was a satisfactory one. Face and figure were perfect; nor was there in the world any thing more graceful and more lovely than the image there, though the one who looked upon it was far too self-distrustful to entertain any such idea as that.

Then she seated herself and waited. The time moved slowly, indeed, as she waited there. After a few minutes she found it impossible to sit any longer. She walked to the door, held it open, and listened. She heard his voice below quite plainly. They had two suits of rooms in the house—the bedrooms up stairs and reception-rooms below. Here Lord Hawbury was, now, within hearing of Ethel. Well she knew that voice. She listened and frowned. The tone was too flippant. He talked like a man without a care—like a butterfly of society—and that was a class which she scorned. Here he was, keeping her waiting. Here he was, keeping up a hateful clatter of small-talk, while her heart was aching with suspense.

Ethel stood there listening. Minute succeeded to minute. There was no request for her. How strong was the contrast between the cool indifference of the man below, and the feverish impatience of that listener above! A wild impulse came to her to go down, under the pretense of looking for something; then another to go down and out for a walk, so that he might see her. But in either case pride held her back. How could she? Had he not already seen her? Must he not know perfectly well that she was there? No; if he did not call for her she could not go. She could not make advances.

Minute succeeded to minute, and Ethel stood burning with impatience, racked with suspense, a prey to the bitterest feelings. Still no message. Why did he delay? Her heart ached now worse than ever, the choking feeling in her throat returned, and her eyes grew moist. She steadied herself by holding to the door. Her fingers grew white at the tightness of her grasp; eyes and ears were strained in their intent watchfulness over the room below.

Of course the caller below was in a perfect state of ignorance about all this. He had not the remotest idea of that one who now stood so near. He came as a martyr. He came to make a call. It was a thing he detested. It bored him. To a man like him the one thing to be avoided on earth was a bore. To be bored was to his mind the uttermost depth of misfortune. This he had voluntarily accepted. He was being bored, and bored to death.

Certainly no man ever accepted a calamity more gracefully than Hawbury. He was charming, affable, easy, chatty. Of course he was known to Lady Dalrymple. The Dowager could make herself as agreeable as any lady living, except young and beautiful ones. The conversation, therefore, was easy and flowing. Hawbury excelled in this.

Now there are several variations in the great art of expression, and each of these is a minor art by itself. Among these may be enumerated:

First, of course, the art of novel-writing.

Second, the art of writing editorials.

Third, the art of writing paragraphs.

After these come all the arts of oratory, letter-writing, essay-writing, and all that sort of thing, among which there is one to which I wish particularly to call attention, and this is:

The art of small-talk.

Now this art Hawbury had to an extraordinary degree of perfection. He knew how to beat out the faintest shred of an idea into an illimitable surface of small-talk. He never took refuge in the weather. He left that to bunglers and beginners. His resources were of a different character, and were so skillfully managed that he never failed to leave a very agreeable impression. Small-talk! Why, I've been in situations sometimes where I would have given the power of writing like Dickens (if I had it) for perfection in this last art.

But this careless, easy, limpid, smooth, natural, pleasant, and agreeable flow of chat was nothing but gall and wormwood to the listener above. She ought to be there. Why was she so slighted? Could it be possible that he would go away without seeing her?

She was soon to know.

She heard him rise. She heard him saunter to the door.

"Thanks, yes. Ha, ha, you're too kind—really—yes—very happy, you know. To-morrow, is it? Good-morning."

And with these words he went out.

With pale face and staring eyes Ethel darted back to the window. He did not see her. His back was turned. He mounted his horse and gayly cantered away. For full five minutes Ethel stood, crouched in the shadow of the window, staring after him, with her dark eyes burning and glowing in the intensity of their gaze. Then she turned away with a bewildered look. Then she locked the door. Then she flung herself upon the sofa, buried her head in her hands, and burst into a convulsive passion of tears. Miserable, indeed, were the thoughts that came now to that poor stricken girl as she lay there prostrate. She had waited long, and hoped fondly, and all her waiting and all her hope had been for this. It was for this that she had been praying—for this that she had so fondly cherished his memory. He had come at last, and he had gone;

but for her he had certainly shown nothing save an indifference as profound as it was inexplicable.

Ethel's excuse for not appearing at the dinner-table was a severe headache. Her friends insisted on seeing her and ministering to her sufferings. Among other things, they tried to cheer her by telling her of Hawbury. Lady Dalrymple was full of him. She told all about his family, his income, his habits, and his mode of life. She mentioned, with much satisfaction, that he had made inquiries after Minnie, and that she had promised to introduce him to her the next time he called. Upon which he had laughingly insisted on calling the next day. All of which led Lady Dalrymple to conclude that he had seen Minnie somewhere, and had fallen in love with her.

This was the pleasing strain of conversation into which the ladies were led off by Lady Dalrymple. When I say the ladies, I mean Lady Dalrymple and Minnie. Mrs. Willoughby said nothing, except once or twice when she endeavored to give a turn to the conversation, in which she was signally unsuccessful. Lady Dalrymple and Minnie engaged in an animated argument over the interesting subject of Hawbury's intentions, Minnie taking her stand on the ground of his indifference, the other maintaining the position that he was in love. Minnie declared that she had never seen him. Lady Dalrymple asserted her belief that he had seen her. The latter also asserted that Hawbury would no doubt be a constant visitor, and gave Minnie very sound advice as to the best mode of treating him.

"THEN SHE FLUNG HERSELF UPON THE SOFA."

On the following day Hawbury called, and was introduced to Minnie. He chatted with her in his usual style, and Lady Dalrymple was more than ever confirmed in her first belief. He suggested a ride, and the suggestion was taken up.

If any thing had been needed to complete Ethel's despair it was this second visit and the project of a ride. Mrs. Willoughby was introduced to him; but he took little notice of her, treating her with a kind of reserve that was a little unusual with him. The reason of this was his strong sympathy with his friend, and his detestation of Mrs. Willoughby's former history. Mrs. Willoughby, however, had to ride with them when they went out, and thus she was thrown a little more into Hawbury's way.

Ethel never made her appearance. The headaches which she avouched were not pretended. They were real, and accompanied with heartaches that were far more painful. Hawbury never saw her, nor did he ever hear her mentioned. In general he himself kept the conversation in motion; and as he never asked questions, they, of course, had no opportunity to answer. On the other hand, there was no occasion to volunteer any remarks about the number or the character of their party. When he talked it was usually with Lady Dalrymple and Minnie: and with these the conversation turned always upon glittering generalities, and the airy nothings of pleasant gossip. All this, then, will very easily account for the fact that Hawbury, though visiting there constantly, never once saw Ethel, never heard her name mentioned, and had not the faintest idea that she was so near. She, on the other hand, feeling now sure that he was utterly false and completely forgetful, proudly and calmly held aloof, and kept out of his way with the most jealous care, until at last she staid indoors altogether, for fear, if she went out, that she might meet him somewhere. For such a meeting she did not feel sufficiently strong.

Often she thought of quitting Naples and returning to England. Yet, after all, she found a strange comfort in being there. She was near him. She heard his voice every day, and saw his face. That was something. And it was better than absence.

Minnie used always to come to her and pour forth long accounts of Lord Hawbury—how he looked, what he said, what he did, and what he proposed to do. Certainly there was not the faintest approach to love-making, or even sentiment, in Hawbury's attitude toward Minnie. His words were of the world of small-talk—a world where sentiment and love-making have but little place. Still there was the evident fact of his attentions, which were too frequent to be overlooked.

Hawbury rapidly became the most prominent subject of Minnie's conversation. She used to prattle away for hours about him. She alluded admiringly to his long whiskers. She thought them "lovely." She said that he was "awfully nice." She told Mrs. Willoughby that "he was nicer than any of them; and then, Kitty darling," she added, "it's so awfully good of him not to be coming and saving my life, and carrying me on his back down a mountain, like an ogre, and then pretending that he's my father, you know.

"For you know, Kitty pet, I've always longed so awfully to see some really nice person, you know, who wouldn't go and save my life and bother me. Now he doesn't seem a bit like proposing. I do *hope* he won't. Don't you, Kitty dearest? It's so *much* nicer not to propose. It's so horrid when they go and propose. And then, you know, I've had so much of that sort of thing. So, Kitty, I think he's really the nicest person that I ever saw, and I really think I'm beginning to like him."

Far different from these were the conversations which Mrs. Willoughby had with Ethel. She was perfectly familiar with Ethel's story. It had been confided to her long ago. She alone knew why it was that Ethel had walked untouched through crowds of admirers. The terrible story of her rescue was memorable to her for other reasons; and the one who had taken the prominent part in that rescue could not be without interest for her.

"There is no use, Kitty—no use in talking about it any more," said Ethel one day, after Mrs. Willoughby had been urging her to show herself. "I can not. I will not. He has forgotten me utterly."

"Perhaps he has no idea that you are here. He has never seen you."

"Has he not been in Naples as long as we have? He must have seen me in the streets. He saw Minnie."

"Do you think it likely that he would come to this house and slight you? If he had forgotten you he would not come here."

"Oh yes, he would. He comes to see Minnie. He knows I am here, of course. He doesn't care one atom whether I make my appearance or not. He doesn't even give me a thought. It's so long since *that time* that he has forgotten even my existence. He has been all over the world since then, and has had a hundred adventures. I have been living quietly, cherishing the remembrance of that one thing."

"Ethel, is it not worth trying? Go down and try him."

"I can not bear it. I can not look at him. I lose all self-command when he is near. I should make a fool of myself. He would look at me with a smile of pity. Could I endure that? No, Kitty; my weakness must never be known to him."

"Oh, Ethel, how I wish you could try it!"

"Kitty, just think how utterly I am forgotten. Mark this now. He knows I was at *your* house. He must remember your name. He wrote to me there, and I answered him from there. He sees you now, and your name must be associated with mine in his memory of me, if he has any. Tell me now, Kitty, has he ever mentioned me? has he ever asked you about me? has he ever made the remotest allusion to me?"

Ethel spoke rapidly and impetuously, and as she spoke she raised herself from the sofa where she was reclining, and turned her large, earnest eyes full upon her friend with anxious and eager watchfulness. Mrs. Willoughby looked back at her with a face full of sadness, and mournfully shook her head.

"You see," said Ethel, as she sank down again—"you see how true my impression is."

"I must say," said Mrs. Willoughby, "that I thought of this before. I fully expected that he would make some inquiry after you. I was so confident in the noble character of the man, both from your story and the description of others, that I could not believe you were right. But you are right, my poor Ethel. I wish I could comfort you, but I can not. Indeed, my dear, not only has he not questioned me about you, but he evidently avoids me. It is not that he is engrossed with Minnie, for he is not so; but he certainly has some reason of his own for avoiding me. Whenever he speaks to me there is an evident effort on his part, and though perfectly courteous, his manner leaves a certain disagreeable impression. Yes, he certainly has some reason for avoiding me."

"The reason is plain enough," murmured Ethel. "He wishes to prevent you from speaking about a painful subject, or at least a distasteful one. He keeps you off at a distance by an excess of formality. He will give you no opportunity whatever to introduce any mention of me. And now let me also ask you this—does he ever take any notice of any allusion that may be made to me?"

"I really don't remember hearing any allusion to you."

"Oh, that's scarcely possible! You and Minnie must sometimes have alluded to 'Ethel.'"

"Well, now that you put it in that light, I do remember hearing Minnie allude to you on several occasions. Once she wondered why 'Ethel' did not ride. Again she remarked how 'Ethel' would enjoy a particular view."

"And he heard it?"

"Oh, of course."

"Then there is not a shadow of a doubt left. He knows I am here. He has forgotten me so totally, and is so completely indifferent, that he comes here and pays attention to another who is in the very same house with me. It is hard. Oh, Kitty, is it not? Is it not bitter? How could I have thought this of *him*?"

A high-hearted girl was Ethel, and a proud one; but at this final confirmation of her worst fears there burst from her a sharp cry, and she buried her face in her hands, and moaned and wept.

CHAPTER XII.

GIRASOLE AGAIN.

ONE day Mrs. Willoughby and Minnie were out driving. Hawbury was riding by the carriage on the side next Minnie, when suddenly their attention was arrested by a gentleman on horseback who was approaching them at an easy pace, and staring hard at them. Minnie's hand suddenly grasped her sister's arm very tightly, while her color came and went rapidly.

"Oh dear!" sighed Mrs. Willoughby.

"Oh, what *shall* I do?" said Minnie, in a hasty whisper. "Can't we pretend not to see him?"

"Nonsense, you little goose," was the reply. "How can you think of such rudeness?"

By this time the gentleman had reached them, and Mrs. Willoughby stopped the carriage, and spoke to him in a tone of gracious suavity, in which there was a sufficient recognition of his claims upon her attention, mingled with a slight hauteur that was intended to act as a check upon his Italian demonstrativeness.

For it was no other than the Count Girasole, and his eyes glowed with excitement and delight, and his hat was off and as far away from his head as possible, and a thousand emotions contended together for expression upon his swarthy and handsome countenance. As soon as he could speak he poured forth a torrent of exclamations with amazing volubility, in the midst of which his keen black eyes scrutinized very closely the faces of the ladies, and finally turned an interrogative glance upon Hawbury, who sat on his horse regarding the new-comer with a certain mild surprise not unmingled with superciliousness. Hawbury's chin was in the air, his eyes rested languidly upon the stranger, and his left hand toyed with his left whisker. He really meant no offense whatever. He knew absolutely nothing about the stranger, and had not the slightest intention of giving offense. It was simply a way he had. It was merely the normal attitude of the English swell before he is introduced. As it was, that first glance which Girasole threw at the English lord inspired him with the bitterest hate, which was destined to produce important results afterward.

Mrs. Willoughby was too good-natured and too wise to slight the Count in any way. After introducing the two gentlemen she spoke a few more civil words, and then bowed him away. But Girasole did not at all take the hint. On the contrary, as the carriage started, he turned his horse and rode along with it on the side next Mrs. Willoughby. Hawbury elevated his eyebrows, and stared for an instant, and then went on talking with Minnie. And now

Minnie showed much more animation than usual. She was much agitated and excited by this sudden appearance of one whom she hoped to have got rid of, and talked rapidly, and laughed nervously, and was so terrified at the idea that Girasole was near that she was afraid to look at him, but directed all her attention to Hawbury. It was a slight, and Girasole showed that he felt it; but Minnie could not help it. After a time Girasole mastered his feelings, and began an animated conversation with Mrs. Willoughby in very broken English. Girasole's excitement at Minnie's slight made him somewhat incoherent, his idioms were Italian rather than English, and his pronunciation was very bad; he also had a fashion of using an Italian word when he did not know the right English one, and so the consequence was that Mrs. Willoughby understood not much more than one-quarter of his remarks.

Mrs. Willoughby did not altogether enjoy this state of things, and so she determined to put an end to it by shortening her drive. She therefore watched for an opportunity to do this so as not to make it seem too marked, and finally reached a place which was suitable. Here the carriage was turned, when, just as it was half-way round, they noticed a horseman approaching. It was Scone Dacres, who had been following them all the time, and who had not expected that the carriage would turn. He was therefore taken completely by surprise, and was close to them before he could collect his thoughts so as to do any thing. To evade them was impossible, and so he rode on. As he approached, the ladies saw his face. It was a face that one would remember afterward. There was on it a profound sadness and dejection, while at the same time the prevailing expression was one of sternness. The ladies both bowed. Scone Dacres raised his hat, and disclosed his broad, massive brow. He did not look at Minnie. His gaze was fixed on Mrs. Willoughby. Her veil was down, and he seemed trying to read her face behind it. As he passed he threw a quick, vivid glance at Girasole. It was not a pleasant glance by any means, and was full of quick, fierce, and insolent scrutiny—a "Who-the-devil-are-you?" glance. It was for but an instant, however, and then he glanced at Mrs. Willoughby again, and then he had passed.

The ladies soon reached their home, and at once retired to Mrs. Willoughby's room. There Minnie flung herself upon the sofa, and Mrs. Willoughby sat down, with a perplexed face.

"What in the world *are* we to do?" said she.

"I'm sure *I* don't know," said Minnie. "I *knew* it was going to be so. I said that he would find me again."

"He is *so* annoying."

"Yes, but, Kitty dear, we can't be rude to him, you know, for he saved my life. But it's horrid, and I really begin to feel quite desperate."

"I certainly will not let him see you. I have made up my mind to that."

"And oh! how he *will* be coming and calling, and tease, tease, teasing. Oh dear! I do wonder what Lord Hawbury thought. He looked *so* amazed. And then—oh, Kitty dear, it was so awfully funny!—did you notice that other man?"

Mrs. Willoughby nodded her head.

"Did you notice how awfully black he looked? He wouldn't look at me at all. *I* know why."

Mrs. Willoughby said nothing.

"He's awfully jealous. Oh, *I* know it. I saw it in his face. He was as black as a thunder-cloud. Oh dear! And it's all about me. Oh, Kitty darling, what *shall* I do? There will be something dreadful, I know. And how shocking to have it about me. And then the newspapers. They'll all have it. And the reporters. Oh dear! Kitty, why *don't* you say something?"

"Why, Minnie dearest, I really don't know what to say."

"But, darling, you must say something. And then that Scone Dacres. I'm more afraid of him than any body. Oh, I know he's going to *kill* some one. He is so big. Oh, if *you* had only been on his back, Kitty darling, and had him run down a steep mountain-side, you'd be as awfully afraid of him as I am. Oh, how I *wish* Lord Hawbury would drive them off, or somebody do something to save me."

"Would you rather that Lord Hawbury would stay, or would you like him to go too?"

"Oh dear! I don't care. If he would only go quietly and nicely, I should like to have him go too, and never, never see a man again except dear papa. And I think it's a shame. And I don't see why I should be so persecuted. And I'm tired of staying here. And I don't want to stay here any more. And, Kitty darling, why shouldn't we all go to Rome?"

"To Rome?"

"Yes."

"Would you prefer Rome?" asked Mrs. Willoughby, thoughtfully.

"Well, yes—for several reasons. In the first place, I must go somewhere, and I'd rather go there than any where else. Then, you know, that dear, delightful holy-week will soon be here, and I'm dying to be in Rome."

"I think it would be better for all of us," said Mrs. Willoughby, thoughtfully—"for all of us, if we were in Rome."

"Of course it would, Kitty sweetest, and especially me. Now if I am in Rome, I can pop into a convent whenever I choose."

"A convent!" exclaimed Mrs. Willoughby, in surprise.

"Oh yes—it's going to come to that. They're all so horrid, you know. Besides, it's getting worse. I got a letter yesterday from Captain Kirby, written to me in England. He didn't know I was here. He has just arrived at London, and was leaving for our place on what he called the wings of the wind. I expect him here at almost any time. Isn't it dreadful, Kitty dearest, to have so many? As fast as one goes another comes, and then they all come together; and do you know, darling, it really makes one feel quite dizzy. I'm sure *I* don't know what to do. And that's why I'm thinking of a convent, you know."

"But you're not a Catholic."

"Oh yes, I am, you know. Papa's an Anglo-Catholic, and I don't see the difference. Besides, they're all the time going over to Rome; and why shouldn't I? I'll be a novice—that is, you know, I'll only go for a time, and not take the vows. The more I think of it, the more I see that it's the only thing there is for me to do."

"Well, Minnie, I really think so too, and not only for you, but for all of us. There's Ethel, too; poor dear girl, her health is very miserable, you know. I think a change would do her good."

"Of course it would; I've been talking to her about it. But she won't hear of leaving Naples. I *wish* she wouldn't be so awfully sad."

"Oh yes; it will certainly be the best thing for dear Ethel, and for you and me and all of us. Then we must be in Rome in holy-week. I wouldn't miss that for any thing."

"And then, too, you know, Kitty darling, there's another thing," said Minnie, very confidentially, "and it's very important. In Rome, you know, all the gentlemen are clergymen—only, you know, the clergymen of the Roman Church can't marry; and so, you know, of course, they can never propose, no matter if they were to save one's life over and over again. And oh! what a relief that would be to find one's self among those dear, darling, delightful priests, and no chance of having one's life saved and having an instant proposal following! It would be *so* charming."

Mrs. Willoughby smiled.

"Well, Minnie dearest," said she, "I really think that we had better decide to go to Rome, and I don't see any difficulty in the way."

"The only difficulty that I can see," said Minnie, "is that I shouldn't like to hurt their feelings, you know."

"Their feelings!" repeated her sister, in a doleful voice.

"Yes; but then, you see, some one's feelings *must* be hurt eventually, so that lessens one's responsibility, you know; doesn't it, Kitty darling?"

While saying this Minnie had risen and gone to the window, with the intention of taking her seat by it. No sooner had she reached the place, however, than she started back, with a low exclamation, and, standing on one side, looked cautiously forth.

"Come here," she said, in a whisper.

Mrs. Willoughby went over, and Minnie directed her attention to some one outside. It was a gentleman on horseback, who was passing at a slow pace. His head was bent on his breast. Suddenly, as he passed, he raised his head and threw over the house a quick, searching glance. They could see without being seen. They marked the profound sadness that was over his face, and saw the deep disappointment with which his head fell.

"Scone Dacres!" said Minnie, as he passed on. "How *aw*fully sad he is!"

Mrs. Willoughby said nothing.

"But, after all, I don't believe it's *me*."

"Why not?"

"Because he didn't look at me a bit when he passed to-day. He looked at you, though."

"Nonsense!"

"Yes, and his face had an *aw*fully hungry look. I know what makes him sad."

"What?"

"He's in love with you."

Mrs. Willoughby stared at Minnie for a moment. Then a short laugh burst from her.

"Child!" she exclaimed, "you have no idea of any thing in the world but falling in love. You will find out some day that there are other feelings than that."

"But, Kitty dear," said Minnie, "didn't you notice something very peculiar about him?"

"What?"

"I noticed it. I had a good look at him. I saw that he fixed his eyes on you with—oh! *such* a queer look. And he was awfully sad too. He looked as if he would like to seize you and lift you on his horse and carry you off, just like young Lochinvar."

"Me!" said Mrs. Willoughby, with a strange intonation.

"Yes, you—oh yes; really now."

"Oh, you little goose, you always think of people rushing after one and carrying one off."

"Well, I'm sure I've had reason to. So many people have always been running after me, and snatching me up as if I were a parcel, and carrying me every where in all sorts of places. And I think it's too bad, and I really wish they'd stop it. But, Kitty dear—"

"What?"

"About this Scone Dacres. Don't you really think there's something very peculiarly sad, and very delightfully interesting and pathetic, and all that sort of thing, in his poor dear old face?"

"I think Scone Dacres has suffered a great deal," said Mrs. Willoughby, in a thoughtful tone. "But come now. Let us go to Ethel. She's lonely."

Soon after they joined the other ladies, and talked over the project of going to Rome. Lady Dalrymple offered no objection; indeed, so far as she had any choice, she preferred it. She was quite willing at all times to do whatever the rest proposed, and also was not without some curiosity as to the proceedings during holy-week. Ethel offered no objections either. She had fallen into a state of profound melancholy, from which nothing now could rouse her, and so she listened listlessly to the discussion about the subject. Mrs. Willoughby and Minnie had the most to say on this point, and offered the chief reasons for going; and thus it was finally decided to take their departure, and to start as soon as possible.

Meanwhile Girasole had his own thoughts and experiences. He had already, some time before, been conscious that his attentions were not wanted, but it was only on the part of the other ladies that he noticed any repugnance to himself. On Minnie's part he had not seen any. In spite of their graciousness and their desire not to hurt his feelings, they had not been able to avoid showing that, while they felt grateful for his heroism in the rescue of Minnie, they could not think of giving her to him. They had manœuvred well enough to get rid of him, but Girasole had also manœuvred on his part to find them again. He had fallen off from them at first when he saw that they were determined on effecting this; but after allowing a sufficient time to elapse, he had no difficulty in tracking them, and finding them at Naples, as we have seen.

But here he made one or two discoveries.

One was that Minnie already had an accepted lover in the person of Lord Hawbury. The lofty superciliousness of the British nobleman seemed to Girasole to be the natural result of his position, and it seemed the attitude of the successful lover toward the rejected suitor.

The other discovery was that Minnie herself was more pleased with the attentions of the English lord than with his own. This was now evident, and he could not help perceiving that his difficulties were far more formidable from the presence of such a rival.

But Girasole was not easily daunted. In the first place, he had unbounded confidence in his own fascinations; in the second place, he believed that he had a claim on Minnie that no other could equal, in the fact that he had saved her life; in the third place, apart from the question of love, he believed her to be a prize of no common value, whose English gold would be welcome indeed to his Italian need and greed; while, finally, the bitter hate with which Lord Hawbury had inspired him gave an additional zest to the pursuit, and made him follow after Minnie with fresh ardor.

Once or twice after this he called upon them. On the first occasion only Lady Dalrymple was visible. On the second, none of the ladies were at home. He was baffled, but not discouraged. Returning from his call, he met Minnie and Mrs. Willoughby. Hawbury was with them, riding beside Minnie. The ladies bowed, and Girasole, as before, coolly turned his horse and rode by the carriage, talking with Mrs. Willoughby, and trying to throw at Minnie what he intended to be impassioned glances. But Minnie would not look at him. Of course she was frightened as usual, and grew excited, and, as before, talked with unusual animation to Hawbury. Thus she overdid it altogether, and more than ever confirmed Girasole in the opinion that she and Hawbury were affianced.

Two days after this Girasole called again.

A bitter disappointment was in store for him.

They were not there—they had gone.

Eagerly he inquired where.

"To Rome," was the reply.

"To Rome!" he muttered, between his set teeth; and mounting his horse hurriedly, he rode away.

He was not one to be daunted. He had set a certain task before himself, and could not easily be turned aside. He thought bitterly of the ingratitude with which he had been treated. He brought before his mind the "stony British stare," the supercilious smile, and the impertinent and insulting expression of Hawbury's face as he sat on his saddle, with his chin up, stroking his whiskers, and surveyed him for the first time. All these things combined to stimulate the hate as well as the love of Girasole. He felt that he himself was not one who could be lightly dismissed, and determined that they should learn this.

"'TO ROME!' HE MUTTERED, BETWEEN HIS SET TEETH."

CHAPTER XIII.

VAIN REMONSTRANCES.

HAWBURY had immolated himself for as much as half a dozen times to gratify Dacres. He had sacrificed himself over and over upon the altar of friendship, and had allowed himself to be bored to death because Dacres so wished it. The whole number of his calls was in reality only about five or six; but that number, to one of his taste and temperament, seemed positively enormous, and represented an immense amount of human suffering.

One day, upon reaching his quarters, after one of these calls, he found Dacres there, making himself, as usual, very much at home.

"Well, my dear fellow," said Hawbury, cheerfully, "how waves the flag now? Are you hauling it down, or are you standing to your guns? Toss over the cigars, and give an account of yourself."

"Do you know any thing about law, Hawbury?" was Dacres's answer.

"Law?"

"Yes."

"No, not much. But what in the world makes you ask such a question as that? Law! No—not I."

"Well, there's a point that I should like to ask somebody about."

"Why not get a lawyer?"

"An Italian lawyer's no use."

"Well, English lawyers are to be found. I dare say there are twenty within five minutes' distance of this place."

"Oh, I don't want to bother. I only wanted to ask some one's opinion in a general way."

"Well, what's the point?"

"Why this," said Dacres, after a little hesitation. "You've heard of outlawry?"

"Should think I had—Robin Hood and his merry men, Lincoln green, Sherwood Forest, and all that sort of thing, you know. But what the mischief sets you thinking about Robin Hood?"

"Oh, I don't mean that rot. I mean real outlawry—when a fellow's in debt, you know."

"Well?"

"Well; if he goes out of the country, and stays away a certain number of years, the debt's outlawed, you know."

"The deuce it is! Is it, though? *I've* been in debt, but I always managed to pull through without getting so far. But that's convenient for some fellows too."

"I'm a little muddy about it, but I've heard something to this effect. I think the time is seven years. If the debt is not acknowledged during the interval, it's outlawed. And now, 'pon my life, my dear fellow, I really don't know but that I've jumbled up some fragments of English law with American. I felt that I was muddy, and so I thought I'd ask you."

"Don't know any more about it than about the antediluvians."

"It's an important point, and I should like to have it looked up."

"Well, get a lawyer here; half London is on the Continent. But still, my dear fellow, I don't see what you're driving at. You're not in debt?"

"No—this isn't debt; but it struck me that this might possibly apply to other kinds of contracts."

"Oh!"

"Yes."

"How—such as what, for instance?"

"Well, you see, I thought, you know, that all contracts might be included under it; and so I thought that if seven years or so annulled all contracts, it might have some effect, you know, upon—the—the—the marriage contract, you know."

At this Hawbury started up, stared at Dacres, gave a loud whistle, and then exclaimed,

"By Jove!"

"I may be mistaken," said Dacres, modestly.

"Mistaken? Why, old chap, you're mad. Marriage? Good Lord! don't you know nothing can abrogate that? Of course, in case of crime, one can get a divorce; but there is no other way. Seven years? By Jove! A good idea that. Why, man, if that were so, the kingdom would be depopulated. Husbands running off from wives, and wives from husbands, to pass the required seven years abroad. By Jove! You see, too, there's another thing, my boy. Marriage is a sacrament, and you've not only got to untie the civil knot, but the clerical one, my boy. No, no; there's no help for it. You gave your word, old chap, 'till death do us part,' and you're in for it."

At this Dacres said nothing; it appeared to dispel his project from his mind. He relapsed into a sullen sort of gloom, and remained so for some time. At last he spoke:

"Hawbury!"

"Well?"

"Have you found out who that fellow is?"

"What fellow?"

"Why that yellow Italian that goes prowling around after my wife."

"Oh yes; I heard something or other today."

"What was it?"

"Well, it seems that he saved her life, or something of that sort."

"Saved her life!" Dacres started. "How? where? Cool, too!"

"Oh, on the Alps somewhere."

"On the Alps! saved her life! Come now, I like that," said Dacres, with bitter intonation. "Aha! don't I know her? I warrant you she contrived all that. Oh, she's deep! But how did it happen? Did you hear?"

"Well, I didn't hear any thing very definite. It was something about a precipice. It was Lady Dalrymple that told me. It seems she was knocked over a precipice by an avalanche."

"Was what? Knocked where? Over a precipice? By a what—an avalanche? Good Lord! I don't believe it. I swear I don't. She invented it all. It's some of her infernal humbug. She slid off over the snow, so as to get him to go after her. Oh, don't I know her and her ways!"

"Well, come now, old man, you shouldn't be too hard on her. You never said that flirtation was one of her faults."

"Well, neither it was; but, as she is a demon, she's capable of any thing; and now she has sobered down, and all her vices have taken this turn. Oh yes. I know her. No more storms now—no rage, no fury—all quiet and sly. Flirtation! Ha, ha! That's the word. And my wife! And going about the country, tumbling over precipices, with devilish handsome Italians going down to save her life! Ha, ha, ha! I like that!"

"See here, old boy, I swear you're too suspicious. Come now. You're going too far. If she chooses, she may trump up the same charge against you and the child-angel at Vesuvius. Come now, old boy, be just. You can afford to.

Your wife may be a fiend in human form; and if you insist upon it, I've nothing to say. But this last notion of yours is nothing but the most wretched absurdity. It's worse. It's lunacy."

"Well, well," said Dacres, in a milder tone; "perhaps she didn't contrive it. But then, you know," he added, "it's just as good for her. She gets the Italian. Ha, ha, ha!"

His laugh was forced, feverish, and unnatural. Hawbury didn't like it, and tried to change the subject.

"Oh, by-the-way," said he, "you needn't have any further trouble about any of them. You don't seem inclined to take any definite action, so the action will be taken for you."

"What do you mean?"

"I mean that they are all going to leave Naples."

"To leave Naples!"

Dacres uttered this in a voice of grief and surprise which astonished Hawbury and touched him.

"Yes," he said. "You know they've been here long enough. They want to see Rome. Holy-week, you know. No end of excitement. Illumination of St. Peter's, and all that sort of thing, you know."

Dacres relapsed into sombre silence. For more than half an hour he did not say a word. Hawbury respected his mood, and watched him with something approaching to anxiety.

"Hawbury," said he at last.

"Well, old man?"

"I'm going to Rome."

"You—to Rome!"

"Yes, me, to Rome."

"Oh, nonsense! See here, old boy. You'd really better not, you know. Break it up. You can't do any thing."

"I'm going to Rome," repeated Dacres, stolidly. "I've made up my mind."

"But, really," remonstrated Hawbury. "See here now, my dear fellow; look here, you know. By Jove! you don't consider, really."

"Oh yes, I do. I know every thing; I consider every thing."

"But what good will it do?"

"It won't do any good; but it may prevent some evil."

"Nothing but evil can ever come of it."

"Oh, no evil need necessarily come of it."

"By Jove!" exclaimed Hawbury, who began to be excited. "Really, my dear fellow, you don't think. You see you can't gain any thing. She's surrounded by friends, you know. She never can be yours, you know. There's a great gulf between you, and all that sort of thing, you know."

"Yes," repeated Dacres, catching his last words—"yes, a great gulf, as deep as the bottomless abyss, never to be traversed, where she stands on one side, and I on the other, and between us hate, deep and pitiless hate, undying, eternal!"

"Then, by Jove! my dear fellow, what's the use of trying to fight against it? You can't do any thing. If this were Indiana, now, or even New York, I wouldn't say any thing, you know; but you know an Indiana divorce wouldn't do *you* any good. Her friends wouldn't take you on those terms—and she wouldn't. Not she, by Jove!"

"I *must* go. I must follow her," continued Dacres. "The sight of her has roused a devil within me that I thought was laid. I'm a changed man, Hawbury."

"I should think so, by Jove!"

"A changed man," continued Dacres. "Oh, Heavens, what power there is in a face! What terrific influence it has over a man! Here am I; a few days ago I was a free man; now I am a slave. But, by Heaven! I'll follow her to the world's end. She shall not shake me off. She thinks to be happy without me. She shall not. I will silently follow as an avenging fate. I can not have her, and no one else shall. The same cursed fate that severs her from me shall keep her away from others. If I am lonely and an exile, she shall not be as happy as she expects. I shall not be the only one to suffer."

"See here, by Jove!" cried Hawbury. "Really. You're going too far, my dear boy, you know. You are, really. Come now. This is just like a Surrey theatre, you know. You're really raving. Why, my poor old boy, you *must* give her up. You can't do any thing. You daren't call on her. You're tied hand and foot. You may worship her here, and rave about your child-angel till you're black in the face, but you never can see her; and as to all this about stopping her from marrying any other person, that's all rot and bosh. What do you suppose any other man would care for your nonsensical ravings? Lonely and an exile! Why, man, she'll be married and done for in three months."

"You don't understand me," said Dacres, dryly.

"I'm glad that I don't; but it's no wonder, old man, for really you were quite incoherent."

"And so they're going to Rome," said Dacres. "Well, they'll find that I'm not to be shaken off so easily."

"Come now, old man, you *must* give up that."

"And I suppose," continued Dacres, with a sneer, "our handsome, dark-eyed little Italian cavalier is going with us. Ha, ha, ha! He's at the house all the time, no doubt."

"Well, yes; he was there once."

"Ah! of course—quite devoted."

"Oh yes; but don't be afraid. It was not to the child-angel. She appears to avoid him. That's really quite evident. It's an apparent aversion on her part."

Dacres drew a long breath.

"Oh," said he; "and so I suppose it's not *her* that *he* goes after. I did not suppose that it was. Oh no. There's another one—more piquant, you know—ha, ha!—a devoted lover—saved her life—quite devoted—and she sits and accepts his attentions. Yet she's seen me, and knows that I'm watching her. Don't she know *me*? Does she want any further proof of what I am ready to do? The ruins of Dacres Grange should serve her for life. She tempts fate when she carries on her gallantries and her Italian cicisbeism under the eyes of Scone Dacres. It'll end bad. By Heaven, it will!"

Scone Dacres breathed hard, and, raising his head, turned upon Hawbury a pair of eyes whose glow seemed of fire.

"Bad!" he repeated, crashing his fist on the table. "Bad, by Heaven!"

Hawbury looked at him earnestly.

"My dear boy," said he, "you're getting too excited. Be cool. Really, I don't believe you know what you're saying. I don't understand what you mean. Haven't the faintest idea what you're driving at. You're making ferocious threats against some people, but, for my life, I don't know who they are. Hadn't you better try to speak so that a fellow can understand the general drift, at least, of what you say?"

"Well, then, you understand this much—I'm going to Rome."

"I'm sorry for it, old boy."

"And see here, Hawbury, I want you to come with me."

"Me? What for?"

"Well, I want you. I may have need of you."

As Dacres said this his face assumed so dark and gloomy an expression that Hawbury began to think that there was something serious in all this menace.

"'Pon my life," said he, "my dear boy, I really don't think you're in a fit state to be allowed to go by yourself. You look quite desperate. I wish I could make you give up this infernal Roman notion."

"I'm going to Rome!" repeated Dacres, resolutely.

Hawbury looked at him.

"You'll come, Hawbury, won't you?"

"Why, confound it all, of course. I'm afraid you'll do something rash, old man, and you'll have to have me to stand between you and harm."

"Oh, don't be concerned about me," said Dacres. "I only want to watch her, and see what her little game is. I want to look at her in the midst of her happiness. She's most infernally beautiful, too; hasn't added a year or a day to her face; more lovely than ever; more beautiful than she was even when I first saw her. And there's a softness about her that she never had before. Where the deuce did she get that? Good idea of hers, too, to cultivate the soft style. And there's sadness in her face, too. Can it be real? By Heavens! if I thought it could be real I'd—but pooh! what insanity! It's her art. There never was such cunning. She cultivates the soft, sad style so as to attract lovers—lovers—who adore her—who save her life—who become her obedient slaves! Oh yes; and I—what am I? Why they get together and laugh at me; they giggle; they snicker—"

"Confound it all, man, what are you going on at that rate for?" interrupted Hawbury. "Are you taking leave of your senses altogether? By Jove, old man, you'd better give up this Roman journey."

"No, I'll keep at it."

"What for? Confound it! I don't see your object."

"My object? Why, I mean to follow her. I can't give her up. I won't give her up. I'll follow her. She shall see me every where. I'll follow her. She sha'n't go any where without seeing me on her track. She shall see that she is mine. She shall know that she's got a master. She shall find herself cut off from that butterfly life which she hopes to enter. I'll be her fate, and she shall know it."

"By Jove!" cried Hawbury. "What the deuce is all this about? Are you mad, or what? Look here, old boy, you're utterly beyond me, you know. What the mischief do you mean? Whom are you going to follow? Whose fate are you going to be? Whose track are you talking about?"

"Who?" cried Dacres. "Why, my wife!"

As he said this he struck his fist violently on the table.

"The deuce!" exclaimed Hawbury, staring at him; after which he added, thoughtfully, "by Jove!"

Not much more was said. Dacres sat in silence for a long time, breathing hard, and puffing violently at his cigar. Hawbury said nothing to interrupt his meditation. After an hour or so Dacres tramped off in silence, and Hawbury was left to meditate over the situation.

And this was the result of his meditations.

He saw that Dacres was greatly excited, and had changed completely from his old self. His state of mind seemed actually dangerous. There was an evil gleam in his eyes that looked like madness. What made it more perplexing still was the new revulsion of feeling that now was manifest. It was not so much love for the child-angel as bitter and venomous hate for his wife. The gentler feeling had given place to the sterner one. It might have been possible to attempt an argument against the indulgence of the former; but what could words avail against revenge? And now there was rising in the soul of Dacres an evident thirst for vengeance, the result of those injuries which had been carried in his heart and brooded over for years. The sight of his wife had evidently kindled all this. If she had not come across his path he might have forgotten all; but she had come, and all was revived. She had come, too, in a shape which was adapted in the highest degree to stimulate all the passion of Dacres's soul—young, beautiful, fascinating, elegant, refined, rich, honored, courted, and happy. Upon such a being as this the homeless wanderer, the outcast, looked, and his soul seemed turned to fire as he gazed. Was it any wonder?

All this Hawbury thought, and with full sympathy for his injured friend. He saw also that Dacres could not be trusted by himself. Some catastrophe would be sure to occur. He determined, therefore, to accompany his friend, so as to do what he could to avert the calamity which he dreaded.

And this was the reason why he went with Dacres to Rome.

As for Dacres, he seemed to be animated by but one motive, which he expressed over and over again:

"She stood between me and my child-angel, and so will I stand between her and her Italian!"

CHAPTER XIV.

THE ZOUAVE OFFICER.

WHATEVER trouble Ethel had experienced at Naples from her conviction that Hawbury was false was increased and, if possible, intensified by the discovery that he had followed them to Rome. His true motives for this could not possibly be known to her, so she, of course, concluded that it was his infatuation for Minnie, and his determination to win her for himself. She felt confident that he knew that she belonged to the party, but was so utterly indifferent to her that he completely ignored her, and had not sufficient interest in her to ask the commonest question about her. All this, of course, only confirmed her previous opinion, and it also deepened her melancholy. One additional effect it also had, and that was to deprive her of any pleasure that might be had from drives about Rome. She felt a morbid dread of meeting him somewhere; she did not yet feel able to encounter him; she could not trust herself; she felt sure that if she saw him she would lose all self-control, and make an exhibition of humiliating weakness. The dread of this was sufficient to detain her at home; and so she remained indoors, a prisoner, refusing her liberty, brooding over her troubles, and striving to acquire that indifference to him which she believed he had toward her. Now going about was the very thing which would have alleviated her woes, but this was the very thing that she was unwilling to do; nor could any persuasion shake her resolve.

One day Mrs. Willoughby and Minnie were out driving, and in passing through a street they encountered a crowd in front of one of the churches. Another crowd was inside, and, as something was going on, they stopped the carriage and sat looking. The Swiss Guards were there in their picturesque costume, and the cardinals in their scarlet robes and scarlet coaches, and military officers of high rank, and carriages of the Roman aristocracy filled with beautiful ladies. Something of importance was going on, the nature of which they did not know. A little knot of Englishmen stood near; and from their remarks the ladies gathered that this was the Church of the Jesuits, and that the Pope in person was going to perform high-mass, and afterward hold a reception.

Soon there arose a murmur and a bustle among the crowd, which was succeeded by a deep stillness. The Swiss Guards drove the throng to either side, and a passage-way was thus formed through the people to the church. A carriage drove up in great state. In this was seated an elderly gentleman in rich pontifical robes. He had a mild and gentle face, upon which was a sweet and winning smile. No face is more attractive than that of Pio Nono.

"Oh, look!" cried Minnie; "that must be the Pope. Oh, what a darling!"

Mrs. Willoughby, however, was looking elsewhere.

"Minnie," said she.

"What, Kitty dear?"

"Are you acquainted with any Zouave officer?"

"Zouave officer! Why, no; what put such a thing as that into your head, you old silly?"

"Because there's a Zouave officer over there in the crowd who has been staring fixedly at us ever since we came up, and trying to make signals, and it's my opinion he's signaling to you. Look at him; he's over there on the top of the steps."

"I won't look," said Minnie, pettishly. "How do I know who he is? I declare I'm afraid to look at any body. He'll be coming and saving my life."

"I'm sure this man is an old acquaintance."

"Nonsense! how can he be?"

"It may be Captain Kirby."

"How silly! Why, Captain Kirby is in the Rifles."

"Perhaps he is dressed this way just for amusement. Look at him."

"Now, Kitty, I think you're unkind. You *know* I don't want to look at him; I don't want to see him. I don't care who he is—the great, big, ugly, old horrid! And if you say any thing more, I'll go home."

Mrs. Willoughby was about to say something, but her attention and Minnie's, and that of every one else, was suddenly diverted to another quarter.

Among the crowd they had noticed a tall man, very thin, with a lean, cadaverous face, and long, lanky, rusty black hair. He wore a white neck-tie, and a suit of rusty black clothes. He also held a large umbrella in his hand, which he kept carefully up out of the way of the crowd. This figure was a conspicuous one, even in that crowd, and the ladies had noticed it at the very first.

As the Pope drove up they saw this long, slim, thin, cadaverous man, in his suit of rusty black, edging his way through the crowd, so as to get nearer, until at length he stood immediately behind the line of Swiss Guards, who were keeping the crowd back, and forming a passageway for the Pope. Meanwhile his Holiness was advancing through the crowd. He reached out his hand, and smiled and bowed and murmured a blessing over them. At last his carriage stopped. The door was opened, and several attendants prepared to receive the Pope and assist him out.

At that instant the tall, slim stranger pushed forward his sallow head, with its long, lanky, and rusty black hair, between two Swiss Guards, and tried to squeeze between them. The Swiss at first stood motionless, and the stranger had actually succeeded in getting about half-way through. He was immediately in front of his Holiness, and staring at him with all his might. His Holiness saw this very peculiar face, and was so surprised that he uttered an involuntary exclamation, and stopped short in his descent.

The stranger stopped short too, and quite involuntarily also. For the Swiss Guards, irritated by his pertinacity, and seeing the Pope's gesture, turned suddenly, and two of them grasped the stranger by his coat collar.

It was, of course, an extremely undignified attitude for the Swiss Guards, whose position is simply an ornamental one. Nothing but the most unparalleled outrage to their dignity could have moved them to this. So unusual a display of energy, however, did not last long. A few persons in citizens' clothes darted forward from among the crowd, and secured the stranger; while the Swiss, seeing who they were, resumed their erect, rigid, and ornamental attitude. The Pope found no longer any obstacle, and resumed his descent. For a moment the stranger had created a wide-spread consternation in the breasts of all the different and very numerous classes of men who composed that crowd. The arrest was the signal for a murmur of voices, among which the ladies heard those of the knot of Englishmen who stood near.

"It's some Garibaldian," said they.

And this was the general sentiment.

Several hours after this they were at home, and a caller was announced. It was the Baron Atramonte.

"Atramonte!" said Lady Dalrymple. "Who is that? We're not at home, of course. Atramonte! Some of these Italian nobles. Really, I think we have seen enough of them. Who is he, Kitty?"

"I'm sure I haven't the faintest idea. I never heard of him in my life."

"We're not at home, of course. It's a singular way, and surely can not be Roman fashion. It's not civilized fashion. But the Continental nobility are *so* odd."

In a few minutes the servant, who had been dispatched to say, "Not at home," returned with the statement that the Baron wished particularly to see Miss Fay on urgent business.

"TWO OF THEM GRASPED THE STRANGER BY HIS COAT COLLAR."

At this extraordinary message Lady Dalrymple and Mrs. Willoughby looked first at one another, and then at Minnie, in amazement.

"I'm sure *I* don't know any thing about him," said Minnie. "They *always* tease me so. Oh, do go and see who he is, and send him away—please! Oh, do, please, Dowdy dear!"

"Well, I suppose I had better see the person," said Lady Dalrymple, good-naturedly. "There must be some mistake. How is he dressed?" she asked the servant. "Is he a military gentleman? Most of them seem to belong to the army."

"Yes, my lady. Zouave dress, my lady."

At this Mrs. Willoughby and Minnie looked at one another. Lady Dalrymple went away; and as no other was present, Ethel being, as usual, in her room, Mrs. Willoughby sighed and said,

"I thought that man must know you."

"Well, I'm sure I don't know him," said Minnie. "I never knew a Zouave officer in my life."

"It may be Captain Kirby, under an assumed name and a disguise."

"Oh no, it isn't. I don't believe he would be such a perfect—monster. Oh dear! It's somebody, though. It must be. And he wants me. Oh, what *shall* I do?"

"Nonsense! You need not go. Aunty will see him, and send him off."

"Oh, I do so hope he'll go; but I'm afraid he won't."

After a short time Lady Dalrymple returned.

"Really," said she, "this is a most extraordinary person. He speaks English, but not at all like an Englishman. I don't know who he is. He calls himself a Baron, but he doesn't seem to be a foreigner. I'm puzzled."

"I hope he's gone," said Mrs. Willoughby.

"No—that's the worst of it. He won't go. He says he must see Minnie, and he won't tell his errand. I told him that he could not see you, but that I would tell you what he wanted, and that you were not at home. And what do you think he said?"

"I'm sure I don't know, Dowdy dear."

"Why, he said he had nothing to do, and would wait till you came back. And he took his seat in a way that showed that he meant to wait. Really, I'm quite at a loss what to do. You'll have to see him, Kitty dear."

"What a strange person!" said Mrs. Willoughby. "It's *so* rude. And don't you know what he is? How do you know he isn't an Italian?"

"Oh, his English, you know. He speaks it perfectly, but not like an Englishman, you know, nor like a Scotchman either, or an Irishman. I wonder whether he may not be an American?"

At this Minnie started.

"Oh dear!" she said.

"What's the matter, darling?"

"An American! Oh dear! what *will* become of me!"

"Why," said Lady Dalrymple, "do you know him, then, after all?"

"Oh, I'm *so* afraid that I know him!"

"Who is it, dear?"

"Oh, Dowdy! Oh, Kitty!"

"What's the matter?"

"It must be that man. Oh, was there *ever* such a trouble—"

"Really, Minnie dearest, you are allowing yourself to get too agitated. Who *is* this person?"

"He—he's—an—American."

"An American? Why, I just said that I thought he might be one. I didn't know that you were acquainted with any."

"Oh yes; I did get acquainted with some in—in Canada."

"Oh; and is this man a Canadian?"

"No, Dowdy darling; only an American."

"Well, if he's a friend of yours, I suppose you know something about him. But how singular it is that you have so completely forgotten his name. Atramonte? Why, I'm sure it's a *very* singular name for an American gentleman—at least it seems so to me—but I don't know much about them, you know. Tell me, darling, who is he?"

"He—he saved my life."

"What! saved your life? Why, my precious child, what *are* you talking about? It was the Italian that saved your life, you know, not this one."

"Oh, but he did too," said Minnie, despairingly. "I couldn't help it. He would do it. Papa was washed away. I wish they all wouldn't be so horrid."

Lady Dalrymple looked in an equally despairing manner at Mrs. Willoughby.

"What is it, Kitty dear? *Is* the child insane, or what does she mean? How could this person have saved her life?"

"That's just what distracts me," said Minnie. "They all do it. Every single person comes and saves my life. And now I suppose I must go down and see this person."

"Well, really, since you say he saved your life, perhaps it would be as well not to be uncivil," said Lady Dalrymple; "but, at the same time, he seems to me to act in a very extraordinary manner. And he calls himself a Baron. Do they have nobles in America?"

"I'm sure I don't know, Dowdy dear. I never knew that he was a Baron. He may have been the son of some American Baron; and—and—I'm sure I don't know."

"Nonsense, Minnie dear," said Mrs. Willoughby. "This man's title is a foreign one. He probably obtained it in Italy or Spain, or perhaps Mexico. I think they have titles in Mexico, though I really don't know."

"Why, of course, one isn't expected to know any thing about America," said Lady Dalrymple. "I can mention quite a number of English statesmen, members of the cabinet, and others, who don't know any more about America than I do."

"Do you really intend to go down yourself and see him, Minnie dear?" asked Mrs. Willoughby.

"How can I help it? What am I to do? I must go, Kitty darling. He is so very positive, and—and he insists so. I don't want to hurt his feelings, you know; and I really think there is nothing for me to do but to go. What do you think about it, Dowdy dear?" and she appealed to her aunt.

"Well, Minnie, my child, I think it would be best not to be unkind or uncivil, since he saved your life."

Upon this Minnie accompanied her sister to see the visitor.

Mrs. Willoughby entered the room first, and Minnie was close behind her, as though she sought protection from some unknown peril. On entering the room they saw a man dressed in Zouave uniform. His hair was cropped short; he wore a mustache and no beard; his features were regular and handsome; while a pair of fine dark eyes were looking earnestly at the door, and the face and the eyes had the expression of one who is triumphantly awaiting the result of some agreeable surprise. Mrs. Willoughby at once recognized the stranger as the Zouave officer who had stared at them near the Church of the Jesuits. She advanced with lady-like grace toward him, when suddenly he stepped hastily past her, without taking any notice of her, and catching Minnie in his arms, he kissed her several times.

Mrs. Willoughby started back in horror.

Minnie did not resist, nor did she scream, or faint, or do any thing. She only looked a little confused, and managed to extricate herself, after which she took a seat as far away as she could, putting her sister between her and the Zouave. But the Zouave's joy was full, and he didn't appear to notice it. He settled himself in a chair, and laughed loud in his happiness.

"Only to think of it," said he. "Why, I had no more idea of your being here, Minnie, than *Victory*. Well, here you see me. Only been here a couple of months or so. You got my last favor, of course? And ain't you regular knocked up to see me a Baron? Yes, a Baron—a real, live Baron! I'll tell you all about it. You see I was here two or three years ago—the time of Mentana—and fought on the Pope's side. Odd thing, too, wasn't it, for an American? But so it was. Well, they promoted me, and wanted me to stay. But I couldn't fix it. I had business off home, and was on my way there the time of the shipwreck. Well, I've been dodgin' all round every where since then, but never forgettin' little Min, mind you, and at last I found myself here, all right. I'd been speculatin' in wines and raisins, and just dropped in here to take pot-luck with some old Zouave friends, when, darn me! if they didn't make me stay. It seems there's squally times ahead. They wanted a live man. They knew I was that live man. They offered me any thing I wanted. They offered me the title of Baron Atramonte. That knocked me, I tell you. Says I, I'm your man. So now you see me Baron Atramonte, captain in the Papal Zouaves, ready to go where glory waits me—but fonder than ever of little Min. Oh, I tell you what, I ain't a bit of a brag, but I'm *some* here. The men think I'm a little the tallest lot in the shape of a commander they ever *did* see. When I'm in Rome I do as the Romans do, and so I let fly at them a speech every now and then. Why, I've gone through nearly the whole 'National Speaker' by this time. I've given them Marcellus's speech to the mob, Brutus's to the Romans, and Antony's over Cæsar's dead body. I tried a bit of Cicero against Catiline, but I couldn't remember it very well. You know it, of course. *Quousque tandem*, you know."

"CATCHING MINNIE IN HIS ARMS, HE KISSED HER SEVERAL TIMES."

"Well, Min, how goes it?" he continued. "This *is* jolly; and, what's more, it's real good in you—darn me if it ain't! I knew you'd be regularly struck up all of a heap when you heard of me as a Baron, but I really didn't think you'd come all the way here to see me. And you do look stunning! You do beat all! And this lady? You haven't introduced me, you know."

The Baron rose, and looked expectantly at Mrs. Willoughby, and then at Minnie. The latter faltered forth some words, among which the Baron caught the names Mrs. Willoughby and Rufus K. Gunn, the latter name pronounced, with the middle initial and all, in a queer, prim way.

"Mrs. Willoughby—ah!—Min's sister, I presume. Well, I'm pleased to see you, ma'am. Do you know, ma'am, I have reason to remember your name? It's associated with the brightest hours of my life. It was in your parlor, ma'am, that I first obtained Min's promise of her hand. Your hand, madam."

And, stooping down, he grasped Mrs. Willoughby's hand, which was not extended, and wrung it so hard that she actually gave a little shriek.

"For my part, ma'am," he continued, "I'm not ashamed of my name—not a mite. It's a good, honest name; but being as the Holy Father's gone and made me a noble, I prefer being addressed by my title. All Americans are above titles. They despise them. But being in Rome, you see, we must do as the Romans do; and so you needn't know me as Rufus K. Gunn, but as the Baron Atramonte. As for you, Min—you and I won't stand on ceremony— you may call me 'Roof,' or any other name you fancy. I would suggest some pet name—something a little loving, you know."

In the midst of all this, which was poured forth with extreme volubility, the servant came and handed a card.

"Count Girasole."

"HAWBURY, AS I'M A LIVING SINNER!"

CHAPTER XV.

THE AMERICAN BARON.

AT any other time Mrs. Willoughby would perhaps have manœuvred Minnie out of the room; but on the present occasion the advent of the Italian was an inexpressible relief. Mrs. Willoughby was not prepared for a scene like this. The manners, the language, and the acts of Rufus K. Gunn had filled her with simple horror. She was actually bewildered, and her presence of mind was utterly gone. As for Minnie, she was quite helpless, and sat, looking frightened. The Baron Atramonte might have been one of the excellent of the earth—he might have been brave and loyal and just and true and tender, but his manner was one to which they were unaccustomed, and consequently Mrs. Willoughby was quite overcome.

The arrival of Girasole, therefore, was greeted by her with joy. She at once rose to meet him, and could not help infusing into her greeting a warmth which she had never shown him before. Girasole's handsome eyes sparkled with delight, and when Mrs. Willoughby pointedly made way for him to seat himself next to Minnie his cup of joy was full. Mrs. Willoughby's only idea at that moment was to throw some obstacle between Minnie and that "dreadful person" who claimed her as his own, and had taken such shocking liberties. She did not know that Girasole was in Rome, and now accepted his arrival at that opportune moment as something little less than providential.

And now, actuated still by the idea of throwing further obstacles between Minnie and the Baron, she herself went over to the latter, and began a series of polite remarks about the weather and about Rome; while Girasole, eager to avail himself of his unexpected privilege, conversed with Minnie in a low voice in his broken English.

This arrangement was certainly not very agreeable to the Baron. His flow of spirits seemed to be checked at once, and his volubility ceased. He made only monosyllabic answers to Mrs. Willoughby's remarks, and his eyes kept wandering, over beyond her to Minnie, and scrutinizing the Italian who was thus monopolizing her at the very moment when he was beginning to have a "realizing sense" of her presence. He looked puzzled. He could not understand it at all. He felt that some wrong was done by somebody. He fell into an ungracious mood. He hated the Italian who had thus come between him and his happiness, and who chatted with Minnie, in his abominable broken English, just like an old acquaintance. He couldn't understand it. He felt an unpleasant restraint thrown over him, and began to meditate a departure, and a call at some more favorable time later in the evening. But he wanted to have a few more words with "Min," and so he tried to "sit out" the Italian.

But the Italian was as determined as the American. It was the first chance that he had had to get a word with Minnie since he was in Milan, and he was eager to avail himself of it. Mrs. Willoughby, on her part, having thus discomfited the Baron, was not unmindful of the other danger; so she moved her seat to a position near enough to overlook and check Girasole, and then resumed those formal, chilling, heartless, but perfectly polite remarks which she had been administering to the Baron since Girasole's arrival.

At length Mrs. Willoughby began to be dreadfully bored, and groaned in spirit over the situation in which Minnie had placed herself, and racked her brains to find some way of retreat from these two determined lovers, who thus set at naught the usages of society for their own convenience. She grew indignant. She wondered if they would *ever* go. She wondered if it were not possible to engage the Count and the Baron in a conversation by themselves, and, under cover of it, withdraw. Finally she began to think whether she would not be justified in being rude to them, since they were so inconsiderate. She thought over this, and was rapidly coming to the decision that some act of rudeness was her only hope, when, to her immense relief, the servant entered and announced Lord Hawbury.

The entrance of the welcome guest into the room where the unwelcome ones were seated was to Mrs. Willoughby like light in a dark place. To Minnie also it brought immense relief in her difficult position. The ladies rose, and were about to greet the new-comer, when, to their amazement, the Baron sprang forward, caught Lord Hawbury's hand, and wrung it over and over again with the most astonishing vehemence.

"Hawbury, as I'm a living sinner! Thunderation! Where did you come from? Good again! Darn it all, Hawbury, this is real good! And how well you look! *How* are you? All right, and right side up? Who'd have thought it? It ain't you, really, now, is it? Darn me if I ever was so astonished in my life! You're the last man I'd have expected. Yes, *Sir*. You may bet high on that."

"Ah, really," said Hawbury, "my dear fellow! Flattered, I'm sure. And how goes it with you? Deuced odd place to find you, old boy. And I'm deuced glad to see you, you know, and all that sort of thing."

And he wrung the Baron's hand quite as heartily as the other wrung his; and the expression on his face was of as much cordiality and pleasure as that upon the face of the other. Then Hawbury greeted the ladies, and apologized by stating that the Baron was a very old and tried friend, whom he had not seen for years; which intelligence surprised Mrs. Willoughby greatly, and brought a faint ray of something like peace to poor Minnie.

The ladies were not imprisoned much longer. Girasole threw a black look at Lord Hawbury, and retreated. After a few moments' chat Hawbury also retired, and made the Baron go with him. And the Baron went without any urging. He insisted, however, on shaking hands heartily with both of the ladies, especially Minnie, whose poor little hand he nearly crushed into a pulp; and to the latter he whispered the consoling assurance that he would come to see her on the following day. After which he followed his friend out.

Then he took Hawbury over to his own quarters, and Hawbury made himself very much at home in a rocking-chair, which the Baron regarded as the pride and joy and glory of his room.

"By Jove!" cried Hawbury. "This is deuced odd, do you know, old chap; and I can't imagine how the mischief you got here!"

This led to long explanations, and a long conversation, which was protracted far into the night, to the immense enjoyment of both of the friends.

The Baron was, as Lord Hawbury had said, an old friend. He had become acquainted with him many years before upon the prairies of America, near the Rocky Mountains. The Baron had rescued him from Indians, by whom he had been entrapped, and the two friends had wandered far over those regions, enduring perils, fighting enemies, and roughing it in general. This rough life had made each one's better nature visible to the other, and had led to the formation of a friendship full of mutual appreciation of the other's best qualities. Now it is just possible that if they had not known one another, Hawbury might have thought the Baron a boor, and the Baron might have called Hawbury a "thundering snob;" but as it was, the possible boor and the possible snob each thought the other one of the finest fellows in the world.

"But you're not a Roman Catholic," said Hawbury, as the Baron explained his position among the Zouaves.

"What's the odds? All's fish that comes to their net. To get an office in the Church may require a profession of faith, but we're not so particular in the army. I take the oath, and they let me go. Besides, I have Roman Catholic leanings."

"Roman Catholic leanings?"

"Yes; I like the Pope. He's a fine man, Sir—a fine man. I regard that man more like a father than any thing else. There isn't one of us but would lay down our lives for that old gentleman."

"But you never go to confession, and you're not a member of the Church."

"No; but then I'm a member of the army, and I have long chats with some of the English-speaking priests. There are some first-rate fellows among them, too. Yes, Sir."

"I don't see much of a leaning in all that."

"Leaning? Why, it's all leaning. Why, look here. I remember the time when I was a grim, true-blue Puritan. Well, I ain't that now. I used to think the Pope was the Beast of the 'Pocalypse. Well, now I think he's the finest old gentleman I ever saw. I didn't use to go to Catholic chapel. Well, now I'm there often, and I rather kind o' like it. Besides, I'm ready to argue with them all day and all night, and what more can they expect from a fighting man?

"You see, after our war I got my hand in, and couldn't stop fighting. The Indians wouldn't do—too much throat-cutting and savagery. So I came over here, took a fancy to the Pope, enlisted, was at Mentana, fit there, got promoted, went home, couldn't stand it, and here I am, back again; though how long I'm going to be here is more'n I can tell. The fact is, I feel kind of onsettled."

"Why so?"

"Oh, it's an aggravating place, at the best."

"How?"

"There's such an everlasting waste of resources—such tarnation bad management. Fact is, I've noted that it's always the case wherever you trust ministers to do business. They're sure to make a mess of it. I've known lots of cases. Why, that's always the way with us. Look at our stock-companies of any kind, our religious societies, and our publishing houses—wherever they get a ministerial committee, the whole concern goes to blazes. I *know* that. Yes, *Sir*. Now that's the case here. Here's a fine country. Why, round this here city there's a country, Sir, that, if properly managed, might beat any of our prairies—and look at it.

"Then, again, they complain of poverty. Why, I can tell you, from my own observation, that they've got enough capital locked up, lying useless, in this here city, to regenerate it all, and put it on its feet. This capital wants to be utilized. It's been lying too long without paying interest. It's time that it stopped. Why, I tell you what it is, if they were to sell out what they have here lying idle, and realize, they'd get enough money to form an endowment fund for the Pope and his court so big that his Holiness and every official in the place might get salaries all round out of the interest that would enable them to live like—well, I was going to say like princes, but there's a lot of princes in Rome that live so shabby that the comparison ain't worth nothing.

"Why, see here, now," continued the Baron, warming with his theme, which seemed to be a congenial one; "just look here; see the position of this Roman court. They can actually levy taxes on the whole world. Voluntary contributions, Sir, are a wonderful power. Think of our missionary societies—our Sabbath-school organizations in the States. Think of the wealth, the activity, and the action of all our great charitable, philanthropic, and religious bodies. What supports them all? Voluntary contributions. Now what I mean to say is this—I mean to say that if a proper organization was arranged here, they could get annual receipts from the whole round globe that would make the Pope the richest man on it. Why, in that case Rothschild wouldn't be a circumstance. The Pope might go into banking himself, and control the markets of the world. But no. There's a lot of ministers here, and they haven't any head for it. I wish they'd give me a chance. I'd make things spin.

"Then, again, they've got other things here that's ruining them. There's too much repression, and that don't do for the immortal mind. My idea is that every man was created free and equal, and has a right to do just as he darn pleases; but you can't beat that into the heads of the governing class here. No, Sir. The fact is, what Rome wants is a republic. It'll come, too, some day. The great mistake of his Holiness's life is that he didn't put himself at the head of the movement in '. He had the chance, but he got frightened, and backed down. Whereas if he had been a real, live Yankee, now—if he had been like some of our Western parsons—he'd have put himself on the tiptop of the highest wave, and gone in. Why, he could have had all Italy at his right hand by this time, instead of having it all against him. There's where he made his little mistake. If I were Pope I'd fight the enemy with their own weapons. I'd accept the situation. I'd go in head over heels for a republic. I'd have Rome the capital, myself president, Garibaldi commander-in-chief, Mazzini secretary of state—a man, Sir, that can lick even Bill Seward himself in a regular, old-fashioned, tonguey, subtile, diplomatic note. And in that case, with a few live men at the head of affairs, where would Victor Emanuel be? Emphatically, nowhere!

"Why, Sir," continued the Baron, "I'd engage to take this city as it is, and the office of Pope, and run the whole Roman Catholic Church, till it knocked out all opposition by the simple and natural process of absorbing all opponents. We want a republic here in Rome. We want freedom, Sir. Where is the Church making its greatest triumphs to-day? In the States, Sir. If the Catholic Church made itself free and liberal and go-ahead; if it kept up with the times; if it was imbued with the spirit of progress, and pitched aside all old-fashioned traditions—why, I tell you, Sir, it would be a little the tallest organization on this green globe of ours. Yes, *Sir!*"

While Hawbury and the Baron were thus engaged in high discourse, Mrs. Willoughby and Minnie were engaged in discourses of a less elevated but more engrossing character.

After the ladies had escaped they went up stairs. Lady Dalrymple had retired some time before to her own room, and they had the apartment to themselves. Minnie flung herself into a chair and looked bewildered; Mrs. Willoughby took another chair opposite, and said nothing for a long time.

"Well," said Minnie at last, "you needn't be so cross, Kitty; I didn't bring him here."

"Cross!" said her sister; "I'm not cross."

"Well, you're showing temper, at any rate; and you know you are, and I think it very unkind in you, when I have so much to trouble me."

"Why, really, Minnie darling, I don't know what to say."

"Well, why don't you tell me what you think of him, and all that sort of thing? You *might*, you know."

"Think of him!" repeated Mrs. Willoughby, elevating her eyebrows.

"Yes, think of him; and you needn't go and make faces about him, at any rate."

"Did I make faces? Well, dear," said Mrs. Willoughby, patiently, "I'll tell you what I think of him. I'm afraid of him."

"Well, then," said Minnie, in a tone of triumph, "now you know how I feel. Suppose he saved your life, and then came in his awfully boisterous way to see you; and got you alone, and began that way, and really quite overwhelmed you, you know; and then, when you were really almost stunned, suppose he went and proposed to you? Now, then!"

And Minnie ended this question with the air of one who could not be answered, and knew it.

"He's awful—perfectly awful!" said Mrs. Willoughby. "And the way he treated you! It was *so* shocking."

"I know; and that's just the horrid way he *always* does," said Minnie, in a plaintive tone. "I'm sure *I* don't know what to do with him. And then he's Lord Hawbury's friend. So what *are* we to do?"

"LOOK AT THE MAN!"

"I don't know, unless we leave Rome at once."

"But I don't *want* to leave Rome," said Minnie. "I hate being chased away from places by people—and they'd be sure to follow me, you know—and I don't know what to do. And oh, Kitty darling, I've just thought of something. It would be so nice. What do you think of it?"

"What is it?"

"Why, this. You know the Pope?"

"No, I don't."

"Oh, well, you've seen him, you know."

"Yes; but what has he got to do with it?"

"Why, I'll get you to take me, and I'll go to him, and tell him all about it, and about all these horrid men; and I'll ask him if he can't do something or other to help me. They have dispensations and things, you know, that the Pope gives; and I want him to let me dispense with these awful people."

"Nonsense!" said Mrs. Willoughby.

"I don't see any nonsense in it at all. I'm in earnest," said Minnie; "and I think it's a great shame."

"Nonsense!" said her sister again; "the only thing is for you to stay in your room."

"But I don't want to stay in my room, and I can't."

"Oh dear! what can I do with this child?" exclaimed Mrs. Willoughby, whose patience was giving way.

Upon this Minnie went over and kissed her, and begged to be forgiven; and offered to do any thing that darling Kitty wanted her to do.

After this they talked a good deal over their difficulty, but without being able to see their way out of it more clearly.

That evening they were walking up and down the balcony of the house. It was a quadrangular edifice, and they had a suite of rooms on the second and third stories. They were on the balcony of the third story, which looked down into the court-yard below. A fountain was in the middle of this, and the moon was shining brightly.

The ladies were standing looking down, when Minnie gently touched her sister's arm, and whispered,

"Look at the man!"

"Where?"

"By the fountain."

Mrs. Willoughby looked, and saw the face of a man who was standing on the other side of the fountain. His head rose above it, and his face was turned toward them. He evidently did not know that he was seen, but was watching the ladies, thinking that he himself was unobserved. The moment that Mrs. Willoughby looked at the face she recognized it.

"Come in," said she to Minnie. And drawing her sister after her, she went into the house.

"I knew the face; didn't you, Kitty dear?" said Minnie. "It's so easy to tell it. It was Scone Dacres. But what in the world does he want? Oh dear! I hope *he* won't bother me."

CHAPTER XVI.

THE INTRUDER.

JUDGING from the Baron's own words, it will be perceived that his comprehension of the situation was a little different from the actual fact. His idea was that his last letter had been received by Minnie in England, whereupon she had been seized with such an ungovernable longing to see him that she at once set out for Rome. She had not sent him any message, for she wished to surprise him. She had done so effectually. He was not merely surprised; he was overwhelmed, overjoyed, intoxicated with joy. This was indeed kind, he thought—the true part of a fond girl, who thus cast aside all silly scruples, and followed the dictates of her own noble and loving heart.

Now the fact that he had made a partial failure of his first visit to his charmer did not in the slightest degree disconcert him. He was naturally joyous, hilarious, and sanguine. His courage never faltered, nor could the brightness of his soul be easily dimmed. A disappointment on one day gave him but little trouble. It was quickly thrown off, and then his buoyant spirit looked forward for better fortune on the next day. The little disappointment which he had did not, therefore, prevent him from letting his reason feast and his soul flow with Lord Hawbury; nor, when that festive season was over, did it prevent him from indulging in the brightest anticipations for the following day.

On the afternoon of that day, then, the Baron directed his steps toward the hotel where his charmer resided, his heart beating high, and the generous blood mantling his cheek, and all that sort of thing. But the Baron was not alone. He had a companion, and this companion was an acquaintance whom he had made that morning. This companion was very tall, very thin, very sallow, with long, straggling locks of rusty black hair, white neck-tie, and a suit of rather seedy black clothes. In fact, it was the very stranger who had been arrested almost under his eyes as a Garibaldian. His case had come under the notice of the Baron, who had visited him, and found him not to be a Garibaldian at all, but a fellow-countryman in distress—in short, no less a person than the Reverend Saul Tozer, an esteemed clergyman, who had been traveling through Europe for the benefit of his health and the enlargement of his knowledge. This fellow-countryman in distress had at once been released by the Baron's influence; and, not content with giving him his liberty, he determined to take him under his protection, and offered to introduce him to society; all of which generous offices were fully appreciated by the grateful clergyman.

The Baron's steps were first directed toward the place above mentioned, and the Reverend Saul accompanied him. On reaching it he knocked, and asked for Miss Fay.

"Not at home," was the reply.

"Oh, well," said he, "I'll go in and wait till she comes home. Come along, parson, and make yourself quite at home. Oh, never mind, young man," he continued to the servant; "I know the way. Come along, parson." And with these words he led the way into the reception-room, in which he had been before.

An elderly lady was seated there whom the Baron recognized as having seen before. It was Lady Dalrymple, whose name was, of course, unknown to him, since he had only exchanged a few words on his former visit. But as he was naturally chivalrous, and as he was bent on making friends with all in the house, and as he was also in a glorious state of good-will to the entire human race, he at once advanced to the lady and made a low bow.

"How do you do, ma'am?"

Lady Dalrymple bowed good-naturedly, for she was good-natured to a fault.

"I suppose you remember me, ma'am," said the Baron, in rather a loud voice; for, as the lady was elderly, he had a vague idea that she was deaf—which impression, I may mention, was altogether unfounded—"I suppose you remember me, ma'am? But I haven't had the pleasure of a regular introduction to you; so we'll waive ceremony, if you choose, and I'll introduce myself. I'm the Baron Atramonte, and this is my very particular friend, the Reverend Saul Tozer."

"I'm happy to make your acquaintance," said Lady Dalrymple, with a smile, and not taking the Baron's offered hand—not, however, from pride, but simply from laziness—for she hated the bother, and didn't consider it good taste.

"I called here, ma'am," said the Baron, without noticing that Lady Dalrymple had not introduced *herself*—"I called here, ma'am, to see my young friend, Miss Minnie Fay. I'm very sorry that she ain't at home; but since I *am* here, I rather think I'll just set down and wait for her. I s'pose you couldn't tell me, ma'am, about how long it'll be before she comes in?"

Lady Dalrymple hadn't any idea.

"All right," said the Baron; "the longer she keeps me waiting, the more welcome she'll be when she does come. That's all I've got to say."

So the Baron handed a chair to the Reverend Saul, and then selecting another for himself in a convenient position, he ensconced himself in it as snugly as possible, and sat in silence for a few minutes. Lady Dalrymple took no notice of him whatever, but appeared to be engrossed with some trifle of needle-work.

After about five minutes the Baron resumed the task of making himself agreeable.

He cleared his throat.

"Long in these parts, ma'am?" he asked.

"Not very long," said Lady Dalrymple, with her usual bland good-nature.

"A nice place this," continued the Baron.

"Yes."

"And do you keep your health, ma'am?" inquired the Baron, with some anxiety.

"Thanks," said Lady Dalrymple; which observation set the Baron's mind wondering what she meant by that.

"Pray, ma'am," said he, after a pause, "might you be any relation to a young lady friend of mine that's staying here named Minnie Fay?"

"A little," said Lady Dalrymple; which remark set the Baron again wondering. And he was about to return to the charge with another and more direct question, when his attention was arrested by the sound of footsteps on the stairs; so he sat bolt upright, and stared hard at the door. There was the rustle of a dress. The Baron rose. So did the Reverend Saul Tozer. The lady appeared. It was not Minnie. It was Mrs. Willoughby.

Now during the Baron's visit there had been some excitement up stairs. The ladies had told the servants that they were not at home to any callers that day. They had found with consternation how carelessly the Baron had brushed aside their little cobweb regulation, and had heard his voice as he strove to keep up an easy conversation with their aunt. Whereupon an earnest debate arose. They felt that it was not fair to leave their aunt alone with the Baron, and that one of them should go to the rescue. To Mrs. Willoughby's amazement, Minnie was anxious to go. To this she utterly objected. Minnie insisted, and Mrs. Willoughby was in despair. In vain she reproached that most whimsical of young ladies. In vain she reminded her of the Baron's rudeness on a former occasion. Minnie simply reminded her that the Baron had saved her life. At last Mrs. Willoughby actually had to resort to entreaties, and thus she persuaded Minnie not to go down. So she went down herself, but in fear and trembling, for she did not know at what moment her voluble and utterly unreliable sister might take it into her head to follow her.

The Baron, who had risen, full of expectation, stood looking at her, full of disappointment, which was very strongly marked on his face. Then he recollected that Minnie was "not at home," and that he must wait till she did get home. This thought, and the hope that he would not now have long to wait, brought back his friendly glow, and his calm and his peace and his goodwill toward the whole human race, including the ladies in the room. He therefore bowed very low, and, advancing, he made an effort to shake hands; but Mrs. Willoughby had already known the dread pressure which the Baron gave, and evaded him by a polite bow. Thereupon the Baron introduced the Reverend Saul Tozer.

The Baron took out his watch, looked at it, frowned, coughed, put it back, and then drummed with his fingers on the arm of the chair.

"Will it be long, ma'am," asked the Baron, "before Minnie gets back?"

"She is not out," said Mrs. Willoughby.

"Not out?"

"No."

"Why, the thundering fool of a servant went and told me that she was not at home!"

"She is at home," said Mrs. Willoughby, sweetly.

"What! at home!" cried the Baron. "And does she know *I'm* here?"

"She does."

"Then why in thunder don't she come down?" cried the Baron, wonderingly.

"Because she is indisposed."

"Indisposed?"

"Yes."

This was the information which Mrs. Willoughby had decided to give to the Baron. Minnie had stipulated that his feelings should not be hurt; and this seemed to her to be the easiest mode of dealing with him.

"Indisposed!" cried the Baron.

"Yes."

"Oh dear! Oh, I hope, ma'am—I do hope, ma'am, that she ain't very bad. Is it any thing serious—or what?"

"Not *very* serious; she has to keep her room, though."

"She ain't sick abed, I hope?"

"Oh no—not so bad as that!"

"Oh dear! it's all *me*, I know. *I'm* to blame. She made this journey—the poor little pet!—just to see me; and the fatigue and the excitement have all been too much. Oh, I might have known it! Oh, I remember now how pale she looked yesterday! Oh dear! what'll I do if any thing happens to her? Oh, do tell me—is she better?—did she pass a good night?—does she suffer any pain?—can I do any thing for her?—will you take a little message from me to her?"

"She is quite easy now, thanks," said Mrs. Willoughby; "but we have to keep her perfectly quiet; the slightest excitement may be dangerous."

Meanwhile the Reverend Saul had become wearied with sitting dumb, and began to look around for some suitable means of taking part in the conversation. As the Baron had introduced him to society, he felt that it was his duty to take some part so as to assert himself both as a man, a scholar, and a clergyman. So, as he found the Baron was monopolizing Mrs. Willoughby, he gradually edged over till he came within ear-shot of Lady Dalrymple, and then began to work his way toward a conversation.

"This, ma'am," he began, "is truly an interesting spot."

Lady Dalrymple bowed.

"Yes, ma'am. I've been for the past few days surveying the ruins of antiquity. It is truly a soul-stirring spectacle."

"So I have heard," remarked Lady Dalrymple, cheerfully.

"Every thing around us, ma'am," continued the Reverend Saul, in a dismal voice, "is subject to dissolution, or is actually dissolving. How forcible air the words of the Psalmist: 'Our days air as the grass, or like the morning flower; when blasting winds sweep o'er the vale, they wither in an hour.' Yes, ma'am, I have this week stood in the Roman Forum. The Coliseum, also, ma'am, is a wonderful place. It was built by the Flavian emperors, and when completed could hold eighty thousand spectators seated, with about twenty thousand standing. In hot weather these spectators were protected from the rays of the sun by means of awnings. It is a mighty fabric, ma'am!"

"I should think so," said Lady Dalrymple.

"The arch of Titus, ma'am, is a fine ruin. It was originally built by the emperor of that name to commemorate the conquest of Jerusalem. The arch of Septimius Severus was built by the Emperor of that name, and the arch of Constantine was built by the emperor of *that* name. They are all very remarkable structures."

"I'm charmed to hear you say so."

"It's true, ma'am; but let me add, ma'am, that the ruins of this ancient city do not offer to my eyes a spectacle half so melancholy as the great moral ruin which is presented by the modern city. For, ma'am, when I look around, what do I see? I behold the Babylon of the Apocalypse! Pray, ma'am, have you ever reflected much on that?"

"Not to any great extent," said Lady Dalrymple, who now began to feel bored, and so arose to her feet. The Reverend Saul Tozer was just getting on a full head of conversational steam, and was just fairly under way, when this sad and chilling occurrence took place. She rose and bowed to the gentlemen, and began to retreat.

All this time the Baron had been pouring forth to Mrs. Willoughby his excited interrogatories about Minnie's health, and had asked her to take a message. This Mrs. Willoughby refused at first.

"Oh no!" said she; "it will really disturb her too much. What she wants most is perfect quiet. Her health is really *very* delicate, and I am *excessively* anxious about her."

"But does she—does she—is she—can she walk about her own room?" stammered the Baron.

"A little," said Mrs. Willoughby. "Oh, I hope in a few weeks she may be able to come down. But the very *greatest* care and quiet are needed, for she is in such a *very* delicate state that we watch her night and day."

"A few weeks!" echoed the Baron, in dismay. "Watch her night and day!"

"Oh, you know, it is the only chance for her recovery. She is *so* delicate."

The Baron looked at Mrs. Willoughby with a pale face, upon which there was real suffering and real misery.

"Can't I do something?" he gasped. "Won't you take a message to her? It ought to do her good. Perhaps she thinks I'm neglecting her. Perhaps she thinks I ain't here enough. Tell her I'm ready to give up my office, and even my title of nobility, and come and live here, if it'll be any comfort to her."

"Oh, really, Sir, you *quite* mistake her," said Mrs. Willoughby. "It has no reference to you whatever. It's a nervous affection, accompanied with general debility and neuralgia."

"Oh no, you don't know her," said the Baron, incredulously. "I *know* her. I know what it is. But she walks, don't she?"

"Yes, a little—just across the room; still, even that is too much. She is *very, very* weak, and must be *quite* kept free from excitement. Even the excitement of your visits is bad for her. Her pulse is—is—always—accelerated—and—she—I—Oh, dear me!"

While Mrs. Willoughby had been making up this last sentence she was startled by a rustling on the stairs. It was the rustle of a female's dress. An awful thought occurred to her, which distracted her, and confused her in the middle of her sentence, and made her scarce able to articulate her words. And as she spoke them the rustle drew nearer, and she heard the sound of feet descending the stairs, until at last the footsteps approached the door, and Mrs. Willoughby, to her utter horror, saw Minnie herself.

Now as to the Baron, in the course of his animated conversation with Mrs. Willoughby, and in his excited entreaties to her to carry a message up to the invalid, he had turned round with his back to the door. It was about the time that Lady Dalrymple had begun to beat a retreat. As she advanced the Baron saw her, and, with his usual politeness, moved ever so far to one side, bowing low as he did so. Lady Dalrymple passed, the Baron raised himself, and as Mrs. Willoughby was yet speaking, and had just reached the exclamation which concluded her last remark, he was astounded by the sudden appearance of Minnie herself at the door.

The effect of this sudden appearance was overwhelming. Mrs. Willoughby stood thunder-struck, and the Baron utterly bewildered. The latter recovered his faculties first. It was just as Lady Dalrymple was passing out. With a bound he sprang toward Minnie, and caught her in his arms, uttering a series of inarticulate cries.

"Oh, Min! and you did come down, did you? And you couldn't stay up there, could you? I wanted to send a message to you. Poor little Min! you're so weak. Is it any thing serious? Oh, my darling little Min! But sit down on this here seat. Don't stand; you're too weak. Why didn't you send, and I'd have carried you down? But tell me now, honest, wasn't it *me* that brought this on? Never mind, I'll never leave you again."

This is the style which the gallant Baron adopted to express his sentiments concerning Minnie; and the result was that he succeeded in giving utterance to words that were quite as incoherent as any that Minnie herself, in her most rambling moods, had ever uttered.

The Baron now gave himself up to joy. He took no notice of any body. He sat by Minnie's side on a sofa, and openly held her hand. The Reverend Saul Tozer looked on with an approving smile, and surveyed the scene like a father. Mrs. Willoughby's soul was on fire with indignation at Minnie's folly and the Baron's impudence. She was also indignant that her little conventional falsehoods had been suddenly disproved by the act of Minnie herself. Yet she did not know what to say, and so she went to a chair, and flung herself into it in fierce anger.

As for Minnie herself, she had come down to the Baron, and appeared rather to enjoy the situation. She talked about Rome and Naples, and asked him all about himself, and the Baron explained his whole situation down to the minutest detail. She was utterly indifferent to her sister. Once or twice the Baron made a move to go, but did not succeed. He finally settled himself down apparently for the rest of the day; but Mrs. Willoughby at last interposed. She walked forward. She took Minnie's hand, and spoke to her in a tone which she but seldom used.

"You shall *not* stay here any longer!" she cried. "Come."

And Minnie obeyed at once.

The Baron insisted on a tender adieu. Mrs. Willoughby stood by, with flashing eyes and heaving breast.

Minnie followed her up stairs in silence.

"You silly child!" she cried. "Are you mad? What made you come down? You broke your promise!"

"Well—well—I couldn't help it, and he is so deliciously rude; and do you know, Kitty dearest, I really begin to feel quite fond of him."

"Now listen, child. You shall never see him again."

"I don't see why not," whimpered Minnie.

"And I'm going to telegraph to papa. I wouldn't have the responsibility of you another week for the world."

"Now, Kitty, you're horrid."

CHAPTER XVII.

THE BARON'S ASSAULTS.

ON the eventful afternoon when the Baron had effected an entrance into the heart of the enemy's country, another caller had come there—one equally intent and equally determined, but not quite so aggressive. This was the Count Girasole. The same answer was given to him which had been given to the Baron, but with far different effect. The Baron had carelessly brushed the slight obstacle aside. To the Count it was an impenetrable barrier. It was a bitter disappointment, too; for he had been filled with the brightest hopes and expectations by the reception with which he had met on his last visit. That reception had made him believe that they had changed their sentiments and their attitude toward him, and that for the future he would be received in the same fashion. He had determined, therefore, to make the most of this favorable change, and so he at once repeated his call. This time, however, his hopes were crushed. What made it worse, he had seen the entrance of the Baron and the Reverend Saul, and knew by this that instead of being a favored mortal in the eyes of these ladies, he was really, in their estimation, placed below these comparative strangers. By the language of Lord Hawbury on his previous call, he knew that the acquaintance of the Baron with Mrs. Willoughby was but recent.

The disappointment of the Count filled him with rage, and revived all his old feelings and plans and projects. The Count was not one who could suffer in silence. He was a crafty, wily, subtle, scheming Italian, whose fertile brain was full of plans to achieve his desires, and who preferred to accomplish his aims by a tortuous path, rather than by a straight one. This repulse revived old projects, and he took his departure with several little schemes in his mind, some of which, at least, were destined to bear fruit afterward.

On the following day the Baron called once more. The ladies in the mean time had talked over the situation, but were unable to see what they were to do with a man who insisted on forcing his way into their house. Their treatment would have been easy enough if it had not been for Minnie. She insisted that they should not be unkind to him. He had saved her life, she said, and she could not treat him with rudeness. Lady Dalrymple was in despair, and Mrs. Willoughby at her wit's end, while Ethel, to whom the circumstance was made known, was roused by it from her sadness, and tried to remonstrate with Minnie. All her efforts, however, were as vain as those of her friends. Minnie could not be induced to take any decided stand. She insisted on seeing him whenever he called, on the ground that it would be unkind not to.

"And will you insist on seeing Girasole also?" asked Mrs. Willoughby.

"I don't know. I'm awfully sorry for him," said Minnie.

"Well, then, Captain Kirby will be here next. Of course you will see him?"

"I suppose so," said Minnie, resignedly.

"And how long do you think this sort of thing can go on? They'll meet, and blood will be shed."

"Oh dear! I'm afraid so."

"Then I'm not going to allow it. I've telegraphed to papa. He'll see whether you are going to have your own way or not."

"I'm sure I don't see what dear papa can do."

"He won't let you see those horrid men."

"He won't be cruel enough to lock me up in the house. I do wish he would come and take me away. I don't want them. They're all horrid."

"This last one—this Gunn—is the most terrible man I ever saw."

"Oh, Kitty dearest! How *can* you say so? Why, his rudeness and violence are perfectly irresistible. He's charming. He bullies one so deliciously."

Mrs. Willoughby at this turned away in despair.

Minnie's very peculiar situation was certainly one which required a speedy change. The forced entrance of the Baron had thrown consternation into the family. Ethel herself had been roused, and took a part in the debate. She began to see Minnie in a new light, and Hawbury's attention to her began to assume the appearance of a very mournful joke. To her mind Minnie was now the subject of desperate attention from five men.

Thus:

1. Lord Hawbury.

2. Count Girasole.

3. Scone Dacres.

4. Baron Atramonte.

5. Captain Kirby, of whom Mrs. Willoughby had just told her.

And of these, four had saved her life, and consequently had the strongest possible claims on her.

And the only satisfaction which Ethel could gain out of this was the thought that Hawbury, at least, had not saved Minnie's life.

And now to proceed.

"MIN, IT'S ME!"

The Baron called, as has been said, on the following day. This time he did not bring the Reverend Saul with him. He wished to see Minnie alone, and felt the presence of third persons to be rather unpleasant.

On reaching the place he was told, as before, that the ladies were not at home.

Now the Baron remembered that on the preceding day the servant had said the same, while all the time the ladies were home. He was charitably inclined to suppose that it was a mistake, and not a deliberate lie; and, as he was in a frame of good-will to mankind, he adopted this first theory.

"All right, young man," said he; "but as you lied yesterday—under a mistake—I prefer seeing for myself to-day."

So the Baron brushed by the servant, and went in. He entered the room. No one was there. He waited a little while, and thought. He was too impatient to wait long. He could not trust these lying servants. So he determined to try for himself. Her room was up stairs, somewhere in the story above.

So he went out of the room, and up the stairs, until his head was on a level with the floor of the story above. Then he called:

"*Min!*"

No answer.

"MIN!" in a louder voice.

No answer.

"MIN! it's ME!" still louder.

No answer.

"*MIN!*" a perfect yell.

At this last shout there was a response. One of the doors opened, and a lady made her appearance, while at two other doors appeared two maids. The lady was young and beautiful, and her face was stern, and her dark eyes looked indignantly toward the Baron.

"Who are you?" she asked, abruptly; "and what do you want?"

"Me? I'm the Baron Atramonte; and I want Min. Don't you know where she is?"

"Who?"

"Min."

"Min?" asked the other, in amazement.

"Yes. My Min—Minnie, you know. Minnie Fay."

At this the lady looked at the Baron with utter horror.

"I want her."

"She's not at home," said the lady.

"Well, really, it's too bad. I must see her. Is she out?"

"Yes."

"Really? Honor bright now?"

The lady retired and shut the door.

"Well, darn it all, you needn't be so peppery," muttered the Baron. "I didn't say any thing. I only asked a civil question. Out, hey? Well, she must be this time. If she'd been in, she'd have made her appearance. Well, I'd best go out and hunt her up. They don't seem to me altogether so cordial as I'd like to have them. They're just a leetle too 'ristocratic."

With these observations to himself, the Baron descended the stairs, and made his way to the door. Here he threw an engaging smile upon the servant, and made a remark which set the other on the broad grin for the remainder of the day. After this the Baron took his departure.

The Baron this time went to some stables, and reappeared in a short time mounted upon a gallant steed, and careering down the Corso. In due time he reached the Piazza del Popolo, and then he ascended the Pincian Hill. Here he rode about for some time, and finally his perseverance was rewarded. He was looking down from the summit of the hill upon the Piazza below, when he caught sight of a barouche, in which were three ladies. One of these sat on the front seat, and her white face and short golden hair seemed to indicate to him the one he sought.

In an instant he put spurs to his horse, and rode down the hill as quick as possible, to the great alarm of the crowds who were going up and down. In a short time he had caught up with the carriage. He was right. It was the right one, and Minnie was there, together with Lady Dalrymple and Mrs. Willoughby. The ladies, on learning of his approach, exhibited no emotion. They were prepared for this, and resigned. They had determined that Minnie should have no more interviews with him indoors; and since they could not imprison her altogether, they would have to submit for the present to his advances. But they were rapidly becoming desperate.

Lord Hawbury was riding by the carriage as the Baron came up.

"Hallo!" said he to the former. "How do? and *how* are you all? Why, I've been hunting all over creation. Well, Minnie, how goes it? Feel lively? That's right. Keep out in the open air. Take all the exercise you can, and eat as hard as you can. You live too quiet as a general thing, and want to knock around more. But we'll fix all that, won't we, Min, before a month of Sundays?"

The advent of the Baron in this manner, and his familiar address to Minnie, filled Hawbury with amazement. He had been surprised at finding him with the ladies on the previous day, but there was nothing in his demeanor which was at all remarkable. Now, however, he noticed the very great familiarity of his tone and manner toward Minnie, and was naturally amazed. The Baron had not confided to him his secret, and he could not understand the cause of such intimacy between the representatives of such different classes. He therefore listened with inexpressible astonishment to the Baron's language, and to Minnie's artless replies.

Minnie was sitting on the front seat of the barouche, and was alone in that seat. As the gentlemen rode on each side of the carriage her face was turned toward them. Hawbury rode back, so that he was beside Lady Dalrymple;

but the Baron rode forward, on the other side, so as to bring himself as near to Minnie as possible. The Baron was exceedingly happy. His happiness showed itself in the flush of his face, in the glow of his eyes, and in the general exuberance and all-embracing swell of his manner. His voice was loud, his gestures demonstrative, and his remarks were addressed by turns to each one in the company. The others soon gave up the attempt to talk, and left it all to the Baron. Lady Dalrymple and Mrs. Willoughby exchanged glances of despair. Hawbury still looked on in surprise, while Minnie remained perfectly calm, perfectly self-possessed, and conversed with her usual simplicity.

As the party thus rode on they met a horseman, who threw a rapid glance over all of them. It was Girasole. The ladies bowed, and Mrs. Willoughby wished that he had come a little before, so that he could have taken the place beside the carriage where the Baron now was. But the place was now appropriated, and there was no chance for the Count. Girasole threw a dark look over them, which rested more particularly on Hawbury. Hawbury nodded lightly at the Count, and didn't appear to take any further notice of him. All this took up but a few moments, and the Count passed on.

Shortly after they met another horseman. He sat erect, pale, sad, with a solemn, earnest glow in his melancholy eyes. Minnie's back was turned toward him, so that she could not see his face, but his eyes were fixed upon Mrs. Willoughby. She looked back at him and bowed, as did also Lady Dalrymple. He took off his hat, and the carriage rolled past. Then he turned and looked after it, bareheaded, and Minnie caught sight of him, and smiled and bowed. And then in a few moments more the crowd swallowed up Scone Dacres.

The Baron thus enjoyed himself in a large, exuberant fashion, and monopolized the conversation in a large, exuberant way. He outdid himself. He confided to the ladies his plans for the regeneration of the Roman Church and the Roman State. He told stories of his adventures in the Rocky Mountains. He mentioned the state of his finances, and his prospects for the future. He was as open, as free, and as communicative as if he had been at home, with fond sisters and admiring brothers around him. The ladies were disgusted at it all; and by the ladies I mean only Mrs. Willoughby and Lady Dalrymple. For Minnie was not—she actually listened in delight. It was not conventional. Very well. Neither was the Baron. And for that matter, neither was she. He was a child of nature. So was she. His rudeness, his aggressiveness, his noise, his talkativeness, his egotism, his confidences about himself—all these did not make him so very disagreeable to her as to her sister and aunt.

So Minnie treated the Baron with the utmost complaisance, and Hawbury was surprised, and Mrs. Willoughby and Lady Dalrymple were disgusted; but the Baron was delighted, and his soul was filled with perfect joy. Too soon for him was this drive over. But the end came, and they reached the hotel. Hawbury left them, but the Baron lingered. The spot was too sweet, the charm too dear—he could not tear himself away.

In fact, he actually followed the ladies into the house.

"I think I'll just make myself comfortable in here, Min, till you come down," said the Baron. And with these words he walked into the reception-room, where he selected a place on a sofa, and composed himself to wait patiently for Minnie to come down.

So he waited, and waited, and waited—but Minnie did not come. At last he grew impatient. He walked out, and up the stairs, and listened.

He heard ladies' voices.

He spoke.

"*Min!*"

No answer.

"MIN!" louder.

No answer.

"MIN! HALLO-O-O-O!"

No answer.

"*MIN!*" a perfect shout.

At this a door was opened violently, and Mrs. Willoughby walked out. Her cheeks were flushed, and her eyes glanced fire.

"Sir," she said, "this is intolerable! You must be intoxicated. Go away at once, or I shall certainly have you turned out of the house."

And saying this she went back, shut the door, and locked it.

The Baron was thunder-struck. He had never been treated so in his life. He was cut to the heart. His feelings were deeply wounded.

"Darn it!" he muttered. "What's all this for? I ain't been doing any thing."

He walked out very thoughtfully. He couldn't understand it at all. He was troubled for some time. But at last his buoyant spirit rose superior to this temporary depression. To-morrow would explain all, he thought. Yes, to-morrow would make it all right. To-morrow he would see Min, and get her to tell him what in thunder the row was. She'd have to tell, for he could never find out. So he made up his mind to keep his soul in patience.

That evening Hawbury was over at the Baron's quarters, by special invitation, and the Baron decided to ask his advice. So in the course of the evening, while in the full, easy, and confidential mood that arises out of social intercourse, he told Hawbury his whole story—beginning with the account of his first meeting with Minnie, and his rescue of her, and her acceptance of him, down to this very day, when he had been so terribly snubbed by Mrs. Willoughby. To all this Hawbury listened in amazement. It was completely new to him. He wondered particularly to find another man who had saved the life of this quiet, timid little girl.

The Baron asked his advice, but Hawbury declined giving any. He said he couldn't advise any man in a love-affair. Every man must trust to himself. No one's advice could be of any avail. Hawbury, in fact, was puzzled, but he said the best he could. The Baron himself was fully of Hawbury's opinion. He swore that it was truth, and declared the man that followed another's advice in a love-affair was a "darned fool that didn't deserve to win his gal."

There followed a general conversation on things of a different kind. The Baron again discoursed on church and state. He then exhibited some curiosities. Among other things a skull. He used it to hold his tobacco. He declared that it was the skull of an ancient Roman. On the inside was a paper pasted there, on which he had written the following:

> "Oh, I'm the skull of a Roman bold
> That fit in the ancient war;
>
> From East to West I bore the flag
> Of S. P. Q. and R.
>
> "In East and West, and North and South,
> We made the nations fear us—
>
> Both Nebuchadnezzar and Hannibal,
> And Pharaoh too, and Pyrrhus.
>
> "We took their statutes from the Greeks,
> And lots of manuscripts too;
>
> We set adrift on his world-wide tramp
> The original wandering Jew.
>
> "But at last the beggarly Dutchman came,
> With his lager and sauerkraut;
>
> And wherever that beggarly Dutchman went
> He made a terrible rout.

"Wo ist der Deutscher's Vaterland?
Is it near the ocean wild?

Is it where the feathery palm-trees grow?
Not there, not there, my child.

"But it's somewhere down around the Rhine;
And now that Bismarck's come,

Down goes Napoleon to the ground,
And away goes the Pope from Rome!"

CHAPTER XVIII.

"HE SAVED MY LIFE."

"I CAN'T bear this any longer!" exclaimed Mrs. Willoughby. "Here you are getting into all sorts of difficulties, each one worse than the other. I'm sure I don't see why you should. You're very quiet, Minnie dearest, but you have more unpleasant adventures than any person I ever heard of. You're run away with on horseback, you're shipwrecked, you're swept down a precipice by an avalanche, and you fall into the crater of a burning volcano. Every time there is some horrid man who saves you, and then proposes. As for you, you accept them all with equal readiness, one after another, and what is worse, you won't give any of them up. I've asked you explicitly which of them you'll give up, and you actually refuse to say. My dear child, what are you thinking of? You can't have them all. You can't have any of them. None of them are agreeable to your family. They're horrid. What are you going to do? Oh, how I wish you had dear mamma to take care of you! But she is in a better world. And here is poor dear papa who can't come. How shocked he would be if he knew all. What is worst, here is that dreadful American savage, who is gradually killing me. He certainly will be my death. What *am* I to do, dear? Can't you possibly show a little sense yourself—only a little, dear—and have some consideration for your poor sister? Even Ethel worries about you, though she has troubles of her own, poor darling; and aunty is really quite ill with anxiety. What *are* we going to do? I know one thing. *I'm* not going to put up with it. My mind is made up. I'll leave Rome at once, and go home and tell papa."

"Well, you needn't scold so," said Minnie. "It's my trouble. I can't help it. They would come. I'm sure *I* don't know what to do."

"Well, you needn't be so awfully kind to them all. That's what encourages them so. It's no use for me to try to keep them away if you make them all so welcome. Now there's that dreadful Italian. I'm positive he's going to get up some unpleasant plot. These Italians are so very revengeful. And he thinks you're so fond of him, and I'm so opposed. And he's right, too. You always act as if you're fond of him, and all the rest. As to that terrible American savage, I'm afraid to think of him; I positively am."

"Well, you needn't be so awfully unkind to him. He saved my life."

"That's no reason why he should deprive me of mine, which he will do if he goes on so much longer."

"You were very, very rude to him, Kitty," said Minnie, severely, "and very, very unkind—"

"I intended to be so."

"I really felt like crying, and running out and explaining things."

"I know you did, and ran back and locked the door. Oh, you wretched little silly goose, what *am* I *ever* to do with such a child as you are! You're really not a bit better than a baby."

This conversation took place on the day following the Baron's last eventful call. Poor Mrs. Willoughby was driven to desperation, and lay awake all night, trying to think of some plan to baffle the enemy, but was unsuccessful; and so she tried once more to have some influence over Minnie by a remonstrance as sharp as she could give.

"He's an American savage. I believe he's an Indian."

"I'm sure I don't see any thing savage in him. He's as gentle and as kind as he can be. And he's so awfully fond of me."

"Think how he burst in here, forcing his way in, and taking possession of the house. And then poor dear aunty! Oh, how she *was* shocked and horrified!"

"It's because he is so *awfully* fond of me, and was so perfectly *crazy* to see me."

"And then, just as I was beginning to persuade him to go away quietly, to think of you coming down!"

"Well, I couldn't bear to have him so sad, when he saved my life, and so I just thought I'd show myself, so as to put him at ease."

"A pretty way to show yourself—to let a great, horrid man treat you so."

"Well, that's what they *all* do," said Minnie, plaintively. "I'm sure *I* can't help it."

"Oh dear! was there ever such a child! Why, Minnie darling, you must know that such things are very, very ill-bred, and very, very indelicate and unrefined. And then, think how he came forcing himself upon us when we were driving. Couldn't he see that he wasn't wanted? No, he's a savage. And then, how he kept giving us all a history of his life. Every body could hear him, and people stared so that it was really quite shocking."

"Oh, that's because he is so very, very frank. He has none of the deceit of society, you know, Kitty darling."

"Deceit of society! I should think not. Only think how he acted yesterday—forcing his way in and rushing up stairs. Why, it's actually quite frightful. He's like a madman. We will have to keep all the doors locked, and send for the police. Why, do you know, Ethel says that he was here before, running about and shouting in the same way: 'Min!' 'Min!' 'Min!'—that's what the horrid wretch calls you —'Min! it's me.' 'Come, Min!'"

At this Minnie burst into a peal of merry, musical laughter, and laughed on till the tears came to her eyes. Her sister looked more disgusted than ever.

"He's such a boy," said Minnie; "he's just like a boy. He's so *awfully* funny. If I'm a child, he's a big boy, and the awfullest, funniest boy I ever saw. And then he's *so* fond of me. Why, he worships me. Oh, it's awfully nice."

"A boy! A beast, you mean—a horrid savage. What *can* I do? I must send for a policeman. I'll certainly have the doors all locked. And then we'll all be prisoners."

"Well, then, it'll all be your own fault, for *I* don't want to have any doors locked."

"Oh dear!" sighed her sister.

"Well, I don't. And I think you're very unkind."

"Why, you silly child, he'd come here some day, carry you off, and make you marry him."

"Well, I do wish he would," said Minnie, gravely. "I wish somebody would, for then it would put a stop to all this worry, and I really don't know what else ever will. Do *you*, now, Kitty darling?"

Mrs. Willoughby turned away with a gesture of despair.

An hour or two after some letters were brought in, one of which was addressed to

>   MISS FAY,
>   *Poste Restante,*
>   *Roma.*

Minnie opened this, and looked over it with a troubled air. Then she spoke to her sister, and they both went off to Minnie's room.

"Who do you think this is from?" she asked.

"Oh, I don't know! Of course it's some more trouble."

"It's from Captain Kirby."

"Oh, of course! And of course he's here in Rome?"

"No, he isn't."

"What! Not yet?"

"No; but he wrote this from London. He has been to the house, and learned that we had gone to Italy. He says he has sent off letters to me, directed to every city in Italy, so that I may be sure to get it. Isn't that good of him?"

"Well?" asked Mrs. Willoughby, repressing an exclamation of vexation.

"Well, he says that in three days he will leave, and go first to Rome, as he thinks we will be most likely to be there this season. And so, you see, he's coming on; and he will be here in three days, you know."

"Minnie," said her sister, after some moments' solemn thought.

"Well, Kitty darling?"

"Do you ever think?"

"I don't know."

"Would you like one of these gentlemen of yours to blow one of the others' brains out, or stab him, or any thing of that sort?"

"How shocking you are, Kitty dear! What a dreadful question!"

"Well, understand me now. One of them *will* do that. There will be trouble, and your name will be associated with it."

"Well," said Minnie, "I know who *won't* be shot."

"Who?"

"Why, Rufus K. Gunn," said she, in the funny, prim way in which she always pronounced that name. "If he finds it out, he'll drive all the others away."

"And would you like that?"

"Well, you know, he's awfully fond of me, and he's so like a boy: and if I'm such a child, I could do better with a man, you know, that's like a boy, you know, than—than—"

"Nonsense! He's a madman, and you're a simpleton, you little goose."

"Well, then, we must be well suited to one another," said Minnie.

"Now, child, listen," said Mrs. Willoughby, firmly. "I intend to put a stop to this. I have made up my mind positively to leave Rome, and take you home to papa. I'll tell him all about it, put you under his care, and have no more responsibility with you. I think he'd better send you back to school. I've been too gentle. You need a firm hand. I'll be firm for a few days, till you can go to papa. You need not begin to cry. It's for your own good. If you're indulged any more, you'll simply go to ruin."

Mrs. Willoughby's tone was different from usual, and Minnie was impressed by it. She saw that her sister was resolved. So she stole up to her and twined her arms about her and kissed her.

"There, there," said her sister, kissing her again, "don't look so sad, Minnie darling. It's for your own good. We must go away, or else you'll have another of those dreadful people. You must trust to me now, dearest, and not interfere with me in any way."

"Well, well, you mustn't be unkind to poor Rufus K. Gunn," said Minnie.

"Unkind? Why, we won't be any thing to him at all."

"And am I never to—to—see him again?"

"No!" said her sister, firmly.

Minnie started, and looked at Mrs. Willoughby, and saw in her face a fixed resolution.

"No, never!" repeated Mrs. Willoughby. "I am going to take you back to England. I'm afraid to take any railroad or steamboat. I'll hire a carriage, and we'll all go in a quiet way to Florence. Then we can take the railroad to Leghorn, and go home by the way of Marseilles. No one will know that we've gone away. They'll think we have gone on an excursion. Now we'll go out driving this morning, and this afternoon we must keep the outer door locked, and not let any one in. I suppose there is no danger of meeting him in the morning. He must be on duty then."

"But mayn't I see him at all before we go?"

"No!"

"Just once—only once?"

"No, not once. You've seen that horrid man for the last time."

Minnie again looked at her sister, and again read her resolution in her face. She turned away, her head dropped, a sob escaped from her, and then she burst into tears.

Mrs. Willoughby left the room.

CHAPTER XIX.

JEALOUSY.

LORD Hawbury had come to Rome for the sole purpose of watching over his friend Scone Dacres. But he had not found it so easy to do so. His friend kept by himself more than he used to, and for several days Hawbury had seen nothing of him. Once while with the ladies he had met him, and noticed the sadness and the gloom of his brow. He saw by this that he was still a prey to those feelings the exhibition of which had alarmed him at Naples, and made him resolve to accompany him here.

A few days afterward, while Hawbury was in his room, his friend entered. Hawbury arose and greeted him with unfeigned joy.

"Well, old man," he said, "you've kept yourself close, too. What have you been doing with yourself? I've only had one glimpse of you for an age. Doing Rome, hey? Antiquities, arts, churches, palaces, and all that sort of thing, I suppose. Come now, old boy, sit down and give an account of yourself. Have a weed? Here's Bass in prime order. Light up, my dear fellow, and let me look at you as you compose your manly form for a friendly smoke. And don't speak till you feel inclined."

Dacres took his seat with a melancholy smile, and selecting a cigar, lighted it, and smoked in silence for some time.

"Who was that Zouave fellow?" he asked at length: "the fellow that I saw riding by the carriage the other day?"

"That—oh, an old friend of mine. He's an American named Gunn. He's joined the Papal Zouaves from some whim, and a deuced good thing it is for them to get hold of such a man. I happened to call one day, and found him with the ladies."

"The ladies—ah!" and Dacres's eyes lighted up with a bad, hard light. "I suppose he's another of those precious cavaliers—the scum of all lands—that dance attendance on my charming wife."

"Oh, see here now, my dear fellow, really now," said Hawbury, "none of that, you know. This fellow is a friend of *mine*, and one of the best fellows I ever saw. You'd like him, old chap. He'd suit you."

"Yes, and suit my wife better," said Dacres, bitterly.

"Oh, come now, really, my dear boy, you're completely out. He don't know your wife at all. It's the other one, you know. Don't be jealous, now, if I tell you."

"Jealous!"

"Yes. I know your weakness, you know; but this is an old affair. I don't want to violate confidence, but—"

Dacres looked hard at his friend and breathed heavily. He was evidently much excited.

"But what?" he said, hoarsely.

"Well, you know, it's an old affair. It's the young one, you know—Miss Fay. He rather affects her, you know. That's about it."

"Miss Fay?"

"Yes; your child-angel, you know. But it's an older affair than yours; it is, really; so don't be giving way, man. Besides, his claims on her are as great as yours; yes, greater too. By Jove!"

"Miss Fay! Oh, is that all?" said Dacres, who, with a sigh of infinite relief, shook off all his late excitement, and became cool once more.

Hawbury noted this very thoughtfully.

"You see," said Dacres, "that terrible wife of mine is so cursedly beautiful and fascinating, and so infernally fond of admiration, that she keeps no end of fellows tagging at her heels. And so I didn't know but that this was some new admirer. Oh, she's a deep one! Her new style, which she has been cultivating for ten years, has made her look like an angel of light. Why, there's the very light of heaven in her eyes, and in her face there is nothing, I swear, but gentleness and purity and peace. Oh, had she but been what she now seems! Oh, if even now I could but believe this, I would even now fling my memories to the winds, and I'd lie down in the dust and let her trample on me, if she would only give me that tender and gentle love that now lurks in her face. Good Heavens! can such a change be possible? No; it's impossible! It can't be! Don't I know her? Can't I remember her? Is my memory all a dream? No, it's real; and it's marked deep by this scar that I wear. Never till that scar is obliterated can that woman change."

Dacres had been speaking, as he often did now, half to himself; and as he ended he rubbed his hand over the place where the scar lay, as though to soothe the inflammation that arose from the rush of angry blood to his head.

"Well, dear boy, I can only say I wish from my heart that her nature was like her face. She's no favorite of mine, for your story has made me look on her with your eyes, and I never have spoken to her except in the most distant way; but I must say I think her face has in it a good deal of that gentleness which you mention. Miss Fay treats her quite like an elder sister, and is deuced fond of her, too. I can see that. So she can't be very fiendish to her.

Like loves like, you know, and the one that the child-angel loves ought to be a little of an angel herself, oughtn't she?"

Dacres was silent for a long time.

"There's that confounded Italian," said he, "dangling forever at her heels—the devil that saved her life. He must be her accepted lover, you know. He goes out riding beside the carriage."

"Well, really, my dear fellow, she doesn't seem overjoyed by his attentions."

"Oh, that's her art. She's so infernally deep. Do you think she'd let the world see her feelings? Never. Slimy, Sir, and cold and subtle and venomous and treacherous—a beautiful serpent. Aha! isn't that the way to hit her off? Yes, a beautiful, malignant, venomous serpent, with fascination in her eyes, and death and anguish in her bite. But she shall find out yet that others are not without power. Confound her!"

"Well, now, by Jove! old boy, I think the very best thing you can do is to go away somewhere, and get rid of these troubles."

"Go away! Can I go away from my own thoughts? Hawbury, the trouble is in my own heart. I must keep near her. There's that Italian devil. He shall not have her. I'll watch them, as I have watched them, till I find a chance for revenge."

"You have watched them, then?" asked Hawbury, in great surprise.

"Yes, both of them. I've seen the Italian prowling about where she lives. I've seen her on her balcony, evidently watching for him."

"But have you seen any thing more? This is only your fancy."

"Fancy! Didn't I see her herself standing on the balcony looking down. I was concealed by the shadow of a fountain, and she couldn't see me. She turned her face, and I saw it in that soft, sweet, gentle beauty which she has cultivated so wonderfully. I swear it seemed like the face of an angel, and I could have worshiped it. If she could have seen my face in that thick shadow she would have thought I was an adorer of hers, like the Italian—ha, ha!—instead of a pursuer, and an enemy."

"Well, I'll be hanged if I can tell myself which you are, old boy; but, at any rate, I'm glad to be able to state that your trouble will soon be over."

"How's that?"

"She's going away."

"Going away!"

"Yes."

"She! going away! where?"

"Back to England."

"Back to England! why, she's just come here. What's that for?"

"I don't know. I only know they're all going home. Well, you know, holy week's over, and there is no object for them to stay longer."

"Going away! going away!" replied Dacres, slowly. "Who told you?"

"Miss Fay."

"Oh, I don't believe it."

"There's no doubt about it, my dear boy. Miss Fay told me explicitly. She said they were going in a carriage by the way of Civita Castellana."

"What are they going that way for? What nonsense! I don't believe it."

"Oh, it's a fact. Besides, they evidently don't want it to be known."

"What's that?" asked Dacres, eagerly.

"I say they don't seem to want it to be known. Miss Fay told me in her childish way, and I saw that Mrs. Willoughby looked vexed, and tried to stop her."

"Tried to stop her! Ah! Who were there? Were you calling?"

"Oh no—it was yesterday morning. I was riding, and, to my surprise, met them. They were driving—Mrs. Willoughby and Miss Fay, you know—so I chatted with them a few moments, or rather with Miss Fay, and hoped I would see them again soon, at some *fête* or other, when she told me this."

"And my wife tried to stop her?"

"Yes."

"And looked vexed?"

"Yes."

"Then it was some secret of *hers*. *She* has some reason for keeping dark. The other has none. Aha! don't I understand her? She wants to keep it from *me*. She knows you're my friend, and was vexed that you should know. Aha! she dreads my presence. She knows I'm on her track. She wants to get away with her Italian—away from my sight. Aha! the tables are turned at last. Aha! my lady. Now we'll see. Now take your Italian and fly, and see how far you can get away from me. Take him, and see if you can hold him. Aha! my angel face, my mild, soft eyes of love, but devil's heart—can not I understand it all? I see through it. I've watched, you. Wait till you see Scone Dacres on your track!"

"What's that? You don't really mean it?" cried Hawbury.

"Yes, I do."

"Will you follow her?"

"Yes, I will."

"What for? For a vague fancy of your jealous mind?"

"It isn't a fancy; it's a certainty. I've seen the Italian dogging her, dodging about her house, and riding with her. I've seen her looking very much as if she were expecting him at her balcony. Is all that nothing? She's seen me, and feels conscience-stricken, and longs to get away where she may be free from the terror of my presence. But I'll track her. I'll strike at her—at her heart, too; for I will strike through the Italian."

"By Jove!"

"I will, I swear!" cried Dacres, gloomily.

"You're mad, Dacres. You imagine all this. You're like a madman in a dream."

"It's no dream. I'll follow her. I'll track her."

"Then, by Jove, you'll have to take me with you, old boy! I see you're not fit to take care of yourself. I'll have to go and keep you from harm."

"You won't keep me from harm, old chap," said Dacres, more gently; "but I'd be glad if you would go. So come along."

"I will, by Jove!"

"I WATCHED HIM."

CHAPTER XX.

THE BARON'S WOES.

DACRES was not the only excited visitor that Hawbury had that day. Before its close another made his appearance in the person of the Baron.

"Well, my noble friend," cried Hawbury—"my Baron bold—how goes it? But, by Jove! what's the matter, my boy? Your brow deep scars of thunder have intrenched, and care sits on your faded cheek. Pour forth the mournful tale. I'll sympathize."

"I swear it's too almighty bad!" cried the Baron.

"What?"

"The way I'm getting humbugged."

"Humbugged! Who's been humbugging you?"

"Darn me if I know; and that's the worst of it by a thundering sight."

"Well, my dear fellow, if I can help you, you'd better let me know what it's all about."

"Why, Minnie; that's the row. There ain't another thing on this green earth that would trouble me for five seconds."

"Minnie? Oh! And what has happened—a lover's quarrel?"

"Not a quarrel. *She's* all right."

"What is it, then?"

"Why, she's disappeared."

"Disappeared! What do you mean by that?"

"Darn me if I know. I only know this, that they keep their place bolted and barred, and they've muffled the bell, and there's no servant to be seen, and I can't find out any thing about them. And it's too almighty bad. Now isn't it?"

"It's deuced odd, too—queer, by Jove! I don't understand. Are you sure they're all locked up?"

"Course I am."

"And no servants?"

"Not a darned servant."

"Did you ask the concierge?"

"Course I did; and crossed his palm, too. But he didn't give me any satisfaction."

"What did he say?"

"Why, he said they were at home, for they had been out in the morning, and had got back again. Well, after that I went back and nearly knocked the door down. And that was no good; I didn't get a word. The concierge swore they were in, and they wouldn't so much as answer me. Now I call that too almighty hard, and I'd like to know what in thunder they all mean by it."

"By Jove! odd, too."

"Well, you know, I thought after a while that it would be all explained the next day; so I went home and waited, and came back the next afternoon. I tried it over again. Same result. I spoke to the concierge again, and he swore again that they were all in. They had been out in the morning, he said, and looked well. They had come home by noon, and had gone to their rooms. Well, I really did start the door that time, but didn't get any answer for my pains."

"By Jove!"

"Well, I was pretty hard up, I tell you. But I wasn't going to give up. So I staid there, and began a siege. I crossed the concierge's palm again, and was in and out all night. Toward morning I took a nap in his chair. He thought it was some government business or other, and assisted me all he could. I didn't see any thing at all though, except an infernal Italian—a fellow that came calling the first day I was there, and worked himself in between me and Min. He was prowling about there, with another fellow, and stared hard at me. I watched him, and said nothing, for I wanted to find out his little game. He's up to something, I swear. When he saw I was on the ground, though, he beat a retreat.

"Well, I staid all night, and the next morning watched again. I didn't knock. It wasn't a bit of use—not a darned bit.

"Well, about nine o'clock the door opened, and I saw some one looking out very cautiously. In a minute I was standing before her, and held out my hand to shake hers. It was the old lady. But she didn't shake hands. She looked at me quite coolly.

"'Good-morning, ma'am,' said I, in quite a winning voice. 'Good-morning, ma'am.'

"'Good-morning,' she said.

"'I come to see Minnie,' said I.

"'To see Minnie!' said she: and then she told me she wasn't up.

"'Ain't up?' said I; 'and it so bright and early! Why, what's got her? Well, you just go and tell her *I'm* here, and I'll just step inside and wait till she comes down,' said I.

"But the old lady didn't budge.

"'I'm not a servant,' she said, very stiff; 'I'm her aunt, and her guardian, and I allow no messages to pass between her and strange gentlemen.'

"'Strange gentlemen!' I cried. 'Why, ain't I engaged to her?'

"'I don't know you,' says she.

"'Wasn't I introduced to you?' says I.

"'No,' says she; 'I don't know you.'

"BUT I SAVED HER LIFE."

"'But I'm engaged to Minnie,' says I.

"'I don't recognize you,' says she. 'The family know nothing about you; and my niece is a silly girl, who is going back to her father, who will probably send her to school.'

"'But I saved her life,' says I.

"'That's very possible,' says she; 'many persons have done so; yet that gives you no right to annoy her; and you shall *not* annoy her. Your engagement is an absurdity. The child herself is an absurdity. *You* are an absurdity. Was it not you who was creating such a frightful disturbance here yesterday? Let me inform you, Sir, that if you repeat it, you will be handed over to the police. The police would certainly have been called yesterday had we not wished to avoid hurting your feelings. We now find that you have no feelings to hurt.'

"'Very well, ma'am,' says I; 'these are your views; but as you are not Minnie, I don't accept them. I won't retire from the field till I hear a command to that effect from Minnie herself. I allow no relatives to stand between me and my love. Show me Minnie, and let me hear what she has to say. That's all I ask, and that's fair and square.'

"'You shall not see her at all,' says the old lady, quite mild; 'not at all. You must not come again, for you will not be admitted. Police will be here to put you out if you attempt to force an entrance as you did before.'

"'Force an entrance!' I cried.

"'Yes,' she said, 'force an entrance. You did so, and you filled the whole house with your shouts. Is that to be borne? Not by us, Sir. And now go, and don't disturb us any more.'

"Well, I'll be darned if I ever felt so cut up in my life. The old lady was perfectly calm and cool; wasn't a bit scared—though there was no reason why she should be. She just gave it to me that way. But when she accused me of forcing an entrance and kicking up a row, I was struck all of a heap and couldn't say a word. *Me* force an entrance! *Me* kick up a row! And in Minnie's house! Why, the old woman's mad!

"Well, the old lady shut the door in my face, and I walked off; and I've been ever since trying to understand it, but I'll be darned if I can make head or tail of it. The only thing I see is that they're all keeping Minnie locked up away from me. They don't like me, though why they don't I can't see; for I'm as good as any body, and I've been particular about being civil to all of them. Still they don't like me, and they see that Minnie does, and they're trying to break up the engagement. But by the living jingo!" and the Baron clinched a good-sized and very sinewy fist, which he brought down hard on the table—"by the living jingo, they'll find they can't come it over *me*! No, *Sir*!"

"Is she fond of you—Miss Fay, I mean?"

"Fond! Course she is. She dotes on me."

"Are you sure?"

"Sure! As sure as I am of my own existence. Why, the way she looks at me is enough! She has a look of helpless trust, an innocent confidence, a tender, child-like faith and love, and a beseeching, pleading, imploring way that tells me she is mine through and through."

Hawbury was a little surprised. He thought he had heard something like that before.

"Oh, well," said he, "that's the chief thing, you know. If you're sure of the girl's affections, the battle's half won."

"Half won! Ain't it all won?"

"Well, not exactly. You see, with us English, there are ever so many considerations."

"But with us Americans there is only one consideration, and that is, Do you love me? Still, if her relatives are particular about dollars, I can foot up as many thousands as her old man, I dare say; and then, if they care for rank, why, I'm a Baron!"

"And what's more, old boy," said Hawbury, earnestly, "if they wanted a valiant, stout, true, honest, loyal soul, they needn't go further than Rufus K. Gunn, Baron de Atramonte."

The Baron's face flushed.

"Hawbury," said he, "that's good in you. We've tried one another, haven't we? You're a brick! And I don't need *you* to tell *me* what you think of me. But if you could get a word into the ear of that cantankerous old lady, and just let her know what *you* know about me, it might move her. You see you're after her style, and I'm not; and she can't see any thing but a man's manner, which, after all, varies in all countries. Now if you could speak a word for me, Hawbury—"

"By Jove! my dear fellow, I'd be glad to do so—I swear I would; but you don't appear to know that I won't have the chance. They're all going to leave Rome to-morrow morning."

The Baron started as though he had been shot.

"What!" he cried, hoarsely. "What's that? Leave Rome?"

"Yes."

"And to-morrow morning?"

"Yes; Miss Fay told me herself—"

"Miss Fay told you herself! By Heaven! What do they mean by that?" And the Baron sat trembling with excitement.

"Well, the holy week's over."

"Darn it all, that's got nothing to do with it! It's me! They're trying to get her from me! How are they going? Do you know?"

"They are going in a carriage by the way of Civita Castellana."

"In a carriage by the way of Civita Castellana! Darn that old idiot of a woman! what's she up to now? If she's running away from me, she'll wish herself back before she gets far on that road. Why, there's an infernal nest of brigands there that call themselves Garibaldians; and, by thunder, the woman's crazy! They'll be seized and held to ransom—perhaps worse. Heavens! I'll go mad! I'll run and tell them. But no; they won't see me. What'll I do? And Minnie! I can't give her up. She can't give me up. She's a poor, trembling little creature; her whole life hangs on mine. Separation from me would kill her. Poor little girl! Separation! By thunder, they shall never separate us! What devil makes the old woman go by that infernal road? Brigands all the way! But I'll go after them; I'll follow them. They'll find it almighty hard work to keep her from me! I'll see her, by thunder! and I'll get her out of their clutches! I swear I will! I'll bring her back here to Rome, and I'll get the Pope himself to bind her to me with a knot that all the old women under heaven can never loosen!"

"What! You're going? By Jove! that's odd, for I'm going with a friend on the same road."

"Good again! Three cheers! And you'll see the old woman, and speak a good word for me?"

"If I see her and get a chance, I certainly will, by Jove!"

CHAPTER XXI.

AN EVENTFUL JOURNEY.

ON the day following two carriages rolled out of Rome, and took the road toward Florence by the way of Civita Castellana. One carriage held four ladies; the other one was occupied by four lady's-maids and the luggage of the party.

It was early morning, and over the wide Campagna there still hung mists, which were dissipated gradually as the sun arose. As they went on the day advanced, and with the departing mists there opened up a wide view. On either side extended the desolate Campagna, over which passed lines of ruined aqueducts on their way from the hills to the city. Here and there crumbling ruins arose above the plain—some ancient, others medieval, none modern. Before them, in the distance, arose the Apennines, among which were, here and there, visible the white outlines of some villa or hamlet.

For mile after mile they drove on; and the drive soon proved very monotonous. It was nothing but one long and unvarying plain, with this only change, that every mile brought them nearer to the mountains. As the mountains were their only hope, they all looked forward eagerly to the time when they would arrive there and wind along the road among them.

Formerly Mrs. Willoughby alone had been the confidante of Minnie's secret, but the events of the past few days had disclosed most of her troubles to the other ladies also, at least as far as the general outlines were concerned. The consequence was, that they all knew perfectly well the reason why they were traveling in this way, and Minnie knew that they all knew it. Yet this unpleasant consciousness did not in the least interfere with the sweetness of her temper and the gentleness of her manner. She sat there, with a meek smile and a resigned air, as though the only part now left her in life was the patient endurance of her unmerited wrongs. She blamed no one; she made no complaint; yet there was in her attitude something so touching, so clinging, so pathetic, so forlorn, and in her face something so sweet, so sad, so reproachful, and so piteous, that she enforced sympathy; and each one began to have a half-guilty fear that Minnie had been wronged by her. Especially did Mrs. Willoughby feel this. She feared that she had neglected the artless and simple-minded child; she feared that she had not been sufficiently thoughtful about her; and now longed to do something to make amends for this imaginary neglect. So she sought to make the journey as pleasant as possible by cheerful remarks and lively observations. None of these things, however, produced any effect upon the attitude of Minnie. She sat there, with unalterable sweetness and unvarying patience, just like a holy martyr, who freely forgave all her enemies, and was praying for those who had despitefully used her.

THE PROCESSION ACROSS THE CAMPAGNA.

The exciting events consequent upon the Baron's appearance, and his sudden revelation in the role of Minnie's lover, had exercised a strong and varied effect upon all; but upon one its result was wholly beneficial, and this was Ethel. It was so startling and so unexpected that it had roused her from her gloom, and given her something to think of. The Baron's debut in their parlor had been narrated to her over and over by each of the three who had witnessed it, and each gave the narrative her own coloring. Lady Dalrymple's account was humorous; Mrs. Willoughby's indignant; Minnie's sentimental. Out of all these Ethel gained a fourth idea, compounded of these three, which again blended with another, and an original one of her own, gained from a personal observation of the Baron, whose appearance on the stairs and impatient summons for "Min" were very vividly impressed on her memory. In addition to this there was the memory of that day on which they endeavored to fight off the enemy.

That was, indeed, a memorable day, and was now alluded to by them all as the day of the siege. It was not without difficulty that they had withstood Minnie's earnest protestations, and intrenched themselves. But Mrs. Willoughby was obdurate, and Minnie's tears, which flowed freely, were unavailing.

Then there came the first knock of the impatient and aggressive visitor, followed by others in swift succession, and in ever-increasing power. Every knock went to Minnie's heart. It excited an unlimited amount of sympathy for the one who had saved her life, and was now excluded from her door.

But as the knocks grew violent and imperative, and Minnie grew sad and pitiful, the other ladies grew indignant. Lady Dalrymple was on the point of sending off for the police, and only Minnie's frantic entreaties prevented this. At last the door seemed almost beaten in, and their feelings underwent a change. They were convinced that he was mad, or else intoxicated. Of the madness of love they did not think. Once convinced that he was mad, they became terrified. The maids all hid themselves. None of them now would venture out even to call the police. They expected that the concierge would interpose, but in vain. The concierge was bribed.

After a very eventful day night came. They heard footsteps pacing up and down, and knew that it was their tormentor. Minnie's heart again melted with tender pity for the man whose love for her had turned his head, and she begged to be allowed to speak to him. But this was not permitted. So she went to bed and fell asleep. So, in process of time, did the others, and the night passed without any trouble. Then morning came, and there was a debate as to who should confront the enemy. There was no noise, but they knew that he was there. At last Lady Dalrymple summoned up her energies, and went forth to do battle. The result has already been described in the words of the bold Baron himself.

But even this great victory did not reassure the ladies. Dreading another visit, they hurried away to a hotel, leaving the maids to follow with the luggage as soon as possible. On the following morning they had left the city.

Events so very exciting as these had produced a very natural effect upon the mind of Ethel. They had thrown her thoughts out of their old groove, and fixed them in a new one. Besides, the fact that she was actually leaving the man who had caused her so much sorrow was already a partial relief. She had dreaded meeting him so much that she had been forced to keep herself a prisoner. A deep grief still remained in her heart; but, at any rate, there was now some pleasure to be felt, if only of a superficial kind.

As for Mrs. Willoughby, in spite of her self-reproach about her purely imaginary neglect of Minnie, she felt such an extraordinary relief that it affected all her nature. The others might feel fatigue from the journey. Not she. She was willing to continue the journey for an indefinite period, so long as she had the sweet consciousness that she was bearing Minnie farther and farther away from the grasp of "that horrid man." The consequence was, that she was lively, lovely, brilliant, cheerful, and altogether delightful. She was as tender to Minnie as a mother could be. She was lavish in her promises of what she would do for her. She chatted gayly with Ethel about a thousand things, and was delighted to find that Ethel reciprocated. She rallied Lady Dalrymple on her silence, and congratulated her over and over, in spite of Minnie's frowns, on the success of her generalship. And so at last the weary

Campagna was traversed, and the two carriages began to ascend among the mountains.

Several other travelers were passing over that Campagna road, and in the same direction. They were not near enough for their faces to be discerned, but the ladies could look back and see the signs of their presence. First there was a carriage with two men, and about two miles behind another carriage with two other men; while behind these, again, there rode a solitary horseman, who was gradually gaining on the other travelers.

Now, if it had been possible for Mrs. Willoughby to look back and discern the faces of the travelers who were moving along the road behind her, what a sudden overturn there would have been in her feelings, and what a blight would have fallen upon her spirits! But Mrs. Willoughby remained in the most blissful ignorance of the persons of these travelers, and so was able to maintain the sunshine of her soul.

At length there came over that sunny soul the first cloud.

The solitary horseman, who had been riding behind, had overtaken the different carriages.

The first carriage contained Lord Hawbury and Scone Dacres. As the horseman passed, he recognized them with a careless nod and smile.

Scone Dacres grasped Lord Hawbury's arm.

"Did you see him?" he cried. "The Italian! I thought so! What do you say now? Wasn't I right?"

"By Jove!" cried Lord Hawbury.

Whereupon Dacres relapsed into silence, sitting upright, glaring after the horseman, cherishing in his gloomy soul the darkest and most vengeful thoughts.

The horseman rode on further, and overtook the next carriage. In this there were two men, one in the uniform of the Papal Zouaves, the other in rusty black. He turned toward these, and greeted them with the same nod and smile.

"Do you see that man, parson?" said the Baron to his companion. "Do you recognize him?"

"No."

"Well, you saw him at Minnie's house. He came in."

"No, he didn't."

"Didn't he? No. By thunder, it wasn't that time. Well, at any rate, that man, I believe, is at the bottom of the row. It's my belief that he's trying to cut me out, and he'll find he's got a hard row to hoe before he succeeds in that project."

And with these words the Baron sat glaring after the Italian, with something in his eye that resembled faintly the fierce glance of Scone Dacres.

The Italian rode on. A few miles further were the two carriages. Minnie and her sister were sitting on the front seats, and saw the stranger as he advanced. He soon came near enough to be distinguished, and Mrs. Willoughby recognized Girasole.

Her surprise was so great that she uttered an exclamation of terror, which startled the other ladies, and made them all look in that direction.

"How very odd!" said Ethel, thoughtfully.

"And now I suppose you'll all go and say that I brought *him* too," said Minnie. "That's *always* the way you do. You *never* seem to think that I may be innocent. You *always* blame me for every little mite of a thing that may happen."

No one made any remark, and there was silence in the carriage as the stranger approached. The ladies bowed somewhat coolly, except Minnie, who threw upon him the most imploring look that could possibly be sent from human eyes, and the Italian's impressible nature thrilled before those beseeching, pleading, earnest, unfathomable, tender, helpless, innocent orbs. Removing his hat, he bowed low.

"I haf not been awara," he said, politely, in his broken English, "that youar ladysippa's bin intend to travalla. Ees eet not subito intenzion?"

Mrs. Willoughby made a polite response of a general character, the Italian paused a moment to drink in deep draughts from Minnie's great beseeching eyes that were fixed upon his, and then, with a low bow, he passed on.

"I believe I'm losing my senses," said Mrs. Willoughby.

"Why, Kitty darling?" asked Minnie.

"I don't know how it is, but I actually trembled when that man came up, and I haven't got over it yet."

"I'm sure I don't see why," said Minnie. "You're *always* imagining things, though. Now *isn't* she, Ethel dearest?"

"Well, really, I don't see much in the Count to make one tremble. I suppose poor dear Kitty has been too much agitated lately, and it's her poor nerves."

"I have my lavender, Kitty dear," said Lady Dalrymple. "Won't you take it? Or would you prefer valerian?"

"Thanks, much, but I do not need it," said Mrs. Willoughby. "I suppose it will pass off."

"I'm sure the poor Count never did any body any harm," said Minnie, plaintively; "so you needn't all abuse him so—unless you're all angry at him for saving my life. I remember a time when you all thought very differently, and all praised him up, no end."

"Really, Minnie darling, I have nothing against the Count, only once he was a little too intrusive; but he seems to have got over that; and if he'll only be nice and quiet and proper, I'm sure I've nothing to say against him."

They drove on for some time, and at length reached Civita Castellana. Here they drove up to the hotel, and the ladies got out and went up to their apartments. They had three rooms up stairs, two of which looked out into the street, while the third was in the rear. At the front windows was a balcony.

The ladies now disrobed themselves, and their maids assisted them to perform the duties of a very simple toilet. Mrs. Willoughby's was first finished. So she walked over to the window, and looked out into the street.

It was not a very interesting place, nor was there much to be seen; but she took a lazy, languid interest in the sight which met her eyes. There were the two carriages. The horses were being led to water. Around the carriages was a motley crowd, composed of the poor, the maimed, the halt, the blind, forming that realm of beggars which from immemorial ages has flourished in Italy. With these was intermingled a crowd of ducks, geese, goats, pigs, and ill-looking, mangy, snarling curs.

Upon these Mrs. Willoughby looked for some time, when at length her ears were arrested by the roll of wheels down the street. A carriage was approaching, in which there were two travelers. One hasty glance sufficed, and she turned her attention once more to the ducks, geese, goats, dogs, and beggars. In a few minutes the crowd was scattered by the newly-arrived carriage. It stopped. A man jumped out. For a moment he looked up, staring hard at the windows. That moment was enough. Mrs. Willoughby had recognized him.

She rushed away from the windows. Lady Dalrymple and Ethel were in this room, and Minnie in the one beyond. All were startled by Mrs. Willoughby's exclamation, and still more by her looks.

"Oh!" she cried.

"What?" cried they. "What is it?"

"*He's* there! *He's* there!"

"Who? who?" they cried, in alarm.

"That horrid man!"

Lady Dalrymple and Ethel looked at one another in utter horror.

As for Minnie, she burst into the room, peeped out of the windows, saw "that horrid man," then ran back, then sat down, then jumped up, and then burst into a peal of the merriest laughter that ever was heard from her.

"Oh, I'm *so* glad! I'm *so* glad!" she exclaimed. "Oh, it's so *aw*fully funny. Oh, I'm *so* glad! Oh, Kitty darling, don't, please don't, look so cross. Oh, ple-e-e-e-e-e-ase don't, Kitty darling. You make me laugh worse. It's so *aw*fully funny!"

But while Minnie laughed thus, the others looked at each other in still greater consternation, and for some time there was not one of them who knew what to say.

But Lady Dalrymple again threw herself in the gap.

"You need not feel at all nervous, my dears," said she, gravely. "I do not think that this person can give us any trouble. He certainly can not intrude upon us in these apartments, and on the highway, you know, it will be quite as difficult for him to hold any communication with us. So I really don't see any cause for alarm on your part, nor do I see why dear Minnie should exhibit such delight."

These words brought comfort to Ethel and Mrs. Willoughby. They at once perceived their truth. To force himself into their presence in a public hotel was, of course, impossible, even for one so reckless as he seemed to be; and on the road he could not trouble them in any way, since he would have to drive before them or behind them.

At Lady Dalrymple's reference to herself, Minnie looked up with a bright smile.

"You're awfully cross with me, aunty darling," she said; "but I forgive you. Only I can't help laughing, you know, to see how frightened you all are at poor Rufus K. Gunn. And, Kitty dearest, oh how you *did* run away from the window! It was awfully funny, you know."

Not long after the arrival of the Baron and his friends another carriage drove up. None of the ladies were at the window, and so they did not see the easy nonchalance of Hawbury as he lounged into the house, or the stern face of Scone Dacres as he strode before him.

"AS FOR DANGAIRE—POUF! DERE IS NONE."

CHAPTER XXII.

ADVICE REJECTED.

DURING dinner the ladies conversed freely about "that horrid man," wondering what plan he would adopt to try to effect an entrance among them. They were convinced that some such attempt would be made, and the servants of the inn who waited on them were strictly charged to see that no one disturbed them. However, their dinner was not interrupted and after it was over they began to think of retiring, so as to leave at an early hour on the following morning. Minnie had already taken her departure, and the others were thinking of following her example, when a knock came at the door.

All started. One of the maids went to the door, and found a servant there who brought a message from the Baron Atramonte. He wished to speak to the ladies on business of the most urgent importance. At this confirmation of their expectations the ladies looked at one another with a smile mingled with vexation, and Lady Dalrymple at once sent word that they could not possibly see him.

But the Baron was not to be put off. In a few moments the servant came back again, and brought another message, of a still more urgent character, in which the Baron entreated them to grant him this interview, and assured them that it was a matter of life and death.

"He's beginning to be more and more violent," said Lady Dalrymple. "Well, dears," she added, resignedly, "in my opinion it will be better to see him, and have done with him. If we do not, I'm afraid he will pester us further. I will see him. You had better retire to your own apartments."

Upon this she sent down an invitation to the Baron to come up, and the ladies retreated to their rooms.

The Baron entered, and, as usual, offered to shake hands—an offer which, as usual, Lady Dalrymple did not accept. He then looked earnestly all round the room, and gave a sigh. He evidently had expected to see Minnie, and was disappointed. Lady Dalrymple marked the glance, and the expression which followed.

"Well, ma'am," said he, as he seated himself near to Lady Dalrymple, "I said that the business I wanted to speak about was important, and that it was a matter of life and death. I assure you that it is. But before I tell it I want to say something about the row in Rome. I have reason to understand that I caused a little annoyance to you all. If I did, I'm sure I didn't intend it. I'm sorry. There! Let's say no more about it. 'Tain't often that I say I'm sorry, but I say so now. Conditionally, though—that is, if I really *did* annoy any body."

"Well, Sir?"

"Well, ma'am—about the business I came for. You have made a sudden decision to take this journey. I want to know, ma'am, if you made any inquiries about this road before starting?"

"This road? No, certainly not."

"I thought so," said the Baron. "Well, ma'am, I've reason to believe that it's somewhat unsafe."

"Unsafe?"

"Yes; particularly for ladies."

"And why?"

"Why, ma'am, the country is in a disordered state, and near the boundary line it swarms with brigands. They call themselves Garibaldians, but between you and me, ma'am, they're neither more nor less than robbers. You see, along the boundary it is convenient for them to dodge to one side or the other, and where the road runs there are often crowds of them. Now our papal government means well, but it ain't got power to keep down these brigands. It would like to, but it can't. You see, the scum of all Italy gather along the borders, because they know we *are* weak; and so there it is."

"And you think there is danger on this road?" said Lady Dalrymple, looking keenly at him.

"I do, ma'am."

"Pray have you heard of any recent acts of violence along the road?"

"No, ma'am."

"Then what reason have you for supposing that there is any particular danger now?"

"A friend of mine told me so, ma'am."

"But do not people use the road? Are not carriages constantly passing and repassing? Is it likely that if it were unsafe there would be no acts of violence? Yet you say there have been none."

"Not of late, ma'am."

"But it is of late, and of the present time, that we are speaking."

"I can only say, ma'am, that the road is considered very dangerous."

"Who considers it so?"

"If you had made inquiries at Rome, ma'am, you would have found this out, and never would have thought of this road."

"And you advise us not to travel it?"

"I do, ma'am."

"What would you advise us to do?"

"I would advise you, ma'am, most earnestly, to turn and go back to Rome, and leave by another route."

Lady Dalrymple looked at him, and a slight smile quivered on her lips.

"I see, ma'am, that for some reason or other you doubt my word. Would you put confidence in it if another person were to confirm what I have said?"

"That depends entirely upon who the other person may be."

"The person I mean is Lord Hawbury."

"Lord Hawbury? Indeed!" said Lady Dalrymple, in some surprise. "But he's in Rome."

"No, ma'am, he's not. He's here—in this hotel."

"In this hotel? Here?"

"Yes, ma'am."

"I'm sure I should like to see him very much, and hear what he says about it."

"I'll go and get him, then," said the Baron, and, rising briskly, he left the room.

In a short time he returned with Hawbury. Lady Dalrymple expressed surprise to see him, and Hawbury explained that he was traveling with a friend. Lady Dalrymple, of course, thought this a fresh proof of his infatuation about Minnie, and wondered how he could be a friend to a man whom she considered as Minnie's persecutor and tormentor.

The Baron at once proceeded to explain how the matter stood, and to ask Hawbury's opinion.

"Yes," said Lady Dalrymple, "I should really like to know what you think about it."

"Well, really," said Hawbury, "I have no acquaintance with the thing, you know. Never been on this road in my life. But, at the same time, I can assure you that this gentleman is a particular friend of mine, and one of the best fellows I know. I'd stake my life on his perfect truth and honor. If he says any thing, you may believe it because he says it. If he says there are brigands on the road, they must be there."

"Oh, of course," said Lady Dalrymple. "You are right to believe your friend, and I should trust his word also. But do you not see that perhaps he may believe what he says, and yet be mistaken?"

At this the Baron's face fell. Lord Hawbury's warm commendation of him had excited his hopes, but now Lady Dalrymple's answer had destroyed them.

"For my part," she added, "I don't really think any of us know much about it. I wish we could find some citizen of the town, or some reliable person, and ask him. I wonder whether the inn-keeper is a trust-worthy man."

The Baron shook his head.

"I wouldn't trust one of them. They're the greatest rascals in the country. Every man of them is in league with the Garibaldians and brigands. This man would advise you to take whatever course would benefit himself and his friends most."

"But surely we might find some one whose opinion would be reliable. What do you say to one of my drivers? The one that drove our carriage looks like a good, honest man."

"Well, perhaps so; but I wouldn't trust one of them. I don't believe there's an honest vetturino in all Italy."

Lady Dalrymple elevated her eyebrows, and threw at Hawbury a glance of despair.

"He speaks English, too," said Lady Dalrymple.

"So do some of the worst rascals in the country," said the Baron.

"Oh, I don't think he can be a very bad rascal. We had better question him, at any rate. Don't you think so, Lord Hawbury?"

"Well, yes; I suppose it won't do any harm to have a look at the beggar."

The driver alluded to was summoned, and soon made his appearance. He was a square-headed fellow, with a grizzled beard, and one of those non-committal faces which may be worn by either an honest man or a knave. Lady Dalrymple thought him the former; the Baron the latter. The result will show which of these was in the right.

The driver spoke very fair English. He had been two or three times over the road. He had not been over it later than two years before. He didn't know it was dangerous. He had never heard of brigands being here. He didn't know. There was a signore at the hotel who might know. He was traveling to Florence alone. He was on horseback.

As soon as Lady Dalrymple heard this she suspected that it was Count Girasole. She determined to have his advice about it. So she sent a private request to that effect.

It was Count Girasole. He entered, and threw his usual smile around. He was charmed, in his broken English, to be of any service to miladi.

To Lady Dalrymple's statement and question Girasole listened attentively. As she concluded a faint smile passed over his face. The Baron watched him attentively.

"I know no brigand on dissa road," said he.

Lady Dalrymple looked triumphantly at the others.

"I have travail dissa road many time. No dangaire—alla safe."

Another smile from Lady Dalrymple.

The Count Girasole looked at Hawbury and then at the Baron, with a slight dash of mockery in his face.

"As for dangaire," he said—"pouf! dere is none. See, I go alone—no arms, not a knife—an' yet gold in my porte-monnaie."

And he drew forth his porte-monnaie, and opened it so as to exhibit its contents.

A little further conversation followed. Girasole evidently was perfectly familiar with the road. The idea of brigands appeared to strike him as some exquisite piece of pleasantry. He looked as though it was only his respect for the company which prevented him from laughing outright. They had taken the trouble to summon him for that! And, besides, as the Count suggested, even if a brigand did appear, there would be always travelers within hearing.

Both Hawbury and the Baron felt humiliated, especially the latter; and Girasole certainly had the best of it on that occasion, whatever his lot had been at other times.

The Count withdrew. The Baron followed, in company with Hawbury. He was deeply dejected. First of all, he had hoped to see Minnie. Then he hoped to frighten the party back. As to the brigands, he was in most serious earnest. All that he said he believed. He could not understand the driver and Count Girasole. The former he might consider a scoundrel; but why should Girasole mislead? And yet he believed that he was right. As for Hawbury, he didn't believe much in the brigands, but he did believe in his friend, and he didn't think much of Girasole. He was sorry for his friend, yet didn't know whether he wanted the party to turn back or not. His one trouble was Dacres, who now was watching the Italian like a blood-hound, who had seen him, no doubt, go up to the ladies, and, of course, would suppose that Mrs. Willoughby had sent for him.

As for the ladies, their excitement was great. The doors were thin, and they had heard every word of the conversation. With Mrs. Willoughby there was but one opinion as to the Baron's motive: she thought he had come to get a peep at Minnie, and also to frighten them back to Rome by silly stories. His signal failure afforded her great triumph. Minnie, as usual, sympathized with him, but said nothing. As for Ethel, the sudden arrival of Lord Hawbury was overwhelming, and brought a return of all her former excitement. The sound of his voice again vibrated through her, and at first there began to arise no end of wild hopes, which, however, were as quickly dispelled. The question arose, What brought him there? There seemed to her but one answer, and that was his infatuation for Minnie. Yet to her, as well as to Lady Dalrymple, it seemed very singular that he should be so warm a friend to Minnie's tormentor. It was a puzzling thing. Perhaps he did not know that the Baron was Minnie's lover. Perhaps he thought that his friend would give her up, and he could win her. Amidst these thoughts there came a wild hope that perhaps he did not love Minnie so very much, after all. But this hope soon was dispelled as she recalled the events of the past, and reflected on his cool and easy indifference to every thing connected with her.

Such emotions as these actuated the ladies; and when the guests had gone they joined their aunt once more, and deliberated. Minnie took no part in the debate, but sat apart, looking like an injured being. There was among them all the same opinion, and that was that it was all a clumsy device of the Baron's to frighten them back to Rome. Such being their opinion, they did not occupy much time in debating about their course on the morrow. The idea of going back did not enter their heads.

This event gave a much more agreeable feeling to Mrs. Willoughby and Lady Dalrymple than they had known since they had been aware that the Baron had followed them. They felt that they had grappled with the difficulty. They had met the enemy and defeated him. Besides, the presence of Hawbury was of itself a guarantee of peace. There could be no further danger of any unpleasant scenes while Hawbury was with him. Girasole's presence, also, was felt to be an additional guarantee of safety.

It was felt by all to be a remarkable circumstance that so many men should have followed them on what they had intended as quite a secret journey. These gentlemen who followed them were the very ones, and the only ones, from whom they wished to conceal it. Yet it had all been revealed to them, and lo! here they all were. Some debate arose as to whether it would not be better to go back to Rome now, and defy the Baron, and leave by another route. But this debate was soon given up, and they looked forward to the journey as one which might afford new and peculiar enjoyment.

On the following morning they started at an early hour. Girasole left about half an hour after them, and passed them a few miles along the road. The Baron and the Reverend Saul left next; and last of all came Hawbury and Dacres. The latter was, if possible, more gloomy and vengeful than ever. The visit of the Italian on the preceding evening was fully believed by him to be a scheme of his wife's. Nor could any amount of persuasion or vehement statement on Hawbury's part in any way shake his belief.

"No," he would say, "you don't understand. Depend upon it, she got him up there to feast her eyes on him. Depend upon it, she managed to get some note from him, and pass one to him in return. He had only to run it under the leaf of a table, or stick it inside of some book: no doubt they have it all arranged, and pass their infernal love-letters backward and forward. But I'll soon have a chance. My time is coming. It's near, too. I'll have my vengeance; and then for all the wrongs of all my life that demon of a woman shall pay me dear!"

To all of which Hawbury had nothing to say. He could say nothing; he could do nothing. He could only stand by his friend, go with him, and watch over him, hoping to avert the crisis which he dreaded, or, if it did come, to lessen the danger of his friend.

The morning was clear and beautiful. The road wound among the hills. The party went in the order above mentioned.

First, Girasole, on horseback.

Next, and two miles at least behind, came the two carriages with the ladies and their maids.

Third, and half a mile behind these, came the Baron and the Reverend Saul.

Last of all, and half a mile behind the Baron, came Hawbury and Scone Dacres.

These last drove along at about this distance. The scenery around grew grander, and the mountains higher. The road was smooth and well constructed, and the carriage rolled along with an easy, comfortable rumble.

They were driving up a slope which wound along the side of a hill. At the top of the hill trees appeared on each side, and the road made a sharp turn here.

Suddenly the report of a shot sounded ahead.

Then a scream.

"Good Lord! Dacres, did you hear that?" cried Hawbury. "The Baron was right, after all."

The driver here tried to stop his horses, but Hawbury would not let him.

"Have you a pistol, Dacres?"

"No."

"Get out!" he shouted to the driver; and, kicking him out of the seat, he seized the reins himself, and drove the horses straight forward to where the noise arose.

"It's the brigands, Dacres. The ladies are there."

"My wife! O God! my wife!" groaned Dacres. But a minute before he had been cursing her.

"Get a knife! Get something, man! Have a fight for it!"

Dacres murmured something.

Hawbury lashed the horses, and drove them straight toward the wood.

CHAPTER XXIII.

CAUGHT IN AMBUSH.

THE ladies had been driving on, quite unconscious of the neighborhood of any danger, admiring the beauty of the scenery, and calling one another's attention to the various objects of interest which from time to time became visible. Thus engaged, they slowly ascended the incline already spoken of, and began to enter the forest. They had not gone far when the road took a sudden turn, and here a startling spectacle burst upon their view.

The road on turning descended slightly into a hollow. On the right arose a steep acclivity, covered with the dense forest. On the other side the ground rose more gradually, and was covered over by a forest much less dense. Some distance in front the road took another turn, and was lost to view among the trees. About a hundred yards in front of them a tree had been felled, and lay across the way, barring their progress.

About twenty armed men stood before them close by the place where the turn was. Among them was a man on horseback. To their amazement, it was Girasole.

Before the ladies could recover from their astonishment two of the armed men advanced, and the driver at once stopped the carriage.

Girasole then came forward.

"Miladi," said he, "I haf de honore of to invitar you to descend."

"Pray what is the meaning of this?" inquired Lady Dalrymple, with much agitation.

"It means dat I war wrong. Dere are brigand on dis road."

Lady Dalrymple said not another word.

The Count approached, and politely offered his hand to assist the ladies out, but they rejected it, and got out themselves. First Mrs. Willoughby, then Ethel, then Lady Dalrymple, then Minnie. Three of the ladies were white with utter horror, and looked around in sickening fear upon the armed men; but Minnie showed not even the slightest particle of fear.

"How horrid!" she exclaimed. "And now some one will come and save my life again. It's *always* the way. I'm sure *this* isn't my fault, Kitty darling."

Before her sister could say any thing Girasole approached.

"Pardon, mees," he said; "but I haf made dis recepzion for you. You sall be well treat. Do not fear. I lay down my life."

"Villain!" cried Lady Dalrymple. "Arrest her at your peril. Remember who she is. She has friends powerful enough to avenge her if you dare to injure her."

"You arra mistake," said Girasole, politely. "Se is mine, not yours. I am her best fren. Se is fiancée to me. I save her life—tell her my love—make a proposezion. Se accept me. Se is my fiancée. I was oppose by you. What else sall I do? I mus haf her. Se is mine. I am an Italiano nobile, an' I love her. Dere is no harm for any. You mus see dat I haf de right. But for me se would be dead."

Lady Dalrymple was not usually excitable, but now her whole nature was aroused; her eyes flashed with indignation; her face turned red; she gasped for breath, and fell to the ground. Ethel rushed to assist her, and two of the maids came up. Lady Dalrymple lay senseless.

With Mrs. Willoughby the result was different. She burst into tears.

"Count Girasole," she cried, "oh, spare her! If you love her, spare her. She is only a child. If we opposed you, it was not from any objection to you; it was because she is such a child."

"You mistake," said the Count, shrugging his shoulders. "I love her better than life. Se love me. It will make her happy. You come too. You sall see se is happy. Come. Be my sistaire. It is love—"

Mrs. Willoughby burst into fresh tears at this, and flung her arms around Minnie, and moaned and wept.

"Well, now, Kitty darling, I think it's horrid. You're *never* satisfied. You're always finding fault. I'm sure if you don't like Rufus K. Gunn, you—"

But Minnie's voice was interrupted by the sound of approaching wheels. It was the carriage of the Baron and his friend. The Baron had feared brigands, but he was certainly not expecting to come upon them so suddenly. The brigands had been prepared, and as the carriage turned it was suddenly stopped by the two carriages in front, and at once was surrounded.

The Baron gave one lightning glance, and surveyed the whole situation. He did not move, but his form was rigid, and every nerve was braced, and his eyes gleamed fiercely. He saw it all—the crowd of women, the calm face of Minnie, and the uncontrollable agitation of Mrs. Willoughby.

"Well, by thunder!" he exclaimed.

Girasole rode up and called out:

"Surrender! You arra my prisoner."

"What! it's you, is it?" said the Baron; and he glared for a moment with a vengeful look at Girasole.

"Descend," said Girasole. "You mus be bound."

"Bound? All right. Here, parson, you jump down, and let them tie your hands."

The Baron stood up. The Reverend Saul stood up too. The Reverend Saul began to step down very carefully. The brigands gathered around, most of them being on the side on which the two were about to descend. The Reverend Saul had just stepped to the ground. The Baron was just preparing to follow. The brigands were impatient to secure them, when suddenly, with a quick movement, the Baron gave a spring out of the opposite side of the carriage, and leaped to the ground. The brigands were taken completely by surprise, and before they could prepare to follow him, he had sprung into the forest, and, with long bounds, was rushing up the steep hill and out of sight.

One shot was fired after him, and that was the shot that Hawbury and Dacres heard. Two men sprang after him with the hope of catching him.

In a few moments a loud cry was heard from the woods.

"MIN!"

Minnie heard it; a gleam of light flashed from her eyes, a smile of triumph came over her lips.

"Wha-a-a-t?" she called in reply.

"Wa-a-a-a-a-it!" was the cry that came back—and this was the cry that Hawbury and Dacres had heard.

"Sacr-r-r-r-r-remento!" growled Girasole.

"I'm sure *I* don't know what he means by telling me that," said Minnie. "How can *I* wait if this horrid Italian won't let me? I'm sure he might be more considerate."

Poor Mrs. Willoughby, who had for a moment been roused to hope by the escape of the Baron, now fell again into despair, and wept and moaned and clung to Minnie. Lady Dalrymple still lay senseless, in spite of the efforts of Ethel and the maids. The occurrence had been more to her than a mere encounter with brigands. It was the thought of her own carelessness that overwhelmed her. In an instant the thought of the Baron's warning and his solemn entreaties flashed across her memory. She recollected how Hawbury had commended his friend, and how she had turned from these to put her trust in the driver and Girasole, the very men who had betrayed her. These were the thoughts that overwhelmed her.

But now there arose once more the noise of rolling wheels, advancing more swiftly than the last, accompanied by the lash of a whip and shouts of a human voice. Girasole spoke to his men, and they moved up nearer to the bend, and stood in readiness there.

What Hawbury's motive was it is not difficult to tell. He was not armed, and therefore could not hope to do much; but he had in an instant resolved to rush thus into the midst of the danger. First of all he thought that a struggle might be going on between the drivers, the other travelers, and the brigands; in which event his assistance would be of great value. Though unarmed, he thought he might snatch or wrest a weapon from some one of the enemy. In addition to this, he wished to strike a blow to save the ladies from captivity, even if his blow should be unavailing. Even if he had known how matters were, he would probably have acted in precisely the same way. As for Dacres, he had but one idea. He was sure it was some trick concocted by his wife and the Italian, though why they should do so he did not stop, in his mad mood, to inquire. A vague idea that a communication had passed between them on the preceding evening with reference to this was now in his mind, and his vengeful feeling was stimulated by this thought to the utmost pitch of intensity.

Hawbury thus lashed his horses, and they flew along the road. After the first cry and the shot that they had heard there was no further noise. The stillness was mysterious. It showed Hawbury that the struggle, if there had been any, was over. But the first idea still remained both in his own mind and in that of Dacres. On they went, and now they came to the turn in the road. Round this they whirled, and in an instant the scene revealed itself.

Three carriages stopped; some drivers standing and staring indifferently; a group of women crowding around a prostrate form that lay in the road; a pale, beautiful girl, to whom a beautiful woman was clinging passionately; a crowd of armed brigands with leveled pieces; and immediately before them a horseman—the Italian, Girasole.

One glance showed all this. Hawbury could not distinguish any face among the crowd of women that bent over Lady Dalrymple, and Ethel's face was thus still unrevealed; but he saw Minnie and Mrs. Willoughby and Girasole.

"What the devil's all this about?" asked Hawbury, haughtily, as his horses stopped at the Baron's carriage.

"You are prisoners—" began Girasole.

But before he could say another word he was interrupted by a cry of fury from Dacres, who, the moment that he had recognized him, sprang to his feet, and with a long, keen knife in his hand, leaped from the carriage into the midst of the brigands, striking right and left, and endeavoring to force his way toward Girasole. In an instant Hawbury was by his side. Two men fell beneath the fierce thrusts of Dacres's knife, and Hawbury tore the rifle from a third. With the clubbed end of this he began dealing blows right and left. The men fell back and leveled their pieces. Dacres sprang forward, and was within three steps of Girasole—his face full of ferocity, his eyes flashing, and looking not so much like an English gentleman as one of the old vikings in a Berserker rage. One more spring brought him closer to Girasole. The Italian retreated. One of his men flung himself before Dacres and tried to grapple with him. The next instant he fell with a groan, stabbed to the heart. With a yell of rage the others rushed upon Dacres; but the latter was now suddenly seized with a new idea. Turning for an instant he held his assailants at bay; and then, seizing the opportunity, sprang into the woods and ran. One or two shots were fired, and then half a dozen men gave chase.

Meanwhile one or two shots had been fired at Hawbury, but, in the confusion, they had not taken effect. Suddenly, as he stood with uplifted rifle ready to strike, his enemies made a simultaneous rush upon him. He was seized by a dozen strong arms. He struggled fiercely, but his efforts were unavailing. The odds were too great. Before long he was thrown to the ground on his face, and his arms bound behind him. After this he was gagged.

The uproar of this fierce struggle had roused all the ladies, and they turned their eyes in horror to where the two were fighting against such odds. Ethel raised herself on her knees from beside Lady Dalrymple, and caught sight of Hawbury. For a moment she remained motionless; and then she saw the escape of Dacres, and Hawbury going down in the grasp of his assailants. She gave a loud shriek and rushed forward. But Girasole intercepted her.

"Go back," he said. "De milor is my prisoner. Back, or you will be bound."

And at a gesture from him two of the men advanced to seize Ethel.

"Back!" he said, once more, in a stern voice. "You mus be tentif to miladi."

Ethel shrank back.

The sound of that scream had struck on Hawbury's ears, but he did not recognize it. If he thought of it at all, he supposed it was the scream of common terror from one of the women. He was sore and bruised and fast bound. He was held down also in such a way that he could not see the party of ladies. The Baron's carriage intercepted the view, for he had fallen behind this during the final struggle. After a little time he was allowed to sit up, but still he could not see beyond.

There was now some delay, and Girasole gave some orders to his men. The ladies waited with fearful apprehensions. They listened eagerly to hear if there might not be some sounds of approaching help. But no such sounds came to gladden their hearts. Lady Dalrymple, also, still lay senseless; and Ethel, full of the direst anxiety about Hawbury, had to return to renew her efforts toward reviving her aunt.

Before long the brigands who had been in pursuit of the fugitives returned to the road. They did not bring back either of them. A dreadful question arose in the minds of the ladies as to the meaning of this. Did it mean that the fugitives had escaped, or had been shot down in the woods by their wrathful pursuers? It was impossible for them to find out. Girasole went over to them and conversed with them apart. The men all looked sullen; but whether that arose from disappointed vengeance or gratified ferocity it was impossible for them to discern.

THE MÊLÉE.

The brigands now turned their attention to their own men. Two of these had received bad but not dangerous wounds from the dagger of Dacres, and the scowls of pain and rage which they threw upon Hawbury and the other captives boded nothing but the most cruel fate to all of them. Another, however, still lay there. It was the one who had intercepted Dacres in his rush upon Girasole. He lay motionless in a pool of blood. They turned him over. His white, rigid face, as it became exposed to view, exhibited the unmistakable mark of death, and a gash on his breast showed how his fate had met him.

The brigands uttered loud cries, and advanced toward Hawbury. He sat regarding them with perfect indifference. They raised their rifles, some clubbing them, others taking aim, swearing and gesticulating all the time like maniacs.

Hawbury, however, did not move a muscle of his face, nor did he show the slightest feeling of any kind. He was covered with dust, and his clothes were torn and splashed with mud, and his hands were bound, and his mouth was gagged; but he preserved a coolness that astonished his enemies. Had it not been for this coolness his brains might have been blown out—in which case this narrative would never have been written; but there was something in his look which made the Italians pause, gave Girasole time to interfere, and thus preserved my story from ruin.

Girasole then came up and made his men stand back. They obeyed sullenly.

Girasole removed the gag.

Then he stood and looked at Hawbury. Hawbury sat and returned his look with his usual nonchalance, regarding the Italian with a cold, steady stare, which produced upon the latter its usual maddening effect.

"Milor will be ver glad to hear," said he, with a mocking smile, "dat de mees will be take good care to. Milor was attentif to de mees; but de mees haf been fiancée to me, an' so I take dis occazione to mak her mine. I sall love her, an' se sall love me. I haf save her life, an' se haf been fiancée to me since den."

Now Girasole had chosen to say this to Hawbury from the conviction that Hawbury was Minnie's lover, and that the statement of this would inflict a pang upon the heart of his supposed rival which would destroy his coolness. Thus he chose rather to strike at Hawbury's jealousy than at his fear or at his pride.

But he was disappointed. Hawbury heard his statement with utter indifference.

"Well," said he, "all I can say is that it seems to me to be a devilish odd way of going to work about it."

"Aha!" said Girasole, fiercely. "You sall see. Se sall be mine. Aha!"

Hawbury made no reply, and Girasole, after a gesture of impatience, walked off, baffled.

In a few minutes two men came up to Hawbury, and led him away to the woods on the left.

"THEY SAW A RUINED HOUSE."

CHAPTER XXIV.

AMONG THE BRIGANDS.

GIRASOLE now returned to the ladies. They were in the same position in which he had left them. Mrs. Willoughby with Minnie, and Ethel, with the maids, attending to Lady Dalrymple.

"Miladi," said Girasole, "I beg your attenzion. I haf had de honore to inform you dat dis mees is my fiancée. Se haf give me her heart an' her hand; se love me, an' I love her. I was prevent from to see her, an' I haf to take her in dis mannaire. I feel sad at de pain I haf give you, an' assuir you dat it was inevitabile. You sall not be troubled more. You are free. Mees," he continued, taking Minnie's hand, "you haf promis me dis fair han', an' you are mine. You come to one who loves you bettaire dan life, an' who you love. You owe youair life to me. I sall make it so happy as nevair was."

"I'm sure *I* don't want to be happy," said Minnie. "I don't *want* to leave darling Kitty—and it's a shame—and you'll make me *hate* you if you do so."

"Miladi," said Girasole to Mrs. Willoughby, "de mees says se not want to leaf you. Eef you want to come, you may come an' be our sistaire."

"Oh, Kitty darling, you won't leave me, will you, all alone with this horrid man?" said Minnie.

"My darling," moaned Mrs. Willoughby, "how can I? I'll go. Oh, my sweet sister, what misery!"

"Oh, now that will be really *quite* delightful if you *will* come, Kitty darling. Only I'm afraid you'll find it awfully uncomfortable."

Girasole turned once more to the other ladies.

"I beg you will assura de miladi when she recovaire of my considerazion de mos distingue, an' convey to her de regrettas dat I haf. Miladi," he continued, addressing Ethel, "you are free, an' can go. You will not be molest by me. You sall go safe. You haf not ver far. You sall fin' houses dere—forward—before—not far."

With these words he turned away.

"You mus come wit me," he said to Mrs. Willoughby and Minnie. "Come. Eet ees not ver far."

He walked slowly into the woods on the left, and the two sisters followed him. Of the two Minnie was far the more cool and collected. She was as composed as usual; and, as there was no help for it, she walked on. Mrs.

Willoughby, however, was terribly agitated, and wept and shuddered and moaned incessantly.

"Kitty darling," said Minnie, "I *wish* you wouldn't go on so. You really make me feel quite nervous. I never saw you so bad in my life."

"Poor Minnie! Poor child! Poor sweet child!"

"Well, if I am a child, you needn't go and tell me about it all the time. It's really quite horrid."

Mrs. Willoughby said no more, but generously tried to repress her own feelings, so as not to give distress to her sister.

After the Count had entered the wood with the two sisters the drivers removed the horses from the carriages and went away, led off by the man who had driven the ladies. This was the man whose stolid face had seemed likely to belong to an honest man, but who now was shown to belong to the opposite class. These men went down the road over which they had come, leaving the carriages there with the ladies and their maids.

Girasole now led the way, and Minnie and her sister followed him. The wood was very thick, and grew more so as they advanced, but there was not much underbrush, and progress was not difficult. Several times a wild thought of flight came to Mrs. Willoughby, but was at once dispelled by a helpless sense of its utter impossibility. How could she persuade the impracticable Minnie, who seemed so free from all concern? or, if she could persuade her, how could she accomplish her desire? She would at once be pursued and surrounded, while, even if she did manage to escape, how could she ever find her way to any place of refuge? Every minute, also, drew them deeper and deeper into the woods, and the path was a winding one, in which she soon became bewildered, until at last all sense of her whereabouts was utterly gone. At last even the idea of escaping ceased to suggest itself, and there remained only a dull despair, a sense of utter helplessness and hopelessness—the sense of one who is going to his doom.

Girasole said nothing whatever, but led the way in silence, walking slowly enough to accommodate the ladies, and sometimes holding an overhanging branch to prevent it from springing back in their faces. Minnie walked on lightly, and with an elastic step, looking around with evident interest upon the forest. Once a passing lizard drew from her a pretty little shriek of alarm, thus showing that while she was so calm in the face of real and frightful danger, she could be alarmed by even the most innocent object that affected her fancy. Mrs. Willoughby thought that she understood Minnie before, but this little shriek at a lizard, from one who smiled at the brigands, struck her as a problem quite beyond her power to solve.

The woods now began to grow thinner. The trees were larger and farther apart, and rose all around in columnar array, so that it was possible to see between them to a greater distance. At length there appeared before them, through the trunks of the trees, the gleam of water. Mrs. Willoughby noticed this, and wondered what it might be. At first she thought it was a harbor on the coast; then she thought it was some river; but finally, on coming nearer, she saw that it was a lake. In a few minutes after they first caught sight of it they had reached its banks.

It was a most beautiful and sequestered spot. All around were high wooded eminences, beyond whose undulating summits arose the towering forms of the Apennine heights. Among these hills lay a little lake about a mile in length and breadth, whose surface was as smooth as glass, and reflected the surrounding shores. On their right, as they descended, they saw some figures moving, and knew them to be the brigands, while on their left they saw a ruined house. Toward this Girasole led them.

The house stood on the shore of the lake. It was of stone, and was two stories in height. The roof was still good, but the windows were gone. There was no door, but half a dozen or so of the brigands stood there, and formed a sufficient guard to prevent the escape of any prisoner. These men had dark, wicked eyes and sullen faces, which afforded fresh terror to Mrs. Willoughby. She had thought, in her desperation, of making some effort to escape by bribing the men, but the thorough-bred rascality which was evinced in the faces of these ruffians showed her that they were the very fellows who would take her money and cheat her afterward. If she had been able to speak Italian, she might have secured their services by the prospect of some future reward after escaping; but, as it was, she could not speak a word of the language, and thus could not enter upon even the preliminaries of an escape.

On reaching the house the ruffians stood aside, staring hard at them. Mrs. Willoughby shrank in terror from the baleful glances of their eyes; but Minnie looked at them calmly and innocently, and not without some of that curiosity which a child shows when he first sees a Chinaman or an Arab in the streets. Girasole then led the way up stairs to a room on the second story.

It was an apartment of large size, extending across the house, with a window at each end, and two on the side. On the floor there was a heap of straw, over which some skins were thrown. There were no chairs, nor was there any table.

"Scusa me," said Girasole, "miladi, for dis accommodazion. It gifs me pain, but I promise it sall not be long. Only dis day an' dis night here. I haf to detain you dat time. Den we sall go to where I haf a home fitter for de bride. I haf a home wharra you sall be a happy bride, mees—"

"But I don't want to stay here *at all* in such a horrid place," said Minnie, looking around in disgust.

"Only dis day an' dis night," said Girasole, imploringly. "Aftaire you sall have all you sall wis."

"Well, at any rate, I think it's very horrid in you to shut me up here. You might let me walk outside in the woods. I'm so *aw*fully fond of the woods."

Girasole smiled faintly.

"And so you sall have plenty of de wood—but to-morra. You wait here now. All safe—oh yes—secura—all aright—oh yes—slip to-night, an' in de mornin' early you sall be mine. Dere sall come a priest, an' we sall have de ceremony."

"Well, I think it was very unkind in you to bring me to such a horrid place. And how can I sit down? You *might* have had a chair. And look at poor, darling Kitty. You may be unkind to me, but you needn't make *her* sit on the floor. You never saved *her* life, and you have no right to be unkind to her."

"Unkind! Oh, mees!—my heart, my life, all arra youairs, an' I lay my life at youair foot."

"I think it would be far more kind if you would put a chair at poor Kitty's feet," retorted Minnie, with some show of temper.

"But, oh, carissima, tink—de wild wood—noting here—no, noting—not a chair—only de straw."

"Then you had no business to bring me here. You might have known that there were no chairs here. I can't sit down on nothing. But I suppose you expect me to stand up. And if that isn't horrid, I don't know what is. I'm sure I don't know what poor dear papa would say if he were to see me now."

"WHAT IS THIS FOR?"

"Do not grieve, carissima mia—do not, charming mees, decompose yourself. To-morra you sall go to a bettaire place, an' I will carra you to my castello. You sall haf every want, you sall enjoy every wis, you sall be happy."

"But I don't see how I can be happy without a chair," reiterated Minnie, in whose mind this one grievance now became pre-eminent. "You talk as though you think I am made of stone or iron, and you think I can stand here all day or all night, and you want me to sleep on that horrid straw and those horrid furry things. I suppose this is the castle that you speak of; and I'm sure I wonder why you *ever* thought of bringing me here. I suppose it doesn't make so much difference about a *carpet*; but you will not even let me have a *chair*; and I think you're *very* unkind."

Girasole was in despair. He stood in thought for some time. He felt that Minnie's rebuke was deserved. If she had reproached him with waylaying her and carrying her off, he could have borne it, and could have found a reply. But such a charge as this was unanswerable. It certainly was very hard that she should not be able to sit down. But then how was it possible for him to find a chair in the woods? It was an insoluble problem. How in the world could he satisfy her?

Minnie's expression also was most touching. The fact that she had no chair to sit on seemed to absolutely overwhelm her. The look that she gave

Girasole was so piteous, so reproachful, so heart-rending, that his soul actually quaked, and a thrill of remorse passed all through his frame. He felt a cold chill running to the very marrow of his bones.

"I think you're *very, very* unkind," said Minnie, "and I really don't see how I can *ever* speak to you again."

This was too much. Girasole turned away. He rushed down stairs. He wandered frantically about. He looked in all directions for a chair. There was plenty of wood certainly—for all around he saw the vast forest—but of what use was it? He could not transform a tree into a chair. He communicated his difficulty to some of the men. They shook their heads helplessly. At last he saw the stump of a tree which was of such a shape that it looked as though it might be used as a seat. It was his only resource, and he seized it. Calling two or three of the men, he had the stump carried to the old house. He rushed up stairs to acquaint Minnie with his success, and to try to console her. She listened in coldness to his hasty words. The men who were carrying the stump came up with a clump and a clatter, breathing hard, for the stump was very heavy, and finally placed it on the landing in front of Minnie's door. On reaching that spot it was found that it would not go in.

Minnie heard the noise and came out. She looked at the stump, then at the men and then at Girasole.

"What is this for?" she asked.

"Eet—eet ees for a chair."

"A chair!" exclaimed Minnie. "Why, it's nothing but a great big, horrid, ugly old stump, and—"

Her remarks ended in a scream. She turned and ran back into the room.

"What—what is de mattaire?" cried the Count, looking into the room with a face pale with anxiety.

"Oh, take it away! take it away!" cried Minnie, in terror.

"What? what?"

"Take it away! take it away!" she repeated.

"But eet ees for you—eet ees a seat."

"I don't want it. I won't have it!" cried Minnie. "It's full of horrid ants and things. And it's dreadful—and *very, very* cruel in you to bring them up here just to *tease* me, when you *know* I hate them so. Take it away! take it away! oh, do please take it away! And oh, do please go away yourself, and leave me with dear, darling Kitty. *She* never teases me. She is *always* kind."

Girasole turned away once more, in fresh trouble. He had the stump carried off, and then he wandered away. He was quite at a loss what to do. He was desperately in love, and it was a very small request for Minnie to make, and he was in that state of mind when it would be a happiness to grant her slightest wish; but here he found himself in a difficulty from which he could find no possible means of escape.

"And now, Kitty darling," said Minnie, after Girasole had gone—"now you see how very, very wrong you were to be so opposed to that dear, good, kind, nice Rufus K. Gunn. *He* would never have treated me so. *He* would never have taken me to a place like this—a horrid old house by a horrid damp pond, without doors and windows, just like a beggar's house—and then put me in a room without a chair to sit on when I'm so *aw*fully tired. He was *always* kind to me, and that was the reason you hated him so, because you couldn't bear to have people kind to me. And I'm *so* tired."

"Come, then, poor darling. I'll make a nice seat for you out of these skins."

And Mrs. Willoughby began to fold some of them up and lay them one upon the other.

"What is that for, Kitty dear?" asked Minnie.

"To make you a nice, soft seat, dearest."

"But I don't want them, and I won't sit on the horrid things," said Minnie.

"But, darling, they are as soft as a cushion. See!" And her sister pressed her hand on them, so as to show how soft they were.

"I don't think they're soft *at all*," said Minnie; "and I wish you wouldn't tease me so, when I'm *so* tired."

"Then come, darling; I will sit on them, and you shall sit on my knees."

"But I don't want to go near those horrid furry things. They belong to cows and things. I think *every body's* unkind to me to-day."

"Minnie, dearest, you really wound me when you talk in that way. Be reasonable now. See what pains I take. I do all I can for you."

"But I'm *always* reasonable, and it's *you* that are unreasonable, when you want me to sit on that horrid fur. It's very, *very* disagreeable in you, Kitty dear."

Mrs. Willoughby said nothing, but went on folding some more skins. These she placed on the straw so that a pile was formed about as high as an ordinary chair. This pile was placed against the wall so that the wall served as a support.

Then she seated herself upon this.

"Minnie, dearest," said she.

"Well, Kitty darling."

"It's really quite soft and comfortable. Do come and sit on it; do, just to please me, only for five minutes. See! I'll spread my dress over it so that you need not touch it. Come, dearest, only for five minutes."

"Well, I'll sit on it just for a little mite of a time, if you promise not to tease me."

"Tease you, dear! Why, of course not. Come."

So Minnie went over and sat by her sister's side.

In about an hour Girasole came back. The two sisters were seated there. Minnie's head was resting on her sister's shoulder, and she was fast asleep, while Mrs. Willoughby sat motionless, with her face turned toward him, and such an expression in her dark eyes that Girasole felt awed. He turned in silence and went away.

"ETHEL OBTAINED A PAIR OF SCISSORS."

CHAPTER XXV.

SEEKING FOR HELP.

THE departure of the drivers with their horses had increased the difficulties of the party, and had added to their danger. Of that party Ethel was now the head, and her efforts were directed more zealously than ever to bring back Lady Dalrymple to her senses. At last these efforts were crowned with success, and, after being senseless for nearly an hour, she came to herself. The restoration of her senses, however, brought with it the discovery of all that had occurred, and thus caused a new rush of emotion, which threatened painful consequences. But the consequences were averted, and at length she was able to rise. She was then helped into her carriage, after which the question arose as to their next proceeding.

The loss of the horses and drivers was a very embarrassing thing to them, and for a time they were utterly at a loss what course to adopt. Lady Dalrymple was too weak to walk, and they had no means of conveying her. The maids had simply lost their wits from fright; and Ethel could not see her way clearly out of the difficulty. At this juncture they were roused by the approach of the Rev. Saul Tozer.

This reverend man had been bound as he descended from his carriage, and had remained bound ever since. In that state he had been a spectator of the struggle and its consequences, and he now came forward to offer his services.

"I don't know whether you remember me, ma'am," said he to Lady Dalrymple, "but I looked in at your place at Rome; and in any case I am bound to offer you my assistance, since you are companions with me in my bonds, which I'd be much obliged if one of you ladies would untie or cut. Perhaps it would be best to untie it, as rope's valuable."

At this request Ethel obtained a pair of scissors from one of the maids, and after vigorous efforts succeeded in freeing the reverend gentleman.

"Really, Sir, I am very much obliged for this kind offer," said Lady Dalrymple, "and I avail myself of it gratefully. Can you advise us what is best to do?"

"Well, ma'am, I've been turning it over in my mind, and have made it a subject of prayer; and it seems to me that it wouldn't be bad to go out and see the country."

"There are no houses for miles," said Ethel.

"Have you ever been this road before?" said Tozer.

"No."

"Then how do you know?"

"Oh, I was thinking of the part we had passed over."

"True; but the country in front may be different. Didn't that brigand captain say something about getting help ahead?"

"Yes, so he did; I remember now," said Ethel.

"Well, I wouldn't take his advice generally, but in this matter I don't see any harm in following it; so I move that I be a committee of one to go ahead and investigate the country and bring help."

"Oh, thanks, thanks, very much. Really, Sir, this is very kind," said Lady Dalrymple.

"And I'll go too," said Ethel, as a sudden thought occurred to her. "Would you be afraid, aunty dear, to stay here alone?"

"Certainly not, dear. I have no more fear for myself, but I'm afraid to trust you out of my sight."

"Oh, you need not fear for me," said Ethel. "I shall certainly be as safe farther on as I am here. Besides, if we can find help I will know best what is wanted."

"Well, dear, I suppose you may go."

Without further delay Ethel started off, and Tozer walked by her side. They went under the fallen tree, and then walked quickly along the road.

"Do you speak Italian, miss?" asked Tozer.

"No."

"I'm sorry for that. I don't either. I'm told it's a fine language."

"So I believe; but how very awkward it will be not to be able to speak to any person!"

"Well, the Italian is a kind of offshoot of the Latin, and I can scrape together a few Latin words—enough to make myself understood, I do believe."

"Can you, really? How very fortunate!"

"It is somewhat providential, miss, and I hope I may succeed."

They walked on in silence now for some time. Ethel was too sad to talk, and Tozer was busily engaged in recalling all the Latin at his command. After a while he began to grow sociable.

"Might I ask, miss, what persuasion you are?"

"Persuasion?" said Ethel, in surprise.

"Yes, 'm; de-nomination—religious body, you know."

"Oh! why, I belong to the Church."

"Oh! and what church did you say, 'm?"

"The Church of England."

"H'm. The 'Piscopalian body. Well, it's a high-toned body."

Ethel gave a faint smile at this whimsical application of a name to her church, and then Tozer returned to the charge.

"Are you a professor?"

"A what?"

"A professor."

"A professor?" repeated Ethel. "I don't think I *quite* understand you."

"Well, do you belong to the church? Are you a member?"

"Oh yes."

"I'm glad to hear it. It's a high and a holy and a happy perrivelege to belong to the church and enjoy the means of grace. I trust you live up to your perrivileges?"

"Live what?" asked Ethel.

"Live up to your perrivileges," repeated Tozer—"attend on all the means of grace—be often at the assembling of yourself together."

"The assembling of myself together? I don't think I *quite* get your meaning," said Ethel.

"Meeting, you know—church-meeting."

"Oh yes; I didn't understand. Oh yes, I always go to church."

"That's right," said Tozer, with a sigh of relief; "and I suppose, now, you feel an interest in the cause of missions?"

"Missions? Oh, I don't know. The Roman Catholics practice that to some extent, and several of my friends say they feel benefit from a mission once a year; but for my part I have not yet any very decided leanings to Roman Catholicism."

"Oh, dear me, dear me!" cried Tozer, "that's not what I mean at all; I mean Protestant missions to the heathen, you know."

"I beg your pardon," said Ethel. "I thought you were referring to something else."

Tozer was silent now for a few minutes, and then asked her, abruptly,

"What's your opinion about the Jews?"

"The Jews?" exclaimed Ethel, looking at him in some surprise, and thinking that her companion must be a little insane to carry on such an extraordinary conversation with such very abrupt changes—"the Jews?"

"Yes, the Jews."

"Oh, I don't like them at all."

"But they're the chosen people."

"I can't help that. I don't like them. But then, you know, I never really saw much of them."

"I refer to their future prospects," said Tozer—"to prophecy. I should like to ask you how you regard them in that light. Do you believe in a spiritual or a temporal Zion?"

"Spiritual Zion? Temporal Zion?"

"Yes, 'm."

"Well, really, I don't know. I don't think I believe any thing at all about it."

"But you *must* believe in either one or the other—you've *got* to," said Tozer, positively.

"But I *don't*, you know; and how can I?"

Tozer threw at her a look of commiseration, and began to think that his companion was not much better than a heathen. In his own home circle he could have put his hand on little girls of ten who were quite at home on all these subjects. He was silent for a time, and then began again.

"I'd like to ask you one thing," said he, "very much."

"What is it?" asked Ethel.

"Do you believe," asked Tozer, solemnly, "that we're living in the Seventh Vial?"

"Vial? Seventh Vial?" said Ethel, in fresh amazement.

"Yes, the Seventh Vial," said Tozer, in a sepulchral voice.

"Living in the Seventh Vial? I really don't know how one can live in a vial."

"The Great Tribulation, you know."

"Great Tribulation?"

"Yes; for instance, now, don't you believe in the Apocalyptic Beast?"

"I don't know," said Ethel, faintly.

"Well, at any rate, you believe in his number—you must."

"His number?"

"Yes."

"What do you mean?"

"Why, the number six, six, six—six hundred and sixty-six."

"I really don't understand this," said Ethel.

"Don't you believe that the Sixth Vial is done?"

"Sixth Vial? What, another vial?"

"Yes; and the drying of the Euphrates."

"The Euphrates? drying?" repeated Ethel in a trembling voice. She began to be alarmed. She felt sure that this man was insane. She had never heard such incoherency in her life. And she was alone with him. She stole a timid look, and saw his long, sallow face, on which there was now a preoccupied expression, and the look did not reassure her.

But Tozer himself was a little puzzled, and felt sure that his companion must have her own opinions on the subject, so he began again:

"Now I suppose you've read Fleming on the Papacy?"

"No, I haven't. I never heard of it."

"Strange, too. You've heard of Elliot's 'Horæ Apocalypticæ?', I suppose?"

"No," said Ethel, timidly.

"Well, it's all in Cumming—and you've read him, of course?"

"Cumming? I never heard of him. Who is he?"

"What, never heard of Cumming?"

"Never."

"And never read his 'Great Tribulation?'"

"No."

"Nor his 'Great Expectation?'"

"No."

"What! not even his 'Apocalyptic Sketches?'"

"I never heard of them."

Tozer looked at her in astonishment; but at this moment they came to a turn in the road, when a sight appeared which drew from Ethel an expression of joy.

"TONITRUENDUM EST MALUM!"

It was a little valley on the right, in which was a small hamlet with a church. The houses were but small, and could not give them much accommodation, but they hoped to find help there.

"I wouldn't trust the people," said Ethel. "I dare say they're all brigands; but there ought to be a priest there, and we can appeal to him."

This proposal pleased Tozer, who resumed his work of collecting among the stores of his memory scraps of Latin which he had once stored away there.

The village was at no very great distance away from the road, and they reached it in a short time. They went at once to the church. The door was open, and a priest, who seemed the village priest, was standing there. He was stout, with a good-natured expression on his hearty, rosy face, and a fine twinkle in his eye, which lighted up pleasantly as he saw the strangers enter.

Tozer at once held out his hand and shook that of the priest.

"Buon giorno," said the priest.

Ethel shook her head.

"Parlate Italiano?" said he.

Ethel shook her head.

"Salve, domine," said Tozer, who at once plunged headlong into Latin.

"Salve bene," said the priest, in some surprise.

"Quomodo vales?" asked Tozer.

"Optime valeo, Dei gratia. Spero vos valere."

Tozer found the priest's pronunciation a little difficult, but managed to understand him.

"Domine," said he, "sumus viatores infelices et innocentes, in quos fures nuper impetum fecerunt. Omnia bona nostra arripuerunt—"

"Fieri non potest!" said the priest.

"Et omnes amicos nostros in captivitatem lachrymabilem tractaverunt—"

"Cor dolet," said the priest; "miseret me vestrum."

"Cujusmodi terra est hæc in qua sustenendum est tot labores?"

The priest sighed.

"Tonitruendum est malum!" exclaimed Tozer, excited by the recollection of his wrongs.

The priest stared.

"In hostium manibus fuimus, et, bonum tonitru! omnia impedimenta amissimus. Est nimis omnipotens malum!"

"Quid vis dicere?" said the priest, looking puzzled. "Quid tibi vis?"

"Est nimis sempiternum durum!"

"In nomine omnium sanctorum apostolorumque," cried the priest, "quid vis dicere?"

"Potes ne juvare nos," continued Tozer, "in hoc lachrymabile tempore? Volo unum verum vivum virum qui possit—"

"Diabolus arripiat me si possim unum solum verbum intelligere!" cried the priest. "Be jabers if I ondherstan' yez at all at all; an' there ye have it."

And with this the priest raised his head, with its puzzled look, and scratched that organ with such a natural air, and with such a full Irish flavor in his brogue and in his face, that both of his visitors were perfectly astounded.

"Good gracious!" cried Tozer; and seizing the priest's hand in both of his, he nearly wrung it off. "Why, what a providence! Why, really, now! And you were an Irishman all the time! And why didn't you speak English?"

"Sure and what made you spake Latin?" cried the priest. "And what was it you were thryin' to say wid yer 'sempiternum durum,' and yer 'tonitruendum malum?' Sure an' ye made me fairly profeen wid yer talk, so ye did."

"Well, I dare say," said Tozer, candidly—"I dare say 'tain't onlikely that I *did* introduce one or two Americanisms in the Latin; but then, you know, I ain't been in practice."

The priest now brought chairs for his visitors, and, sitting thus in the church, they told him about their adventures, and entreated him to do something for them. To all this the priest listened with thoughtful attention, and when they were done he at once promised to find horses for them which would draw the carriages to this hamlet or to the next town. Ethel did not think Lady Dalrymple could go further than this place, and the priest offered to find some accommodations.

He then left them, and in about half an hour he returned with two or three peasants, each of whom had a horse.

"They'll be able to bring the leedies," said the priest, "and haul the impty wagons afther thim."

"I think, miss," said Tozer, "that you'd better stay here. It's too far for you to walk."

"Sure an' there's no use in the wide wurruld for *you* to be goin' back," said the priest to Ethel. "You can't do any gud, an' you'd betther rist till they come. Yer frind'll be enough."

Ethel at first thought of walking back, but finally she saw that it would be quite useless, and so she resolved to remain and wait for her aunt. So Tozer went off with the men and the horses, and the priest asked Ethel all about the affair once more. Whatever his opinions were, he said nothing.

While he was talking there came a man to the door who beckoned him out. He went out, and was gone for some time. He came back at last, looking very serious.

"I've just got a missage from thim," said he.

"A message," exclaimed Ethel, "from them? What, from Girasole?"

"Yis. They want a praste, and they've sint for me."

"A priest?"

"Yis; an' they want a maid-servant to wait on the young leedies; and they want thim immajitly; an' I'll have to start off soon. There's a man dead among thim that wants to be put undherground to-night, for the rist av thim are goin' off in the mornin'; an' accordin' to all I hear, I wouldn't wondher but what I'd be wanted for somethin' else afore mornin'."

"Oh, my God!" cried Ethel; "they're going to kill him, then!"

"Kill him! Kill who? Sure an' it's not killin' they want me for. It's the other—it's marryin'."

"Marrying?" cried Ethel. "Poor, darling Minnie! Oh, you can not—you will not marry them?"

"Sure an' I don't know but it's the best thing I can do—as things are," said the priest.

"Oh, what shall I do! what shall I do!" moaned Ethel.

"Well, ye've got to bear up, so ye have. There's throubles for all of us, an' lots av thim too; an' more'n some av us can bear."

Ethel sat in the darkest and bitterest grief for some time, a prey to thoughts and fears that were perfect agony to her.

At last a thought came to her which made her start, and look up, and cast at the priest a look full of wonder and entreaty. The priest watched her with the deepest sympathy visible on his face.

"We must save them!" she cried.

"Sure an' it's me that made up me moind to that same," said the priest, "only I didn't want to rise yer hopes."

"*We* must save them," said Ethel, with strong emphasis.

"*We?* What can you do?"

Ethel got up, walked to the church door, looked out, came back, looked anxiously all around, and then, resuming her seat, she drew close to the priest, and began to whisper, long and anxiously.

CHAPTER XXVI.

THE AVENGER ON THE TRACK.

WHEN Dacres had sprung aside into the woods in the moment of his fierce rush upon Girasole, he had been animated by a sudden thought that escape for himself was possible, and that it would be more serviceable to his friends. Thus, then, he had bounded into the woods, and with swift steps he forced his way among the trees deeper and deeper into the forest. Some of the brigands had given chase, but without effect. Dacres's superior strength and agility gave him the advantage, and his love of life was a greater stimulus than their thirst for vengeance. In addition to this the trees gave every assistance toward the escape of a fugitive, while they threw every impediment in the way of a pursuer. The consequence was, therefore, that Dacres soon put a great distance between himself and his pursuers, and, what is more, he ran in such a circuitous route that they soon lost all idea of their own locality, and had not the faintest idea where he had gone. In this respect, however, Dacres himself was not one whit wiser than they, for he soon found himself completely bewildered in the mazes of the forest; and when at length the deep silence around gave no further sound of pursuers, he sank down to take breath, with no idea whatever in what direction the road lay.

After a brief rest he arose and plunged deeper still into the forest, so as to put an additional distance between himself and any possible pursuit. He at length found himself at the foot of a precipice about fifty feet in height, which was deep in the recesses of the forest. Up this he climbed, and found a mossy place among the trees at its top, where he could find rest, and at the same time be in a more favorable position either for hearing or seeing any signs of approaching pursuers.

Here, then, he flung himself down to rest, and soon buried himself among thoughts of the most exciting kind. The scene which he had just left was fresh in his mind, and amidst all the fury of that strife there rose most prominent in his memory the form of the two ladies, Minnie standing calm and unmoved, while Mrs. Willoughby was convulsed with agitated feeling. What was the cause of that? Could it be possible that his wife had indeed contrived such a plot with the Italian? Was it possible that she had chosen this way of striking two blows, by one of which she could win her Italian, and by the other of which she could get rid of himself, her husband? Such had been his conjecture during the fury of the fight, and the thought had roused him up to his Berserker madness; but now, as it recurred again, he saw other things to shake his full belief. Her agitation seemed too natural.

Yet, on the other hand, he asked himself, why should she not show agitation? She was a consummate actress. She could show on her beautiful face the softness and the tenderness of an angel of light while a demon reigned in her malignant heart. Why should she not choose this way of keeping up appearances? She had betrayed her friends, and sought her husband's death; but would she wish to have her crime made manifest? Not she. It was for this, then, that she wept and clung to the child-angel.

Such thoughts as these were not at all adapted to give comfort to his mind, or make his rest refreshing. Soon, by such fancies, he kindled anew his old rage, and his blood rose to fever heat, so that inaction became no longer tolerable. He had rest enough. He started up, and looked all around, and listened attentively. No sound arose and no sight appeared which at all excited suspicion. He determined to set forth once more, he scarcely knew where. He had a vague idea of finding his way back to the road, so as to be able to assist the ladies, together with another idea, equally ill defined, of coming upon the brigands, finding the Italian, and watching for an opportunity to wreak vengeance upon this assassin and his guilty partner.

He drew his knife once more from a leathern sheath on the inside of the breast of his coat, into which he had thrust it some time before, and holding this he set forth, watchfully and warily. On the left side of the precipice the ground sloped down, and at the bottom of this there was a narrow valley. It seemed to him that this might be the course of some spring torrent, and that by following its descent he might come out upon some stream. With this intention he descended to the valley, and then walked along, following the descent of the ground, and keeping himself as much as possible among the thickest growths of the trees.

The ground descended very gradually, and the narrow valley wound along among rolling hills that were covered with trees and brush. As he confined himself to the thicker parts of this, his progress was necessarily slow; but at the end of that turn he saw before him unmistakable signs of the neighborhood of some open place. Before him he saw the sky in such a way that it showed the absence of forest trees. He now moved on more cautiously, and, quitting the valley, he crept up the hill-slope among the brush as carefully as possible, until he was at a sufficient height, and then, turning toward the open, he crept forward from cover to cover. At length he stopped. A slight eminence was before him, beyond which all was open, yet concealed from his view. Descending the slope a little, he once more advanced, and finally emerged at the edge of the forest.

He found himself upon a gentle declivity. Immediately in front of him lay a lake, circular in shape, and about a mile in diameter, embosomed among wooded hills. At first he saw no signs of any habitation; but as his eyes wandered round he saw upon his right, about a quarter of a mile away, an old stone house, and beyond this smoke curling up from among the forest trees on the borders of the lake.

The scene startled him. It was so quiet, so lonely, and so deserted that it seemed a fit place for a robber's haunt. Could this be indeed the home of his enemies, and had he thus so wonderfully come upon them in the very midst of their retreat? He believed that it was so. A little further observation showed figures among the trees moving to and fro, and soon he distinguished faint traces of smoke in other places, which he had not seen at first, as though there were more fires than one.

Dacres exulted with a fierce and vengeful joy over this discovery. He felt now not like the fugitive, but rather the pursuer. He looked down upon this as the tiger looks from his jungle upon some Indian village. His foes were numerous, but he was concealed, and his presence unsuspected. He grasped his dagger with a firmer clutch, and then pondered for a few minutes on what he had better do next.

One thing was necessary first of all, and that was to get as near as he possibly could without discovery. A slight survey of the situation showed him that he might venture much nearer; and his eye ran along the border of the lake which lay between him and the old house, and he saw that it was all covered over with a thick fringe of trees and brush-wood. The narrow valley along which he had come ended at the shore of the lake just below him on his right, and beyond this the shore arose again to a height equal to where he now was. To gain that opposite height was now his first task.

Before starting he looked all around, so as to be sure that he was not observed. Then he went back for some distance, after which he descended into the valley, crouching low, and crawling stealthily among the brush-wood. Moving thus, he at length succeeded in reaching the opposite slope without appearing to have attracted any attention from any pursuers. Up this slope he now moved as carefully as ever, not relaxing his vigilance one jot, but, if possible, calling into play even a larger caution as he found himself drawing nearer to those whom he began to regard as his prey.

Moving up this slope, then, in this way, he at length attained the top, and found himself here among the forest trees and underbrush. They were here even denser than they were on the place which he had just left. As he moved along he saw no indications that they had been traversed by human footsteps. Every thing gave indication of an unbroken and undisturbed solitude. After feeling his way along here with all the caution which he could exercise, he finally ventured toward the shore of the lake, and found himself able to go to the very edge without coming to any open space or crossing any path.

On looking forth from the top of the bank he found that he had not only drawn much nearer to the old house, but that he could see the whole line of shore. He now saw that there were some men by the door of the house, and began to suspect that this was nothing else than the headquarters and citadel of the brigands. The sight of the shore now showed him that he could approach very much nearer, and unless the brigands, or whoever they were, kept scouts out, he would be able to reach a point immediately overlooking the house, from which he could survey it at his leisure. To reach this point became now his next aim.

The wood being dense, Dacres found no more difficulty in passing through this than in traversing what lay behind him. The caution which he exercised here was as great as ever, and his progress was as slow, but as sure. At length he found himself upon the desired point, and, crawling cautiously forward to the shore, he looked down upon the very old house which he had desired to reach.

The house stood close by the lake, upon a sloping bank which lay below. It did not seem to be more than fifty yards away. The doors and windows were gone. Five or six ill-looking fellows were near the doorway, some sprawling on the ground, others lolling and lounging about. One glance at the men was sufficient to assure him that they were the brigands, and also to show him that they kept no guard or scout or outpost of any kind, at least in this direction.

Here, then, Dacres lay and watched. He could not wish for a better situation. With his knife in his hand, ready to defend himself in case of need, and his whole form concealed perfectly by the thick underbrush into the midst of which he had crawled, he peered forth through the overhanging leaves, and watched in breathless interest. From the point where he now was he could see the shore beyond the house, where the smoke was rising. He could now see that there were no less than four different columns of smoke ascending from as many fires. He saw as many as twenty or thirty figures moving among the trees, made conspicuous by the bright colors of their costumes. They seemed to be busy about something which he could not make out.

Suddenly, while his eye roved over the scene, it was struck by some fluttering color at the open window of the old house. He had not noticed this before. He now looked at it attentively. Before long he saw a figure cross the window and return. It was a female figure.

The sight of this revived all that agitation which he had felt before, but which had been calmed during the severe efforts which he had been putting forth. There was but one thought in his mind, and but one desire in his heart.

His wife.

He crouched low, with a more feverish dread of discovery at this supreme moment, and a fiercer thirst for some further revelation which might disclose what he suspected. His breathing came thick and hard, and his brow lowered gloomily over his gleaming eyes.

He waited thus for some minutes, and the figure passed again.

He still watched.

Suddenly a figure appeared at the window. It was a young girl, a blonde, with short golden curls. The face was familiar indeed to him. Could he ever forget it? There it was full before him, turned toward him, as though that one, by some strange spiritual sympathy, was aware of his presence, and was thus turning toward him this mute appeal. Her face was near enough for its expression to be visible. He could distinguish the childish face, with its soft, sweet innocence, and he knew that upon it there was now that piteous, pleading, beseeching look which formerly had so thrilled his heart. And it was thus that Dacres saw his child-angel.

A prisoner, turning toward him this appeal! What was the cause, and what did the Italian want of this innocent child? Such was his thought. What could his fiend of a wife gain by the betrayal of that angelic being? Was it possible that even her demon soul could compass iniquity like this? He had thought that he had fathomed her capacity for malignant wickedness; but the presence here of the child-angel in the power of these miscreants showed him that this capacity was indeed unfathomable. At this sudden revelation of sin so enormous his very soul turned sick with horror.

He watched, and still looked with an anxiety that was increasing to positive pain.

And now, after one brief glance, Minnie drew back into the room. There was nothing more to be seen for some time, but at last another figure appeared.

He expected this; he was waiting for it; he was sure of it; yet deep down in the bottom of his heart there was a hope that it might not be so, that his suspicions, in this case at least, might be unfounded. But now the proof came; it was made manifest here before his eyes, and in the light of day.

In spite of himself a low groan escaped him. He buried his face in his hands and shut out the sight. Then suddenly he raised his head again and stared, as though in this face there was an irresistible fascination by which a spell was thrown over him.

It was the face of Mrs. Willoughby—youthful, beautiful, and touching in its tender grace. Tears were now in those dark, luminous eyes, but they were unseen by him. Yet he could mark the despondency of her attitude; he could see a certain wild way of looking up and down and in all directions; he noted how her hands grasped the window-ledge as if for support.

And oh, beautiful demon angel, he thought, if you could but know how near you are to the avenger! Why are you so anxious, my demon wife? Are you impatient because your Italian is delaying? Can you not live for five seconds longer without him? Are you looking in all directions to see where he is? Don't fret; he'll soon be here.

And now there came a confirmation of his thoughts. He was not surprised; he knew it; he suspected it. It was all as it should be. Was it not in the confident expectation of this that he had come here with his dagger—on their trail?

It was Girasole.

He came from the place, further along the shore, where the brigands were around their fires. He was walking quickly. He had a purpose. It was with a renewed agony that Dacres watched his enemy—coming to visit his wife. The intensity of that thirst for vengeance, which had now to be checked until a better opportunity, made his whole frame tremble. A wild desire came to him then and there to bound down upon his enemy, and kill and be killed in the presence of his wife. But the other brigands deterred him. These men might interpose and save the Italian, and make him a prisoner. No; he must wait till he could meet his enemy on something like equal terms—when he could strike a blow that would not be in vain. Thus he overmastered himself.

He saw Girasole enter the house. He watched breathlessly. The time seemed long indeed. He could not hear any thing; the conversation, if there was any, was carried on in a low tone. He could not see any thing; those who conversed kept quiet; no one passed in front of the window. It was all a mystery, and this made the time seem longer. At length Dacres began to think that Girasole would not go at all. A long time passed. Hours went away, and still Girasole did not quit the house.

It was now sundown. Dacres had eaten nothing since morning, but the conflict of passion drove away all hunger or thirst. The approach of darkness was in accordance with his own gloomy wishes. Twilight in Italy is short. Night would soon be over all.

The house was on the slope of the bank. At the corner nearest him the house was sunk into the ground in such a way that it looked as though one might climb into the upper story window. As Dacres looked he made up his mind to attempt it. By standing here on tiptoe he could catch the upper window-ledge with his hands. He was strong. He was tall. His enemy was in the house. The hour was at hand. He was the man.

Another hour passed.

All was still.

There was a flickering lamp in the hall, but the men seemed to be asleep.

Another hour passed.

There was no noise.

Then Dacres ventured down. He moved slowly and cautiously, crouching low, and thus traversing the intervening space.

He neared the house and touched it. Before him was the window of the lower story. Above him was the window of the upper story. He lifted up his hands. They could reach the window-ledge.

He put his long, keen knife between his teeth, and caught at the upper window-ledge. Exerting all his strength, he raised himself up so high that he could fling one elbow over. For a moment he hung thus, and waited to take breath and listen.

There was a rush below. Half a dozen shadowy forms surrounded him. He had been seen. He had been trapped.

He dropped down and, seizing his knife, struck right and left.

In vain. He was hurled to the ground and bound tight.

CHAPTER XXVII.

FACE TO FACE.

HAWBURY, on his capture, had been at once taken into the woods, and led and pushed on by no gentle hands. He had thus gone on until he had found himself by that same lake which others of the party had come upon in the various ways which have been described. Toward this lake he was taken, until finally his party reached the old house, which they entered. It has already been said that it was a two-story house. It was also of stone, and strongly built. The door was in the middle of it, and rooms were on each side of the hall. The interior plan of the house was peculiar, for the hall did not run through, but consisted of a square room, and the stone steps wound spirally from the lower hall to the upper one. There were three rooms up stairs, one taking up one end of the house, which was occupied by Mrs. Willoughby and Minnie; another in the rear of the house, into which a door opened from the upper hall, close by the head of the stairs; and a third, which was opposite the room first mentioned.

Hawbury was taken to this house, and led up stairs into this room in the rear of the house. At the end farthest from the door he saw a heap of straw with a few dirty rugs upon it. In the wall a beam was set, to which an iron ring was fastened. He was taken toward this bed, and here his legs were bound together, and the rope that secured them was run around the iron ring so as to allow of no more motion than a few feet. Having thus secured the prisoner, the men left him to his own meditations.

The room was perfectly bare of furniture, nothing being in it but the straw and the dirty rugs. Hawbury could not approach to the windows, for he was bound in a way which prevented that. In fact, he could not move in any direction, for his arms and legs were fastened in such a way that he could scarcely raise himself from where he was sitting. He therefore was compelled to remain in one position, and threw himself down upon the straw on his side, with his face to the wall, for he found that position easier than any other. In this way he lay for some time, until at length he was roused by the sound of footsteps ascending the stairs. Several people were passing his room. He heard the voice of Girasole. He listened with deep attention. For some time there was no reply. At length there was the sound of a woman's voice—clear, plain, and unmistakable. It was a fretful voice of complaint. Girasole was trying to answer it. After a time Girasole left. Then all was still. Then Girasole returned. Then there was a clattering noise on the stairs, and the bumping of some heavy weight, and the heavy breathing of men. Then he heard Girasole say something, after which arose Minnie's voice, close by, as though she was in the hall, and her words were, "Oh, take it away, take it away!" followed by long reproaches, which Hawbury did not fully understand.

This showed him that Minnie, at least, was a prisoner, and in this house, and in the adjoining room, along with some one whom he rightly supposed was Mrs. Willoughby.

After this there was a further silence for some time, which at last was broken by fresh sounds of trampling and shuffling, together with the confused directions of several voices all speaking at once. Hawbury listened, and turned on his couch of straw so as to see any thing which presented itself. The clatter and the noise approached nearer, ascending the stairs, until at last he saw that they were entering his room. Two of the brigands came first, carrying something carefully. In a few moments the burden which they bore was revealed.

It was a rude litter, hastily made from bushes fastened together. Upon this lay the dead body of a man, his white face upturned, and his limbs stiffened in the rigidity of death. Hawbury did not remember very distinctly any of the particular events of his confused struggle with the brigands; but he was not at all surprised to see that there had been one of the ruffians sent to his account. The brigands who carried in their dead companion looked at the captive with a sullen ferocity and a scowling vengefulness, which showed plainly that they would demand of him a reckoning for their comrade's blood if it were only in their power. But they did not delay, nor did they make any actual demonstrations to Hawbury. They placed the corpse of their comrade upon the floor in the middle of the room, and then went out.

The presence of the corpse only added to the gloom of Hawbury's situation, and he once more turned his face to the wall, so as to shut out the sight. Once more he gave himself up to his own thoughts, and so the time passed slowly on. He heard no sounds now from the room where Miss Fay was confined. He heard no noise from the men below, and could not tell whether they were still guarding the door, or had gone away. Various projects came to him, foremost among which was the idea of escaping. Bribery seemed the only possible way. There was about this, however, the same difficulty which Mrs. Willoughby had found—his ignorance of the language. He thought that this would be an effectual bar to any communication, and saw no other alternative than to wait Girasole's pleasure. It seemed to him that a ransom would be asked, and he felt sure, from Girasole's offensive manner, that the ransom would be large. But there was no help for it. He felt more troubled about Miss Fay; for Girasole's remarks about her seemed to point to views of his own which were incompatible with her liberation.

In the midst of these reflections another noise arose below. It was a steady tramp of two or three men walking. The noise ascended the stairway, and drew nearer and nearer. Hawbury turned once more, and saw two men entering the room, carrying between them a box about six feet long and eighteen inches or two feet wide. It was coarsely but strongly made, and was undoubtedly intended as a coffin for the corpse of the brigand. The men put the coffin down against the wall and retired. After a few minutes they returned again with the coffin lid. They then lifted the dead body into the coffin, and one of them put the lid in its place and secured it with half a dozen screws. After this Hawbury was once more left alone. He found this far more tolerable, for now he had no longer before his very eyes the abhorrent sight of the dead body. Hidden in its coffin, it no longer gave offense to his sensibilities. Once more, therefore, Hawbury turned his thoughts toward projects of escape, and discussed in his mind the probabilities for and against.

The day had been long, and longer still did it seem to the captive as hour after hour passed slowly by. He could not look at his watch, which his captors had spared; but from the shadows as they fell through the windows, and from the general appearance of the sky, he knew that the close of the day was not far off. He began to wonder that he was left so long alone and in suspense, and to feel impatient to know the worst as to his fate. Why did not some of them come to tell him? Where was Girasole? Was he the chief? Were the brigands debating about his fate, or were they thus leaving him in suspense so as to make him despondent and submissive to their terms? From all that he had ever heard of brigands and their ways, the latter seemed not unlikely; and this thought made him see the necessity of guarding himself against being too impatient for freedom, and too compliant with any demands of theirs.

From these thoughts he was at last roused by footsteps which ascended the stairs. He turned and looked toward the door. A man entered.

It was Girasole.

He entered slowly, with folded arms, and coming about half-way, he stood and surveyed the prisoner in silence. Hawbury, with a sudden effort, brought himself up to a sitting posture, and calmly surveyed the Italian.

"Well," asked Hawbury, "I should like to know how long you intend to keep up this sort of thing? What are you going to do about it? Name your price, man, and we'll discuss it, and settle upon something reasonable."

"My price?" repeated Girasole, with peculiar emphasis.

"Yes. Of course I understand you fellows. It's your trade, you know. You've caught me, and, of course, you'll try to make the best of me, and all that sort of thing. So don't keep me waiting."

"Inglis milor," said Girasole, with a sharp, quick accent, his face flushing up as he spoke—"Inglis milor, dere is no price as you mean, an' no ransom. De price is one dat you will not wis to pay."

"Oh, come, now, my good fellow, really you must remember that I'm tied up, and not in a position to be chaffed. Bother your Italian humbug! Don't speak in these confounded figures of speech, you know, but say up and down—how much?"

"De brigands haf talk you ovair, an' dey will haf no price."

"What the devil is all that rot about?"

"Dey will haf youair blood."

"My blood?"

"Yes."

"And pray, my good fellow, what good is that going to do them?"

"It is vengeance," said Girasole.

"Vengeance? Pooh! Nonsense! What rot! What have I ever done?"

"Dat—dere—his blood," said Girasole, pointing to the coffin.

"INGLIS MILOR, I SALL HAF YOUAIR LIFE."

"What! that scoundrel? Why, man alive, are you crazy? That was a fair stand-up fight. That is, it was two English against twenty Italians, if you call that fair; but perhaps it is. His blood! By Jove! Cool, that! Come, I like it."

"An' more," said Girasole, who now grew more excited. "It is not de brigand who condemn you; it is also me. I condemn you."

"You?" said Hawbury, elevating his eyebrows in some surprise, and fixing a cool stare upon Girasole. "And what the devil's *this* row about, I should like to know? I don't know *you*. What have you against *me*?"

"Inglis milor," cried Girasole, who was stung to the quick by a certain indescribable yet most irritating superciliousness in Hawbury's tone—"Inglis milor, you sall see what you sall soffair. You sall die! Dere is no hope. You are condemn by de brigand. You also are condemn by me, for you insult me."

"Well, of all the beastly rot I ever heard, this is about the worst! What do you mean by all this infernal nonsense? Insult you! What would I insult you for? Why, man alive, you're as mad as a March hare! If I thought you were a gentleman, I'd—by Jove, I will, too! See here, you fellow: I'll fight you for it—pistols, or any thing. Come, now. I'll drop all considerations of rank. I'll treat you as if you were a real count, and not a sham one. Come, now. What do you say? Shall we have it out? Pistols—in the woods there. You've got all your infernal crew around you, you know. Well? What? You won't? By Jove!"

Girasole's gesture showed that he declined the proposition.

"Inglis milor," said he, with a venomous glitter in his eyes, "I sall haf youair life—wis de pistol, but not in de duello. I sall blow your brain out myself."

"Blow and be hanged, then!" said Hawbury.

And with these words he fell back on his straw, and took no further notice of the Italian.

CHAPTER XXVIII.

TORN ASUNDER.

When Dacres made his attempt upon the house he was not so unobserved as he supposed himself to be. Minnie and Mrs. Willoughby happened at that time to be sitting on the floor by the window, one on each side, and they were looking out. They had chosen the seat as affording some prospect of the outer world. There was in Mrs. Willoughby a certain instinctive feeling that if any rescue came, it would come from the land side; and, therefore, though the hope was faint indeed, it nevertheless was sufficiently well defined to inspire her with an uneasy and incessant vigilance. Thus, then, she had seated herself by the window, and Minnie had taken her place on the opposite side, and the two sisters, with clasped hands, sat listening to the voices of the night.

At length they became aware of a movement upon the bank just above them and lying opposite. The sisters clasped one another's hands more closely, and peered earnestly through the gloom. It was pretty dark, and the forest threw down a heavy shadow, but still their eyes were by this time accustomed to the dark, and they could distinguish most of the objects there. Among these they soon distinguished a moving figure; but what it was, whether man or beast, they could not make out.

This moving figure was crawling down the bank. There was no cover to afford concealment, and it was evident that he was trusting altogether to the concealment of the darkness. It was a hazardous experiment, and Mrs. Willoughby trembled in suspense.

Minnie, however, did not tremble at all, nor was the suspense at all painful. When Mrs. Willoughby first cautiously directed her attention to it in a whisper, Minnie thought it was some animal.

"Why, Kitty dear," she said, speaking back in a whisper, "why, it's an animal; I wonder if the creature is a wild beast. I'm sure I think it's very dangerous, and no doors or windows. But it's *always* the way. He wouldn't give me a chair; and so I dare say I shall be eaten up by a bear before morning."

Minnie gave utterance to this expectation without the slightest excitement, just as though the prospect of becoming food for a bear was one of the very commonest incidents of her life.

"Oh, I don't think it's a bear."

"Well, then, it's a tiger or a lion, or perhaps a wolf. I'm sure *I* don't see what difference it makes what one is eaten by, when one *has* to be eaten."

"It's a man!" said Mrs. Willoughby, tremulously.

"A man!—nonsense, Kitty darling. A man walks; he doesn't go on all-fours, except when he is very, very small."

"Hush! it's some one coming to help us. Watch him, Minnie dear. Oh, how dangerous!"

"Do you really think so?" said Minnie, with evident pleasure. "Now that is really kind. But I wonder who it *can* be?"

Mrs. Willoughby squeezed her hand, and made no reply. She was watching the slow and cautious movement of the shadowy figure.

"He's coming nearer!" said she, tremulously.

Minnie felt her sister's hand throb at the quick movement of her heart, and heard her short, quick breathing.

"Who *can* it be, I wonder?" said Minnie, full of curiosity, but without any excitement at all.

"Oh, Minnie!"

"What's the matter, darling?"

"It's so terrible."

"What?"

"This suspense. Oh, I'm so afraid!"

"Afraid! Why, I'm not afraid at all."

"Oh! he'll be caught."

"No, he won't," said Minnie, confidently. "I *knew* he'd come. They *always* do. Don't be afraid that he'll be caught, or that he'll fail. They *never* fail. They always *will* save me. Wait till your life has been saved as often as mine has, Kitty darling. Oh, I expected it all! I was thinking a little while ago he ought to be here soon."

"He! Who?"

"Why, any person; the person who is going to save me this time. I don't know, of course, who he is; some horrid man, of course. And then—oh dear!—I'll have it all over again. He'll carry me away on his back, and through those wretched woods, and bump me against the trees and things. Then he'll get me to the road, and put me on a horrid old horse, and gallop away. And by that time it will be morning. And then he'll propose. And so there'll be another. And I don't know what I *shall* do about it. Oh dear!"

Mrs. Willoughby had not heard half of this. All her soul was intent upon the figure outside. She only pressed her sister's hand, and gave a warning "Hus-s-s-h!"

"I know one thing I *do* wish," said Minnie.

Her sister made no reply.

"I do wish it would turn out to be that nice, dear, good, kind Rufus K. Gunn. I don't want any more of them. And I'm sure he's nicer than this horrid Count, who wouldn't take the trouble to get me even a chair. And yet he pretends to be fond of me."

"Hus-s-s-h!" said her sister.

But Minnie was irrepressible.

"I don't want any horrid stranger. But, oh, Kitty darling, it would be so awfully funny if he were to be caught! and then he *couldn't* propose, you know."

By this time the figure had reached the house. Minnie peeped over and looked down. Then she drew back her head and sighed.

"Oh dear!" she said, in a plaintive tone.

"What, darling?"

"Why, Kitty darling, do you know he really looks a little like that great, big, horrid man that ran with me down the volcano, and then pretended he was my dear papa. And here he comes to save me again. Oh, what *shall* I do? Won't you pretend you're me, Kitty darling, and please go yourself? Oh, ple-e-ease do!"

But now Minnie was interrupted by two strong hands grasping the window-sill. A moment after a shadowy head arose above it. Mrs. Willoughby started back, but through the gloom she was able to recognize the strongly marked face of Scone Dacres.

For a moment he stared through the darkness. Then he flung his elbow over.

There arose a noise below. There was a rush. The figure disappeared from the window. A furious struggle followed, in the midst of which arose fierce oaths and deep breathings, and the sound of blows. Then the struggle subsided, and they heard footsteps tramping heavily. They followed the sound into the house. They heard men coming up the stairs and into the hall outside. Then they all moved into the front-room opposite theirs. After a few minutes they heard the steps descending the stairs. By this they judged that the prisoner had been taken to that room which was on the other side of the hall and in the front of the house.

"There dies our last hope!" said Mrs. Willoughby, and burst into tears.

"I'm sure I don't see what you're crying about," said Minnie. "You certainly oughtn't to want me to be carried off again by that person. If he had me, he'd *never* give me up—especially after saving me twice."

Mrs. Willoughby made no reply, and the sisters sat in silence for nearly an hour. They were then aroused by the approach of footsteps which entered the house; after which voices were heard below.

Then some one ascended the stairs, and they saw the flicker of a light. It was Girasole.

He came into the room with a small lamp, holding his hand in front of the flame. This lamp he set down in a corner out of the draught, and then turned to the ladies.

"Miladi," said Girasole, in a gentle voice, "I am ver pained to haf to tella you dat it is necessaire for you to separat dis night—till to-morra."

"To separate?" exclaimed Mrs. Willoughby.

"Only till to-morra, miladi. Den you sall be togeder foravva. But it is now necessaire. Dere haf ben an attemp to a rescue. I mus guard again dis—an' it mus be done by a separazion. If you are togeder you might run. Dis man was almos up here. It was only chance dat I saw him in time."

"Oh, Sir," cried Mrs. Willoughby, "you can not—you will not separate us. You can not have the heart to. I promise most solemnly that we will not escape if you only leave us together."

Girasole shook his head.

"I can not," said he, firmly; "de mees is too precious. I dare not. If you are prisonaire se will not try to fly, an' so I secure her de more; but if you are togeder you will find some help. You will bribe de men. I can not trust dem."

"Oh, do not separate us. Tie us. Bind us. Fasten us with chains. Fasten me with chains, but leave me with her."

"Chains? nonsance; dat is impossibile. Chains? no, miladi. You sall be treat beautiful. No chain, no; notin but affection—till to-morra, an' den de mees sall be my wife. De priest haf come, an' it sall be allaright to-morra, an' you sall be wit her again. An' now you haf to come away; for if you do not be pleasant, I sall not be able to 'low you to stay to-morra wit de mees when se become my Contessa."

Mrs. Willoughby flung her arms about her sister, and clasped her in a convulsive embrace.

"Well, Kitty darling," said Minnie, "don't cry, or you'll make me cry too. It's just what we might have expected, you know. He's been as unkind as he could be about the chair, and of course he'll do all he can to tease me. Don't cry, dear. You must go, I suppose, since that horrid man talks and scolds so about it; only be sure to be back early; but how I am *ever* to pass the night here all alone and standing up, I'm sure *I* don't know."

"Alone? Oh no," said Girasole. "Charming mees, you sall not be alone; I haf guard for dat. I haf sent for a maid."

"But I don't want any of your horrid old maids. I want my own maid, or none at all."

"Se sall be your own maid. I haf sent for her."

"What, my own maid?—Dowlas?"

"I am ver sorry, but it is not dat one. It is anoder—an Italian."

"Well, I think that is *very* unkind, when you *know* I can't speak a word of the language. But you *always* do all you can to tease me. I *wish* I had never seen you."

Girasole looked hurt.

"Charming mees," said he, "I will lay down my life for you."

"But I don't want you to lay down your life. I want Dowlas."

"And you sall haf Dowlas to-morra. An' to-night you sall haf de Italian maid."

"Well, I suppose I must," said Minnie, resignedly.

"Miladi," said Girasole, turning to Mrs. Willoughby, "I am ver sorry for dis leetle accommodazion. De room where you mus go is de one where I haf put de man dat try to safe you. He is tied fast. You mus promis you will not loose him. Haf you a knife?"

"No," said Mrs. Willoughby, in a scarce audible tone.

"Do not mourn. You sall be able to talk to de prisonaire and get consolazion. But come."

With these words Girasole led the way out into the hall, and into the front-room on the opposite side. He carried the lamp in his hand. Mrs. Willoughby saw a figure lying at the other end of the room on the floor. His face was turned toward them, but in the darkness she could not see it plainly. Some straw was heaped up in the corner next her.

"Dere," said Girasole, "is your bed. I am sorra. Do not be trouble."

With this he went away.

Mrs. Willoughby flung herself on her knees, and bowed her head and wept convulsively. She heard the heavy step of Girasole as he went down stairs. Her first impulse was to rush back to her sister. But she dreaded discovery, and felt that disobedience would only make her fate harder.

"ONE ARM WENT AROUND HER NECK."

CHAPTER XXIX.

FOUND AT LAST.

IN a few moments Girasole came back and entered Minnie's room. He was followed by a woman who was dressed in the garb of an Italian peasant girl. Over her head she wore a hood to protect her from the night air, the limp folds of which hung over her face. Minnie looked carelessly at this woman and then at Girasole.

"Charming mees," said Girasole, "I haf brought you a maid for dis night. When we leaf dis you sall haf what maid you wis."

"That horrid old fright!" said Minnie. "I don't want her."

"You sall only haf her for dis night," said Girasole. "You will be taken care for."

"I suppose nobody cares for what *I* want," said Minnie, "and I may as well speak to the wall, for all the good it does."

Girasole smiled and bowed, and put his hand on his heart, and then called down the stairs:

"Padre Patricio!"

A solid, firm step now sounded on the stairs, and in a few moments the priest came up. Girasole led the way into Hawbury's room. The prisoner lay on his side. He was in a deep sleep. Girasole looked in wonder at the sleeper who was spending in this way the last hours of his life, and then pointed to the coffin.

"Here," said he, in Italian, "is the body. When the grave is dug they will tell you. You must stay here. You will not be afraid to be with the dead."

The priest smiled.

Girasole now retreated and went down stairs.

Soon all was still.

The Italian woman had been standing where she had stopped ever since she first came into the room. Minnie had not paid any attention to her, but at last she noticed this.

"I *wish* you wouldn't stand there in that way. You really make me feel quite nervous. And what with the dark, and not having any light, and losing poor dear Kitty, and not having any chair to sit upon, really one's life is scarce worth having. But all this is thrown away, as you can't speak English—and how horrid it is to have no one to talk to."

The woman made no reply, but with a quiet, stealthy step she drew near to Minnie.

"What do you want? You horrid creature, keep away," said Minnie, drawing back in some alarm.

"Minnie dear!" said the woman. "H-s-s-s-h!" she added, in a low whisper.

Minnie started.

"Who are you?" she whispered.

One arm went around her neck, and another hand went over her mouth, and the woman drew nearer to her.

"Not a word. H-s-s-s-h! I've risked my life. The priest brought me."

"Why, my darling, darling love of an Ethel!" said Minnie, who was overwhelmed with surprise.

"H-s-s-s-h!"

"But how can I h-s-s-s-h when I'm so perfectly frantic with delight? Oh, you darling pet!"

"H-s-s-s-h! Not another word. I'll be discovered and lost."

"Well, dear, I'll speak very, very low. But how did you come here?"

"The priest brought me."

"The priest?"

"Yes. He was sent for, you know; and I thought I could help you, and he is going to save you."

"He! Who?"

"The priest, you know."

"The priest! Is he a Roman Catholic priest, Ethel darling?"

"Yes, dear."

"And *he* is going to save me this time, is he?"

"I hope so, dear."

"Oh, how perfectly lovely that is! and it was so kind and thoughtful in you! Now this is really quite nice, for you know I've *longed* so to be saved by a priest. These horrid men, you know, all go and propose the moment they save one's life; but a priest *can't*, you know—no, not if he saved one a thousand times over. Can he now, Ethel darling?"

"Oh no!" said Ethel, in a little surprise. "But stop, darling. You really must *not* say another word—no, not so much as a whisper—for we certainly *will* be heard; and don't notice what I do, or the priest either, for it's very, very important, dear. But you keep as still as a little mouse, and wait till we are all ready."

"Well, Ethel dear, I will; but it's awfully funny to see you here—and oh, *such* a funny figure as you are!"

"H-s-s-s-h!"

Minnie relapsed into silence now, and Ethel withdrew near to the door, where she stood and listened. All was still. Down stairs there was no light and no sound. In the hall above she could see nothing, and could not tell whether any guards were there or not.

Hawbury's room was at the back of the house, as has been said, and the door was just at the top of the stairs. The door where Ethel was standing was there too, and was close by the other, so that she could listen and hear the deep breathing of the sleeper. One or two indistinct sounds escaped him from time to time, and this was all that broke the deep stillness.

She waited thus for nearly an hour, during which all was still, and Minnie said not a word. Then a shadowy figure appeared near her at Hawbury's door, and a hand touched her shoulder.

Not a word was said.

Ethel stole softly and noiselessly into Hawbury's room, where the priest was. She could see the two windows, and the priest indicated to her the position of the sleeper.

Slowly and cautiously she stole over toward him.

She reached the place.

She knelt by his side, and bent low over him. Her lips touched his forehead.

The sleeper moved slightly, and murmured some words.

"All fire," he murmured; "fire—and flame. It is a furnace before us. She must not die."

Then he sighed.

Ethel's heart beat wildly. The words that he spoke told her where his thoughts were wandering. She bent lower; tears fell from her eyes and upon his face.

"My darling," murmured the sleeper, "we will land here. I will cook the fish. How pale! Don't cry, dearest."

The house was all still. Not a sound arose. Ethel still bent down and listened for more of these words which were so sweet to her.

"Ethel!" murmured the sleeper, "where are you? Lost! lost!"

A heavy sigh escaped him, which found an echo in the heart of the listener. She touched his forehead gently with one hand, and whispered,

"My lord!"

Hawbury started.

"What's this?" he murmured.

"A friend," said Ethel.

At this Hawbury became wide awake.

"Who are you?" he whispered, in a trembling voice. "For God's sake—oh, for God's sake, speak again! tell me!"

"Harry," said Ethel.

Hawbury recognized the voice at once.

A slight cry escaped him, which was instantly suppressed, and then a torrent of whispered words followed.

"Oh, my darling! my darling! my darling! What is this? How is this? Is it a dream? Oh, am I awake? Is it you? Oh, my darling! my darling! Oh, if my arms were but free!"

Ethel bent over him, and passed her arm around him till she felt the cords that bound him. She had a sharp knife ready, and with this she cut the cords. Hawbury raised himself, without waiting for his feet to be freed, and caught Ethel in his freed arms in a silent embrace, and pressed her over and over again to his heart.

Ethel with difficulty extricated herself.

"There's no time to lose," said she. "I came to save you. Don't waste another moment; it will be too late. Oh, do not! Oh, wait!" she added, as Hawbury made another effort to clasp her in his arms. "Oh, do what I say, for my sake!"

She felt for his feet, and cut the rest of his bonds.

"What am I to do?" asked Hawbury, clasping her close, as though he was afraid that he would lose her again.

"Escape."

"Well, come! I'll leap with you from the window."

"You can't. The house and all around swarms with brigands. They watch us all closely."

"I'll fight my way through them."

"Then you'll be killed, and I'll die."

"Well, I'll do whatever you say."

"Listen, then. You must escape alone."

"What! and leave you? Never!"

"I'm safe. I'm disguised, and a priest is with me as my protector."

"How can you be safe in such a place as this?"

"I am safe. Do not argue. There is no time to lose. The priest brought me here, and will take me away."

"But there are others here. I can't leave them. Isn't Miss Fay a prisoner? and another lady?"

"Yes; but the priest and I will be able, I hope, to liberate them. We have a plan."

"But can't I go with you and help you?"

"Oh no! it's impossible. You could not. We are going to take them away in disguise. We have a dress. You couldn't be disguised."

"And *must* I go alone?"

"You must."

"I'll do it, then. Tell me what it is. But oh, my darling! how can I leave you, and in such a place as this?"

"I assure you I am not in the slightest danger."

"I shall feel terribly anxious."

"H-s-s-s-h! no more of this. Listen now."

"Well?"

Ethel bent lower, and whispered in his ear, in even lower tones than ever, the plan which she had contrived.

CHAPTER XXX.

A DESPERATE PLAN.

ETHEL's plan was hastily revealed. The position was exceedingly perilous; time was short, and this was the only way of escape.

It was the priest who had concocted it, and he had thought of it as the only plan by which Hawbury's rescue could be effected. This ingenious Irishman had also formed another plan for the rescue of Minnie and her sister, which was to be attempted in due course of time.

Now no ordinary mode of escape was possible for Hawbury. A strict watch was kept. The priest had noticed on his approach that guards were posted in different directions in such a way that no fugitive from the house could elude them. He had also seen that the guard inside the house was equally vigilant. To leap from the window and run for it would be certain death, for that was the very thing which the brigands anticipated. To make a sudden rush down the stairs was not possible, for at the door below there were guards; and there, most vigilant of all, was Girasole himself.

The decision of the Irish priest was correct, as has been proved in the case of Dacres, who, in spite of all his caution, was observed and captured. Of this the priest knew nothing, but judged from what he himself had seen on his approach to the house.

The plan of the priest had been hastily communicated to Ethel, who shared his convictions and adopted his conclusions. She also had noticed the vigilance with which the guard had been kept up, and only the fact that a woman had been sent for and was expected with the priest had preserved her from discovery and its consequences. As it was, however, no notice was taken of her, and her pretended character was assumed to be her real one. Even Girasole had scarcely glanced at her. A village peasant was of no interest in his eyes. His only thought was of Minnie, and the woman that the priest brought was only used as a desperate effort to show a desire for her comfort. After he had decided to separate the sisters the woman was of more importance; but he had nothing to say to her, and thus Ethel had effected her entrance to Minnie's presence in safety, with the result that has been described.

The priest had been turning over many projects in his brain, but at last one suggested itself which had originated in connection with the very nature of his errand.

One part of that errand was that a man should be conveyed out of the house and carried away and left in a certain place. Now the man who was thus to be carried out was a dead man, and the certain place to which he was to be borne and where he was to be left was the grave; but these stern facts did not at all deter the Irish priest from trying to make use of this task that lay before him for the benefit of Hawbury.

Here was a problem. A prisoner anxious for escape, and a dead man awaiting burial; how were these two things to be exchanged so that the living man might pass out without going to the grave?

The Irish priest puzzled and pondered and grew black in the face with his efforts to get to the solution of this problem, and at length succeeded—to his own satisfaction, at any rate. What is more, when he explained his plan to Ethel, she adopted it. She started, it is true; she shuddered, she recoiled from it at first, but finally she adopted it. Furthermore, she took it upon herself to persuade Hawbury to fall in with it.

So much with regard to Hawbury. For Minnie and her sister the indefatigable priest had already concocted a plan before leaving home. This was the very commonplace plan of a disguise. It was to be an old woman's apparel, and he trusted to the chapter of accidents to make the plan a success. He noticed with pleasure that some women were at the place, and thought that the prisoners might be confounded with them.

When at length Ethel had explained the plan to Hawbury he made a few further objections, but finally declared himself ready to carry it out.

The priest now began to put his project into execution. He had brought a screw-driver with him, and with this he took out the screws from the coffin one by one, as quietly as possible.

Then the lid was lifted off, and Hawbury arose and helped the priest to transfer the corpse from the coffin to the straw. They then put the corpse on its side, with the face to the wall, and bound the hands behind it, and the feet also. The priest then took Hawbury's handkerchief and bound it around the head of the corpse. One or two rugs that lay near were thrown over the figure, so that it at length looked like a sleeping man.

Hawbury now got into the coffin and lay down on his back at full length. The priest had brought some bits of wood with him, and these he put on the edge of the coffin in such a way that the lid would be kept off at a distance of about a quarter of an inch. Through this opening Hawbury could have all the air that was requisite for breathing.

Then Ethel assisted the priest to lift the lid on.

Thus far all had been quiet; but now a slight noise was heard below. Some men were moving. Ethel was distracted with anxiety, but the priest was as cool as a clock. He whispered to her to go back to the room where she belonged.

"Will you be able to finish it?" she asked.

"Sure an' I will—only don't you be afther stayin' here any longer."

At this Ethel stole back to Minnie's room, and stood listening with a quick-beating heart.

But the priest worked coolly and dextrously. He felt for the holes to which the screws belonged, and succeeded in putting in two of them.

Then there was a noise in the hall below.

The priest began to put in the third screw.

There were footsteps on the stairs.

He screwed on.

Nearer and nearer came the steps.

The priest still kept to his task.

At last a man entered the room. Ethel, who had heard all, was faint with anxiety. She was afraid that the priest had not finished his task.

Her fears were groundless.

Just as the foremost of the men entered the room the priest finished screwing, and stood by the coffin, having slipped the screw-driver into his pocket, as calm as though nothing had happened. Three of the screws were in, and that was as many as were needed.

The men brought no light with them, and this circumstance was in the priest's favor.

"You've been keeping me waiting long," said the priest, in Italian.

"You may be glad it wasn't longer," said one of them, in a sullen tone. "Where is it?"

"Here," said the priest.

The men gathered around the coffin, and stooped down over it, one at each corner. Then they raised it up. Then they carried it out; and soon the heavy steps of the men were heard as they went down the stairs with their burden.

Ethel still stood watching and listening.

As she listened she heard some one ascending the stairs. New terror arose. Something was wrong, and all would be discovered. But the man who came up had no light, and that was one comfort. She could not see who it was.

The man stopped for a moment in front of Minnie's door, and stood so close to her that she heard his breathing. It was quick and heavy, like the breathing of a very tired or a very excited man. Then he turned away and went to the door of the front-room opposite. Here he also stood for a few moments.

All was still.

Then he came back, and entered Hawbury's room.

Now the crisis had come—the moment when all might be discovered. And if so, they all were lost. Ethel bent far forward and tried to peer through the gloom. She saw the dark figure of the new-comer pass by one of the windows, and by the outline she knew that it was Girasole. He passed on into the shadow, and toward the place where the straw was. She could not see him any more.

Girasole stepped noiselessly and cautiously, as though fearful of waking the sleeper. At every step he paused and listened. The silence reassured him.

He drew nearer and nearer, his left hand groping forward, and his right hand holding a pistol. His movements were perfectly noiseless.

His own excitement was now intense, his heart throbbed fiercely and almost painfully as he approached his victim.

At last he reached the spot, and knelt on one knee. He listened for a moment. There was no noise and no movement on the part of the figure before him.

In the gloom he could see the outline of that figure plainly. It lay on its side, curled up in the most comfortable attitude which could be assumed, where arms and legs were bound.

"How soundly he sleeps!" thought Girasole.

He paused for a moment, and seemed to hesitate; but it was only for a moment. Then, summing up his resolution, he held his pistol close to the head of the figure, and fired.

"HE HELD HIS PISTOL CLOSE TO THE HEAD, AND FIRED."

The loud report echoed through the house. A shriek came from Minnie's room, and a cry came from Mrs. Willoughby, who sprang toward the hall. But Girasole came out and intercepted her.

"Eet ees notin," said he, in a tremulous voice. "Eet ees all ovair. Eet ees only a false alarm."

Mrs. Willoughby retreated to her room, and Minnie said nothing. As for Ethel, the suspense with her had passed away as the report of the pistol came to her ears.

Meanwhile the coffin was carried out of the house, and the men, together with the priest, walked on toward a place further up the shore and on the outskirts of the woods. They reached a place where a grave was dug.

At this moment a pistol-shot sounded. The priest stopped, and the men stopped also. They did not understand it. The priest did not know the cause of the shot, but seeing the alarm of the men he endeavored to excite their fears. One of the men went back, and was cursed by Girasole for his pains. So he returned to the grave, cursing every body.

The coffin was now lowered into the grave, and the priest urged the men to go away and let him finish the work; but they refused. The fellows seemed to have some affection for their dead comrade, and wished to show it by putting him underground, and doing the last honors. So the efforts of the

Irish priest, though very well meant, and very urgent, and very persevering, did not meet with that success which he anticipated.

Suddenly he stopped in the midst of the burial service, which he was prolonging to the utmost.

"Hark!" he cried, in Italian.

"What?" they asked.

"It's a gun! It's an alarm!"

"There's no gun, and no alarm," said they.

All listened, but there was no repetition of the sound, and the priest went on.

He had to finish it.

He stood trembling and at his wit's end. Already the men began to throw in the earth.

But now there came a real alarm.

CHAPTER XXXI.

DISCOVERED.

THE report of the pistol had startled Minnie, and for a moment had greatly agitated her. The cry of Mrs. Willoughby elicited a response from her to the effect that all was right, and would, no doubt, have resulted in a conversation, had it not been prevented by Girasole.

Minnie then relapsed into silence for a time, and Ethel took a seat by her side on the floor, for Minnie would not go near the straw, and then the two interlocked their arms in an affectionate embrace.

"Ethel darling," whispered Minnie, "do you know I'm beginning to get awfully tired of this?"

"I should think so, poor darling!"

"If I only had some place to sit on," said Minnie, still reverting to her original grievance, "it wouldn't be so very bad, you know. I could put up with not having a bed, or a sofa, or that sort of thing, you know; but really I must say not to have any kind of a seat seems to me to be very, very inconsiderate, to say the least of it."

"Poor darling!" said Ethel again.

"And now do you know, Ethel dear, I'm beginning to feel as though I should really like to run away from this place, if I thought that horrid man wouldn't see me?"

"Minnie darling," said Ethel, "that's the very thing I came for, you know."

"Oh yes, I know! And that dear, nice, good, kind, delightful priest! Oh, it was so nice of you to think of a priest, Ethel dear! I'm so grateful! But when is he coming?"

"Soon, I hope. But *do* try not to talk so."

"But I'm only whispering."

"Yes, but your whispers are too loud, and I'm afraid they'll hear."

"Well, I'll try to keep still; but it's so *awfully* hard, you know, when one has *so* much to say, Ethel dear."

Minnie now remained silent for about five minutes.

"How did you say you were going to take me away?" she asked at length.

"In disguise," said Ethel.

"But *what* disguise?"

"In an old woman's dress—but hu-s-s-s-sh!"

"But I don't *want* to be dressed up in an old woman's clothes; they make me *such* a figure. Why, I'd be a perfect fright."

"Hu-s-s-s-sh! Dear, dear Minnie, you're talking too loud. They'll certainly hear us," said Ethel, in a low, frightened whisper.

"But *do*—*do* promise you won't take me in an old woman's clothes!"

"Oh, there—there it is again!" said Ethel. "Dear, dear Minnie, there's some one listening."

"Well, I don't see what harm there is in what I'm saying. I only wanted—"

Here there was a movement on the stairs just outside. Ethel had heard a sound of that kind two or three times, and it had given her alarm; but now Minnie herself heard it, and stopped speaking.

And now a voice sounded from the stairs. Some Italian words were spoken, and seemed to be addressed to them. Of course they could make no reply. The words were repeated, with others, and the speaker seemed to be impatient. Suddenly it flashed across Ethel's mind that the speaker was Girasole, and that the words were addressed to her.

Her impression was correct, and the speaker was Girasole. He had heard the sibilant sounds of the whispering, and, knowing that Minnie could not speak Italian, it had struck him as being a very singular thing that she should be whispering. Had her sister joined her? He thought he would go up and see. So he went up softly, and the whispering still went on. He therefore concluded that the "Italian woman" was not doing her duty, and that Mrs. Willoughby had joined her sister. This he would not allow; but as he had already been sufficiently harsh he did not wish to be more so, and therefore he called to the "Italian woman."

"Hallo, you woman there! didn't I tell you not to let the ladies speak to one another?"

Of course no answer was given, so Girasole grew more angry still, and cried out again, more imperatively:

"Why do you not answer me? Where are you? Is this the way you watch?"

Still there was no answer. Ethel heard, and by this time knew what his suspicion was; but she could neither do nor say any thing.

"Come down here at once, you hag!"

But the "hag" did not come down, nor did she give any answer. The "hag" was trembling violently, and saw that all was lost. If the priest were only here! If she could only have gone and returned with him! What kept him?

Girasole now came to the top of the stairs, and spoke to Minnie.

"Charming mees, are you awake?"

"Yes," said Minnie.

"Ees your sistaire wit you?"

"No. How can *she* be with me, I should like to know, when you've gone and put her in some horrid old room?"

"Ah! not wit you? Who are you whisperin' to, den?"

Minnie hesitated.

"To my maid," said she.

"WHAT DIT YOU COME FOR?"—"FOR HER."

"Does de maid spik Inglis?" asked Girasole.

"Yes," said Minnie.

"Ah! I did not know eet. I mus have a look at de contadina who spiks Inglis. Come here, Italiana. You don't spik Italiano, I tink. Come here."

Ethel rose to her feet.

Girasole ran down, and came back after a few minutes with a lamp. Concealment was useless, and so Ethel did not cover her face with the hood. It had fallen off when she was sitting by Minnie, and hung loosely down her shoulders from the strings which were around her neck. Girasole recognized her at one glance.

"Ah!" said he; and then he stood thinking. As for Ethel, now that the suspense was over and the worst realized, her agitation ceased. She stood looking at him with perfect calm.

"What dit you come for?" he asked.

"For *her*," said Ethel, making a gesture toward Minnie.

"What could you do wit her?"

"I could see her and comfort her."

"Ah! an' you hope to make her escape. Ha, ha! ver well. You mus not complain eef you haf to soffair de consequence. Aha! an' so de priest bring you here—ha?"

Ethel was silent.

"Ah! you fear to say—you fear you harma de priest—ha?"

Minnie had thus far said nothing, but now she rose and looked at Girasole, and then at Ethel. Then she twined one arm around Ethel's waist, and turned her large, soft, childish eyes upon Girasole.

"What do you mean," she said, "by *always* coming here and teasing, and worrying, and firing off pistols, and frightening people? I'm sure it was horrid enough for you to make me come to this wretched place, when you *know* I don't like it, without annoying me so. Why did you go and take away poor darling Kitty? And what do you mean now, pray, by coming here? I never was treated so unkindly in my life. I did not think that *any one* could be so very, very rude."

"Charming mees," said Girasole, with a deprecating air, "it pains me to do any ting dat you do not like."

"It don't pain you," said Minnie—"it don't pain you *at all*. You're *always* teasing me. You *never* do what I want you to. You wouldn't even give me a chair."

"Alas, carissima mia, to-morra you sall haf all! But dis place is so remote."

"It is *not* remote," said Minnie. "It's close by roads and villages and things. Why, here is Ethel; she has been in a village where there are houses, and people, and as many chairs as she wants."

"Oh, mees, eef you will but wait an' be patient—eef you will but wait an' see how tender I will be, an' how I lof you."

"You *don't* love me," said Minnie, "one bit. Is this love—not to give me a chair? I have been standing up till I am nearly ready to drop. And you have nothing better than some wretched promises. I don't care for to-morrow; I want to be comfortable to-day. You won't let me have a single thing. And now you come to tease me again, and frighten poor, dear, darling Ethel."

"Eet ees because she deceif me—she come wit a plot—she steal in here. Eef she had wait, all would be well."

"You mustn't *dare* to touch her," said Minnie, vehemently. "You *shall* leave her here. She *shall* stay with me."

"I am ver pain—oh, very; but oh, my angel—sweet—charming mees—eet ees dangaire to my lof. She plot to take you away. An' all my life is in you. Tink what I haf to do to gain you!"

Minnie looked upon Girasole, with her large eyes dilated with excitement and resentment.

"You are a horrid, horrid man," she exclaimed. "I *hate* you."

"Oh, my angel," pleaded Girasole, with deep agitation, "take back dat word."

"I'm sorry you ever saved my life," said Minnie, very calmly; "and I'm sorry I ever saw you. I *hate* you."

"Ah, you gif me torment. You do not mean dis. You say once you lof me."

"*I* did not say I loved *you*. It was *you* who said you loved *me*. *I* never liked *you*. And I don't really see how I *could* be engaged to you when I was engaged to another man before. He is the only one whom I recognize now. I don't know you at all. For I couldn't be bound to two men; could I, Ethel dear?"

Ethel did not reply to this strange question.

But upon Girasole its effect was very great. The manner of Minnie had been excessively perplexing to him all through this eventful day. If she had stormed and gone into a fine frenzy he could have borne it. It would have been natural. But she was perfectly unconcerned, and her only complaint was about trifles. Such trifles too! He felt ashamed to think that he could have subjected to such annoyances a woman whom he so dearly loved. And now he was once more puzzled. Minnie confronted him, looking at him fixedly, without one particle of fear, with her large, earnest, innocent eyes fastened upon his—with the calm, cool gaze, of some high-minded child rebuking a younger child-companion. This was a proceeding which he was not prepared for. Besides, the child-innocence of her face and of her words actually daunted him. She seemed so fearless, because she was so innocent. She became a greater puzzle than ever. He had never seen much of her before, and this day's experience of her had actually daunted him and confounded him. And what was the worst to him of all her words was her calm and simple declaration, "I hate you!"

"Yes," said Minnie, thoughtfully, "it must be so; and dear Kitty would have said the same, only she was so awfully prejudiced. And I always thought he was so nice. Yes, I think I really must be engaged to him. But as for you," she said, turning full upon Girasole, "I hate you!"

Girasole's face grew white with rage and jealousy.

"Aha!" said he. "You lof *him*. Aha! An' you were engage to *him*. Aha!"

"Yes, I really think so."

"Aha! Well, listen," cried Girasole, in a hoarse voice—"listen. He—he—de rival—de one you say you are engage—he is dead!"

And with this he fastened upon Minnie his eyes that now gleamed with rage, and had an expression in them that might have made Ethel quiver with horror, but she did not, for she knew that Girasole was mistaken on that point.

As for Minnie, she was not at all impressed by his fierce looks.

"I don't think you really know what you're talking about," said she; "and you're very, very unpleasant. At any rate, you are altogether in the wrong when you say he is dead."

"Dead! He is dead! I swear it!" cried Girasole, whose manner was a little toned down by Minnie's coolness.

"This is getting to be awfully funny, you know," said Minnie. "I really think we don't know what one another is talking about. I'm sure *I* don't, and I'm sure *he* don't, either; does he, Ethel darling?"

"De Inglis milor," said Girasole. "He is dead."

"Well, but I don't mean him at all," said Minnie.

"Who—who?" gasped Girasole. "Who—who—who?"

"Why, the person I mean," said Minnie, very placidly, "is Rufus K. Gunn."

Girasole uttered something like a howl, and retreated.

CHAPTER XXXII.

UNDER ARREST.

GIRASOLE retreated half-way down the stairs, and then he stopped for some time and thought. Then he came back and motioned to Ethel.

"You must come," he said, gruffly.

"You shall not," said Minnie.

"No, no, darling," said Ethel; "I had better go. It will only get you into fresh trouble. And I'll be back as soon as I can."

"Oh, how I *hate* you!" said Minnie to Girasole. The latter said nothing. Ethel kissed Minnie, and descended the stairs after him.

The Irish priest was standing over the grave bathed in a cold perspiration, his heart throbbing violently, every new thud of the earth, as it sounded violently against the coffin, sending a cold chill of horror through every nerve. Already enough earth had been thrown to cover three-quarters of the lid, and at the foot it was heaped up some distance. He tried to frame some excuse to get the men away. His brain whirled; his mind was confused; his thoughts refused to be collected.

And now, in the midst of this, the attention of all was attracted by a loud stern voice, which sounded from some one near. The priest looked around. The men stopped shoveling, and turned to see the cause of the noise.

Girasole was seen approaching, and was already near enough to be distinguished. Behind him followed a female form. At this sight the priest's mind misgave him.

Girasole came up, and now the priest saw that the female was no other than Ethel.

"Where is this priest?" asked Girasole, angrily, speaking, of course, in Italian.

The priest advanced.

"I am here," said he, with quiet dignity.

At this change in the state of affairs the priest regained his presence of mind. The cessation in the work gave him relief, and enabled him to recall his scattered and confused thoughts. The men stood looking at the speakers, and listening, leaning on their shovels.

"You were sent for?"

"Yes."

"And a maid?"

"Yes."

"You brought this lady?"

"Yes."

"You put her in disguise; you passed her off as an Italian?"

"Yes."

The priest made no attempt at denial or equivocation. He knew that this would be useless. He waited for an opportunity to excuse himself, and to explain rather than to deny. But every answer of his only served to increase the fury of Girasole, who seemed determined to visit upon the head of the priest and Ethel the rage that he felt at his last interview with Minnie.

"Then why," cried Girasole, "did you try to trick us? Don't you know the punishment we give to spies and traitors?"

"I have nothing to do with spies and traitors."

"You are one yourself."

"I am not."

"You lie!"

"I do not," said the priest, mildly. "Hear me, and let me tell my story, and you will see that I am not a traitor; or, if you don't wish to listen, then question me."

"There is but one question. What made you bring this lady?"

"That is simply answered," said the priest, with unfaltering calmness. "This lady and her friends arrived at my village and claimed hospitality. They were in distress. Some of their friends had been taken from them. A message came from you requesting my presence, and also a lady's-maid. There was no stipulation about the kind of one. This lady was the intimate friend of the captive, and entreated me to take her, so that she should see her friend, and comfort her, and share her captivity. I saw no harm in the wish. She proposed to become a lady's-maid. I saw no harm in that."

"Why did she disguise herself?"

"So as to pass without trouble. She didn't want to be delayed. She wanted to see her friends as soon as possible. If you had questioned her, you would no doubt have let her pass."

"I would, no doubt, have done nothing of the kind."

"I don't see any objection," said the priest.

"Objection? She is a spy!"

"A spy? Of what, pray?"

"She came to help her friend to escape."

"To escape? How could she possibly help her to escape? Do you think it so easy to escape from this place?"

Girasole was silent.

"Do you think a young lady, who has never been out of the care of her friends before, could do much to assist a friend like herself in an escape?"

"She might."

"But how? This is not the street of a city. That house is watched, I think. There seem to be a few men in these woods, if I am not mistaken. Could this young lady help her friend to elude all these guards? Why, you know very well that she could not."

"Yes; but then there is—"

"Who?"

"Yourself."

"Myself?"

"Yes."

"What of me?"

"What do I know about your designs?"

"What designs could *I* have? Do you think *I* could plan an escape?"

"Why not?"

"Why not? What! living here close beside you? *I* be a traitor? *I*, with my life at your mercy at all times—with my throat within such easy reach of any assassin who might choose to revenge my treachery?"

"We are not assassins," said Girasole, angrily.

"And I am not a traitor," rejoined the priest, mildly.

UNDER GUARD.

Girasole was silent, and stood in thought. The men at the grave had heard every word of this conversation. Once they laughed in scorn when the priest alluded to the absurdity of a young girl escaping. It was too ridiculous. Their sympathies were evidently with the priest. The charge against him could not be maintained.

"Well," said Girasole at length, "I don't trust you. You may be traitors, after all. I will have you guarded, and if I find out any thing that looks like treason, by Heaven I will have your life, old man, even if you should be the Holy Father himself; and as to the lady—well, I will find plenty of ways," he added, with a sneer, "of inflicting on her a punishment commensurable with her crime. Here, you men, come along with me," he added, looking at the men by the grave.

"But we want to finish poor Antonio's grave," remonstrated one of the men.

"Bah! he'll keep," said Girasole, with a sneer.

"Can't one of us stay?" asked the man.

"No, not one; I want you all. If they are traitors, they are deep ones. They must be guarded; and, mind you, if they escape, you shall suffer."

With these words he led the way, and the priest and Ethel followed him. After these came the men, who had thrown down their shovels beside the grave. They all walked on in silence, following Girasole, who led the way to a place beyond the grave, and within view of one of the fires formerly alluded to. The place was about half-way between the grave and the fire. It was a little knoll bare of trees, and from it they could be seen by those at the nearest fire. Here Girasole paused, and, with some final words of warning to the guards, he turned and took his departure.

The priest sat down upon the grass, and urged Ethel to do the same. She followed his advice, and sat down by his side. The guards sat around them so as to encircle them, and, mindful of Girasole's charge, they kept their faces turned toward them, so as to prevent even the very thought of flight. The priest addressed a few mild parental words to the men, who gave him very civil responses, but relaxed not a particle of their vigilance.

In the priest's mind there was still some anxiety, but much greater hope than he had dared to have for some time. He remembered that the coffin was not all covered over, and hoped that the inmate might be able to breathe. The fact that the work had been so unexpectedly interrupted was one which filled him with joy, and gave rise to the best hopes. The only offset to all this was his own captivity, but that was a very serious one. Besides, he knew that his life hung upon a thread. Before the next day Girasole would certainly discover all, and in that case he was a doomed man. But his nature was of a kind that could not borrow trouble, and so the fact of the immediate safety of Hawbury was of far more importance, and attracted far more of his thoughts, than his own certain but more remote danger.

As for Ethel, she was now a prey to the deepest anxiety. All was discovered except the mere fact of Hawbury's removal, and how long that would remain concealed she could not know. Every moment she expected to hear the cry of those who might discover the exchange. And Hawbury, so long lost, so lately found—Hawbury, whom she had suspected of falsity so long and so long avoided, who now had proved himself so constant and so true—what was his fate? She had gazed with eyes of horror at that grave wherein he lay, and had seen the men shoveling in the earth as she came up. The recollection of this filled her with anguish. Had they buried him?—how deep was the earth that lay over him?—could there, indeed, be any hope?

All depended on the priest. She hoped that he had prevented things from going too far. She had seen him watching the grave, and motionless. What did that inactivity mean? Was it a sign that Hawbury was safe, or was it merely because he could not do any thing?

She was distracted by such fearful thoughts as these. Her heart once more throbbed with those painful pulsations which she had felt when approaching Hawbury. For some time she sat supporting her agony as best she could, and not daring to ask the priest, for fear their guards might suspect the truth, or perhaps understand her words.

But at last she could bear it no longer.

She touched the priest's arm as he sat beside her, without looking at him.

The priest returned the touch.

"Is he safe?" she asked, in a tremulous voice, which was scarce audible from grief and anxiety.

"He is," said the priest.

And then, looking at the man before him, he added immediately, in an unconcerned tone,

"She wants to know what time it is, and I told her two o'clock. That's right, isn't it?"

"About right," said the man.

Now that was a lie, but whether it was justifiable or not may be left to others to decide.

As for Ethel, an immense load of anxiety was lifted off her mind, and she began to breathe more freely.

CHAPTER XXXIII.

THE DEMON WIFE.

WHEN Dacres was overpowered by his assailants no mercy was shown him. His hands were bound tight behind him, and kicks and blows were liberally bestowed during the operation. Finally, he was pushed and dragged into the house, and up stairs to the room already mentioned. There he was still further secured by a tight rope around his ankles, after which he was left to his own meditations.

Gloomy and bitter and fierce, indeed, were those meditations. His body was covered with bruises, and though no bones were broken, yet his pain was great. In addition to this the cords around his wrists and ankles were very tight, and his veins seemed swollen to bursting. It was difficult to get an easy position, and he could only lie on his side or on his face. These bodily pains only intensified the fierceness of his thoughts and made them turn more vindictively than ever upon the subject of his wife.

She was the cause of all this, he thought. She had sacrificed every thing to her love for her accursed paramour. For this she had betrayed him, and her friends, and the innocent girl who was her companion. All the malignant feelings which had filled his soul through the day now swelled within him, till he was well-nigh mad. Most intolerable of all was his position now—the baffled enemy. He had come as the avenger, he had come as the destroyer; but he had been entrapped before he had struck his blow, and here he was now lying, defeated, degraded, and humiliated! No doubt he would be kept to afford sport to his enemy—perhaps even his wife might come to gloat over his sufferings, and feast her soul with the sight of his ruin. Over such thoughts as these he brooded, until at last he had wrought himself into something like frenzy, and with the pain that he felt, and the weariness that followed the fatigues of that day, these thoughts might finally have brought on madness, had they gone on without any thing to disturb them.

But all these thoughts and ravings were destined to come to a full and sudden stop, and to be changed to others of a far different character. This change took place when Girasole, after visiting the ladies, came, with Mrs. Willoughby, to his room. As Dacres lay on the floor he heard the voice of the Italian, and the faint, mournful, pleading tones of a woman's voice, and, finally, he saw the flash of a light, and knew that the Italian was coming to his room, and perhaps this woman also. He held his breath in suspense. What did it mean? The tone of Girasole was not the tone of love. The light drew nearer, and the footsteps too—one a heavy footfall, the tread of a man; the other lighter, the step of a woman. He waited almost breathless.

At last she appeared. There she was before him, and with the Italian; but oh, how changed from that demon woman of his fancies, who was to appear before him with his enemy and gloat over his sufferings! Was there a trace of a fiend in that beautiful and gentle face? Was there thought of joy or exultation over him in that noble and mournful lady, whose melancholy grace and tearful eyes now riveted his gaze? Where was the foul traitor who had done to death her husband and her friend? Where was the miscreant who had sacrificed all to a guilty passion? Not there; not with that face; not with those tears: to think that was impossible—it was unholy. He might rave when he did not see her, but now that his eyes beheld her those mad fancies were all dissipated.

There was only one thing there—a woman full of loveliness and grace, in the very bloom of her life, overwhelmed with suffering which this Italian was inflicting on her. Why? Could he indulge the unholy thought that the Italian had cast her off, and supplied her place with the younger beauty? Away with such a thought! It was not jealousy of that younger lady that Dacres perceived; it was the cry of a loving, yearning heart that clung to that other one, from whom the Italian had violently severed her. There was no mistake as to the source of this sorrow. Nothing was left to the imagination. Her own words told all.

Then the light was taken away, and the lady crouched upon the floor. Dacres could no longer see her amidst that gloom; but he could hear her; and every sob, and every sigh, and every moan went straight to his heart and thrilled through every fibre of his being. He lay there listening, and quivering thus as he listened with a very intensity of sympathy that shut out from his mind every other thought except that of the mourning, stricken one before him.

Thus a long time passed, and the lady wept still, and other sounds arose, and there were footsteps in the house, and whisperings, and people passing to and fro; but to all these Dacres was deaf, and they caused no more impression on his senses than if they were not. His ears and his sense of hearing existed only for these sobs and these sighs.

At last a pistol-shot roused him. The lady sprang up and called in despair. A cry came back, and the lady was about to venture to the other room, when she was driven back by the stern voice of Girasole. Then she stood for a moment, after which she knelt, and Dacres heard her voice in prayer. The prayer was not audible, but now and then words struck upon his ears which gave the key to her other words, and he knew that it was no prayer of remorse for guilt, but a cry for help in sore affliction.

Had any thing more been needed to destroy the last vestige of Dacres's former suspicions it was furnished by the words which he now heard.

"Oh, Heaven!" he thought; "can this woman be what I have thought her? But if not, what a villain am I! Yet now I must rather believe myself to be a villain than her!"

In the midst of this prayer Girasole's voice sounded, and then Minnie's tones came clearly audible. The lady rose and listened, and a great sigh of relief escaped her. Then Girasole descended the stairs, and the lady again sank upon her knees.

Thus far there seemed a spell upon Dacres; but this last incident and the clear child-voice of Minnie seemed to break it. He could no longer keep silence. His emotion was as intense as ever, but the bonds which had bound his lips seemed now to be loosened.

"Oh, Arethusa!" he moaned.

At the sound of his voice Mrs. Willoughby started, and rose to her feet. So great had been her anxiety and agitation that for some time she had not thought of another being in the room, and there had been no sound from him to suggest his existence. But now his voice startled her. She gave no answer, however.

"Arethusa!" repeated Dacres, gently and longingly and tenderly.

"Poor fellow!" thought Mrs. Willoughby; "he's dreaming."

"Arethusa! oh, Arethusa!" said Dacres once more. "Do not keep away. Come to me. I am calm now."

"Poor fellow!" thought Mrs. Willoughby. "He doesn't seem to be asleep. He's talking to me. I really think he is."

"Arethusa," said Dacres again, "will you answer me one question?"

Mrs. Willoughby hesitated for a moment, but now perceived that Dacres was really speaking to her. "He's in delirium," she thought. "Poor fellow, I must humor him, I suppose. But what a funny name to give me!"

So, after a little preparatory cough, Mrs. Willoughby said, in a low voice,

"What question?"

Dacres was silent for a few moments. He was overcome by his emotions. He wished to ask her one question—the question of all questions in his mind. Already her acts had answered it sufficiently; but he longed to have the answer in her own words. Yet he hesitated to ask it. It was dishonor to her to ask it. And thus, between longing and hesitation, he delayed so long that

Mrs. Willoughby imagined that he had fallen back into his dreams or into his delirium, and would say no more.

But at last Dacres staked every thing on the issue, and asked it:

"Arethusa! oh, Arethusa! do you—do you love—the—the Italian?"

"The Italian!" said Mrs. Willoughby—"love the Italian! me!" and then in a moment she thought that this was his delirium, and she must humor it. "Poor fellow!" she sighed again; "how he fought them! and no doubt he has had fearful blows on his head."

"Do you? do you? Oh, answer, I implore you!" cried Dacres.

"No!" said Mrs. Willoughby, solemnly. "I hate him as I never hated man before." She spoke her mind this time, although she thought the other was delirious.

A sigh of relief and of happiness came from Dacres, so deep that it was almost a groan.

"And oh," he continued, "tell me this—have you ever loved him at all?"

"I always disliked him excessively," said Mrs. Willoughby, in the same low and solemn tone. "I saw something bad—altogether bad—in his face."

"Oh, may Heaven forever bless you for that word!" exclaimed Dacres, with such a depth of fervor that Mrs. Willoughby was surprised. She now believed that he was intermingling dreams with realities, and tried to lead him to sense by reminding him of the truth.

"It was Minnie, you know, that he was fond of."

"What! Minnie Fay?"

"Yes; oh yes. I never saw any thing of him."

"Oh, Heavens!" cried Dacres; "oh, Heavens, what a fool, beast, villain, and scoundrel I have been! Oh, how I have misjudged *you*! And can *you* forgive me? Oh, can you? But no—you can not."

At this appeal Mrs. Willoughby was startled, and did not know what to say or to do. How much of this was delirium and how much real she could not tell. One thing seemed evident to her, and that was that, whether delirious or not, he took her for another person. But she was so full of pity for him, and so very tender-hearted, that her only idea was to "humor" him.

"Oh," he cried again, "can this all be true, and have all my suspicions been as mad as these last? And *you*—how *you* have changed! How beautiful you are! What tenderness there is in your glance—what a pure and gentle and touching grace there is in your expression! I swear to you, by Heaven! I have stood gazing at you in places where you have not seen me, and thought I saw heaven in your face, and worshiped you in my inmost soul. This is the reason why I have followed you. From the time I saw you when you came into the room at Naples till this night I could not get rid of your image. I fought against the feeling, but I can not overcome it. Never, never were you half so dear as you are now!"

Now, of course, that was all very well, considered as the language of an estranged husband seeking for reconciliation with an estranged wife; but when one regards it simply as the language of a passionate lover directed to a young and exceedingly pretty widow, one will perceive that it was *not* all very well, and that under ordinary circumstances it might create a sensation.

Upon Mrs. Willoughby the sensation was simply tremendous. She had begun by "humoring" the delirious man; but now she found his delirium taking a course which was excessively embarrassing. The worst of it was, there was truth enough in his language to increase the embarrassment. She remembered at once how the mournful face of this man had appeared before her in different places. Her thoughts instantly reverted to that evening on the balcony when his pale face appeared behind the fountain. There was truth in his words; and her heart beat with extraordinary agitation at the thought. Yet at the same time there was some mistake about it all; and he was clearly delirious.

"Oh, Heavens!" he cried. "Can you ever forgive me? Is there a possibility of it? Oh, can you forgive me? Can you—can you?"

He was clearly delirious now. Her heart was full of pity for him. He was suffering too. He was bound fast. Could she not release him? It was terrible for this man to lie there bound thus. And perhaps he had fallen into the hands of these ruffians while trying to save *her* and her sister. She must free him.

"Would you like to be loosed?" she asked, coming nearer. "Shall I cut your bonds?"

She spoke in a low whisper.

"Oh, tell me first, I implore you! Can you forgive me?"

He spoke in such a piteous tone that her heart was touched.

"Forgive you?" she said, in a voice full of sympathy and pity. "There is nothing for *me* to forgive."

"Now may Heaven forever bless you for that sweet and gentle word!" said Dacres, who altogether misinterpreted her words, and the emphasis she placed on them; and in his voice there was such peace, and such a gentle, exultant happiness, that Mrs. Willoughby again felt touched.

"Poor fellow!" she thought; "how he *must* have suffered!"

"Where are you fastened?" she whispered, as she bent over him. Dacres felt her breath upon his cheek; the hem of her garment touched his sleeve, and a thrill passed through him. He felt as though he would like to be forever thus, with *her* bending over him.

"My hands are fastened behind me," said he.

"I have a knife," said Mrs. Willoughby. She did not stop to think of danger. It was chiefly pity that incited her to this. She could not bear to see him lying thus in pain, which he had perhaps, as she supposed, encountered for her. She was impulsive, and though she thought of his assistance toward the escape of Minnie and herself, yet pity and compassion were her chief inspiring motives.

Mrs. Willoughby had told Girasole that she had no knife; but this was not quite true, for she now produced one, and cut the cords that bound his wrists. Again a thrill flashed through him at the touch of her little fingers; she then cut the cords that bound his ankles.

Dacres sat up. His ankles and wrists were badly swollen, but he was no longer conscious of pain. There was rapture in his soul, and of that alone was he conscious.

"Be careful!" she whispered, warningly; "guards are all around, and listeners. Be careful! If you can think of a way of escape, do so."

Dacres rubbed his hand over his forehead.

"Am I dreaming?" said he; "or is it all true? A while ago I was suffering from some hideous vision; yet now you say you forgive me!"

Mrs. Willoughby saw in this a sign of returning delirium. "But the poor fellow must be humored, I suppose," she thought.

"Oh, there is nothing for *me* to forgive," said she.

"But if there were any thing, would you?"

"Yes."

"Freely?" he cried, with a strong emphasis.

"Yes, freely."

"Oh, could you answer me one more question? Oh, could you?"

"No, no; not now—not now, I entreat you," said Mrs. Willoughby, in nervous dread. She was afraid that his delirium would bring him upon delicate ground, and she tried to hold him back.

"But I must ask you," said Dacres, trembling fearfully—"I must—now or never. Tell me my doom; I have suffered so much. Oh, Heavens! Answer me. Can you? Can you feel toward me as you once did?"

"He's utterly mad," thought Mrs. Willoughby; "but he'll get worse if I don't soothe him. Poor fellow! I ought to answer him."

"Yes," she said, in a low voice.

"Oh, my darling!" murmured Dacres, in rapture inexpressible; "my darling!" he repeated; and grasping Mrs. Willoughby's hand, he pressed it to his lips. "And you will love me again—you will love me?"

Mrs. Willoughby paused. The man was mad, but the ground was so dangerous! Yes, she must humor him. She felt his hot kisses on her hand.

"You *will*—you *will* love me, will you not?" he repeated. "Oh, answer me! Answer me, or I shall die!"

"Yes," whispered Mrs. Willoughby, faintly.

As she said this a cold chill passed through her. But it was too late. Dacres's arms were around her. He had drawn her to him, and pressed her against his breast, and she felt hot tears upon her head.

"Oh, Arethusa!" cried Dacres.

"Well," said Mrs. Willoughby, as soon as she could extricate herself, "there's a mistake, you know."

"A mistake, darling?"

"Oh dear, what *shall* I do?" thought Mrs. Willoughby; "he's beginning again. I must stop this, and bring him to his senses. How terrible it is to humor a delirious man!"

"Oh, Arethusa!" sighed Dacres once more.

Mrs. Willoughby arose.

"I'm not Arethusa at all," said she; "that isn't my name. If you *can* shake off your delirium, I wish you would. I really do."

"What!" cried Dacres, in amazement.

"I'm not Arethusa at all; that isn't my name."

"Not your name?"

"No; my name's Kitty."

"Kitty!" cried Dacres, starting to his feet.

At that instant the report of a gun burst upon their ears, followed by another and another; then there were wild calls and loud shouts. Other guns were heard.

Yet amidst all this wild alarm there was nothing which had so tremendous an effect upon Dacres as this last remark of Mrs. Willoughby's.

"THE PRIEST FLUNG HIMSELF FORWARD."

CHAPTER XXXIV.

THE CRISIS OF LIFE.

WHEN the Irish priest conjectured that it was about two o'clock in the morning he was not very far astray in his calculation. The short remarks that were exchanged between him and Ethel, and afterward between him and the men, were followed by a profound silence. Ethel sat by the side of the priest, with her head bent forward and her eyes closed as though she were asleep; yet sleep was farther from her than ever it had been, and the thrilling events of the night afforded sufficient material to keep her awake for many a long hour yet to come. Her mind was now filled with a thousand conflicting and most exciting fancies, in the midst of which she might again have sunk into despair had she not been sustained by the assurance of the priest.

Sitting near Ethel, the priest for some time looked fixedly ahead of him as though he were contemplating the solemn midnight scene, or meditating upon the beauties of nature. In truth, the scene around was one which was deserving even of the close attention which the priest appeared to give. Immediately before him lay the lake, its shore not far beneath, and almost at their feet. Around it arose the wooded hills, whose dark forms, darker from the gloom of night, threw profound shadows over the opposite shores. Near by the shore extended on either side. On the right there were fires, now burning low, yet occasionally sending forth flashes; on the left, and at some distance, might be seen the dusky outline of the old stone house. Behind them was the forest, vast, gloomy, clothed in impenetrable shade, in which lay their only hope of safety, yet where even now there lurked the watchful guards of the brigands. It was close behind them. Once in its shelter, and they might gain freedom; yet between them and it was an impassable barrier of enemies, and there also lay a still more impassable barrier in the grave where Hawbury lay. To fly, even if they could fly, would be to give him up to death; yet to remain, as they must remain, would be to doom him to death none the less, and themselves too.

Seated there, with his eyes directed toward the water, the priest saw nothing of the scene before him; his eyes were fixed on vacancy; his thoughts were endeavoring to grapple with the situation and master it. Yet so complicated was that situation, and so perplexing the dilemma in which he found himself—a dilemma where death perched upon either horn—that the good priest found his faculties becoming gradually more and more unable to deal with the difficulty, and he felt himself once more sinking down deeper and deeper into that abyss of despair from which he had but recently extricated himself.

And still the time passed, and the precious moments, laden with the fate not only of Hawbury, but of all the others—the moments of the night during which alone any escape was to be thought of—moved all too swiftly away.

Now in this hour of perplexity the good priest bethought him of a friend whose fidelity had been proved through the varied events of a life—a friend which, in his life of celibacy, had found in his heart something of that place which a fond and faithful wife may hold in the heart of a more fortunate man. It was a little friend, a fragrant friend, a tawny and somewhat grimy friend; it was in the pocket of his coat; it was of clay; in fact, it was nothing else than a dudeen.

Where in the world had the good priest who lived in this remote corner of Italy got that emblem of his green native isle? Perhaps he had brought it with him in the band of his hat when he first turned his back upon his country, or perhaps he had obtained it from the same quarter which had supplied him with that very black plug of tobacco which he brought forth shortly afterward. The one was the complement of the other, and each was handled with equal love and care. Soon the occupation of cutting up the tobacco and rubbing it gave a temporary distraction to his thoughts, which distraction was prolonged by the further operation of pressing the tobacco into the bowl of the dudeen.

Here the priest paused and cast a longing look toward the fire, which was not far away.

"Would you have any objection to let me go and get a coal to light the pipe?" said he to one of the men.

The man had an objection, and a very strong one.

"Would one of you be kind enough to go and get me a brand or a hot coal?"

This led to an earnest debate, and finally one of the men thought that he might venture. Before doing so, however, a solemn promise was extorted from the priest that he would not try to escape during his absence. This the priest gave.

"Escape!" he said—"it's a smoke I want. Besides, how can I escape with three of ye watching me? And then, what would I want to escape for? I'm safe enough here."

The man now went off, and returned in a short time with a brand. The priest gave him his blessing, and received the brand with a quiet exultation that was pleasing to behold.

"Matches," said he, "ruin the smoke. They give it a sulphur taste. There's nothing like a hot coal."

Saying this, he lighted his pipe. This operation was accomplished with a series of those short, quick, hard, percussive puffs with which the Irish race in every clime on this terrestrial ball perform the solemn rite.

And now the thoughts of the priest became more calm and regular and manageable. His confusion departed, and gradually, as the smoke ascended to the skies, there was diffused over his soul a certain soothing and all-pervading calm.

He now began to face the full difficulty of his position. He saw that escape was impossible and death inevitable. He made up his mind to die. The discovery would surely be made in the morning that Hawbury had been substituted for the robber; he would be found and punished, and the priest would be involved in his fate. His only care now was for Ethel; and he turned his thoughts toward the formation of some plan by which he might obtain mercy for her.

He was in the midst of these thoughts—for himself resigned, for Ethel anxious—and turning over in his mind all the various modes by which the emotion of pity or mercy might be roused in a merciless and pitiless nature; he was thinking of an appeal to the brigands themselves, and had already decided that in this there lay his best hope of success—when all of a sudden these thoughts were rudely interrupted and dissipated and scattered to the winds by a most startling cry.

Ethel started to her feet.

"Oh Heavens!" she cried, "what was that?"

"Down! down!" cried the men, wrathfully; but before Ethel could obey the sound was repeated, and the men themselves were arrested by it.

The sound that thus interrupted the meditations of the priest was the explosion of a rifle. As Ethel started up another followed. This excited the men themselves, who now listened intently to learn the cause.

They did not have to wait long.

Another rifle explosion followed, which was succeeded by a loud, long shriek.

"An attack!" cried one of the men, with a deep curse. They listened still, yet did not move away from the place, for the duty to which they had been assigned was still prominent in their minds. The priest had already risen to his feet, still smoking his pipe, as though in this new turn of affairs its assistance might be more than ever needed to enable him to preserve his presence of mind, and keep his soul serene in the midst of confusion.

And now they saw all around them the signs of agitation. Figures in swift motion flitted to and fro amidst the shade, and others darted past the smouldering fires. In the midst of this another shot sounded, and another, and still another. At the third there was a wild yell of rage and pain, followed by the shrill cry of a woman's voice. The fact was evident that some one of the brigands had fallen, and the women were lamenting.

The confusion grew greater. Loud cries arose; calls of encouragement, of entreaty, of command, and of defiance. Over by the old house there was the uproar of rushing men, and in the midst of it a loud, stern voice of command. The voices and the rushing footsteps moved from the house to the woods. Then all was still for a time.

It was but for a short time, however. Then came shot after shot in rapid succession. The flashes could be seen among the trees. All around them there seemed to be a struggle going on. There was some unseen assailant striking terrific blows from the impenetrable shadow of the woods. The brigands were firing back, but they fired only into thick darkness. Shrieks and yells of pain arose from time to time, the direction of which showed that the brigands were suffering. Among the assailants there was neither voice nor cry. But, in spite of their losses and the disadvantage under which they labored, the brigands fought well, and resisted stubbornly. From time to time a loud, stern voice arose, whose commands resounded far and wide, and sustained the courage of the men and directed their movements.

The men who guarded the priest and Ethel were growing more and more excited every moment, and were impatient at their enforced inaction.

"They must be soldiers," said one.

"Of course," said another.

"They fight well."

"Ay; better than the last time."

"How did they learn to fight so well under cover?"

"They've improved. The last time we met them we shot them like sheep, and drove them back in five minutes."

"They've got a leader who understands fighting in the woods. He keeps them under cover."

"Who is he?"

"Diavolo! who knows? They get new captains every day."

"Was there not a famous American Indian—"

"True. I heard of him. An Indian warrior from the American forests. Guiseppe saw him when he was at Rome."

"Bah!—you all saw him."

"Where?"

"On the road."

"We didn't."

"You did. He was the Zouave who fled to the woods first."

"He?"

"Yes."

"Diavolo!"

These words were exchanged between them as they looked at the fighting. But suddenly there came rapid flashes and rolling volleys beyond the fires that lay before them, and the movement of the flashes showed that a rush had been made toward the lake. Wild yells arose, then fierce returning fires, and these showed that the brigands were being driven back.

The guards could endure this no longer.

"They are beating us," cried one of the men, with a curse. "We must go and fight."

"What shall we do with these prisoners?"

"Tie them and leave them."

"Have you a rope?"

"No. There is one by the grave."

"Let's take the prisoners there and bind them."

This proposition was accepted; and, seizing the priest and Ethel, the four men hurried them back to the grave. The square hole lay there just beside them, with the earth by its side. Ethel tried to see into it, but was not near enough to do so. One of the men found the rope, and began in great haste to bind the arms of the priest behind him. Another began to bind Ethel in the same way.

But now there came loud cries, and the rush of men near them. A loud, stern voice was encouraging the men.

"On! on!" he cried. "Follow me! We'll drive them back!"

Saying this, a man hurried on, followed by a score of brigands.

It was Girasole.

He had been guarding the woods at this side when he had seen the rush that had been made farther up. He had seen his men driven in, and was now hurrying up to the place to retrieve the battle. As he was running on he came up to the party at the grave.

He stopped.

"What's this?" he cried.

"The prisoners—we were securing them."

It was now lighter than it had been, and dawn was not far off. The features of Girasole were plainly distinguishable. They were convulsed with the most furious passion, which was not caused so much by the rage of conflict as by the sight of the prisoners. He had suspected treachery on their part, and had spared them for a time only so as to see whether his suspicions were true or not. But now this sudden assault by night, conducted so skillfully, and by such a powerful force, pointed clearly to treachery, as he saw it, and the ones who to him seemed most prominent in guilt were the priest and Ethel.

His suspicions were quite reasonable under the circumstances. Here was a priest whom he regarded as his natural enemy. These brigands identified themselves with republicans and Garibaldians whenever it suited their purposes to do so, and consequently, as such, they were under the condemnation of the Pope; and any priest might think he was doing the Pope good service by betraying those who were his enemies. As to this priest, every thing was against him. He lived close by; every step of the country was no doubt familiar to him; he had come to the camp under very suspicious circumstances, bringing with him a stranger in disguise. He had given plausible answers to the cross-questioning of Girasole; but those were empty words, which went for nothing in the presence of the living facts that now stood before him in the presence of the enemy.

These thoughts had all occurred to Girasole, and the sight of the two prisoners kindled his rage to madness. It was the deadliest purpose of vengeance that gleamed in his eyes as he looked upon them, and they knew it. He gave one glance, and then turned to his men.

"On! on!" he cried; "I will join you in an instant; and you," he said to the guards, "wait a moment."

The brigands rushed on with shouts to assist their comrades in the fight, while the other four waited.

All this time the fight had not ceased. The air was filled with the reports of rifle-shots, the shouts of men, the yells of the wounded. The flashes seemed to be gradually drawing nearer, as though the assailants were still driving the brigands. But their progress was slow, for the fighting was carried on among the trees, and the brigands resisted stubbornly, retreating from cover to cover, and stopping every moment to make a fresh stand. But the assailants had gained much ground, and were already close by the borders of the lake, and advancing along toward the old stone house.

The robbers had not succeeded in binding their prisoners. The priest and Ethel both stood where they had encountered Girasole, and the ropes fell from the robbers' hands at the new interruption. The grave with its mound was only a few feet away.

Girasole had a pistol in his left hand and a sword in his right. He sheathed his sword and drew another pistol, keeping his eyes fixed steadily all the while upon his victims.

"You needn't bind these prisoners," said Girasole, grimly; "I know a better way to secure them."

"In the name of God," cried the priest, "I implore you not to shed innocent blood!"

"Pooh!" said Girasole.

"This lady is innocent; you will at least spare her!"

"She shall die first!" said Girasole, in a fury, and reached out his hand to grasp Ethel. The priest flung himself forward between the two. Girasole dashed him aside.

"Give us time to pray, for God's sake—one moment to pray!"

"Not a moment!" cried Girasole, grasping at Ethel.

Ethel gave a loud shriek and started away in horror. Girasole sprang after her. The four men turned to seize her. With a wild and frantic energy, inspired by the deadly terror that was in her heart, she bounded away toward the grave.

CHAPTER XXXV.

BURIED ALIVE.

HAWBURY last vanished from the scene to a place which is but seldom resorted to by a living man. Once inside of his terrible retreat he became a prey to feelings of the most varied and harrowing character, in the midst of which there was a suspense, twofold, agonizing, and intolerable. First of all, his suspense was for Ethel, and then for himself. In that narrow and restricted retreat his senses soon became sharpened to an unusual degree of acuteness. Every touch against it communicated itself to his frame, as though the wood of his inclosure had become part of himself; and every sound intensified itself to an extraordinary degree of distinctness, as though the temporary loss of vision had been compensated for by an exaggeration of the sense of hearing. This was particularly the case as the priest drove in the screws. He heard the shuffle on the stairs, the whisper to Ethel, her retreat, and the ascending footsteps; while at the same time he was aware of the unalterable coolness of the priest, who kept calmly at his work until the very last moment. The screws seemed to enter his own frame, and the slight noise which was made, inaudible as it was to others, to him seemed loud enough to rouse all in the house.

Then he felt himself raised and carried down stairs. Fortunately he had got in with his feet toward the door, and as that end was carried out first, his descent of the stairs was not attended with the inconvenience which he might have felt had it been taken down in an opposite direction.

One fact gave him very great relief, for he had feared that his breathing would be difficult. Thanks, however, to the precautions of the priest, he felt no difficulty at all in that respect. The little bits of wood which prevented the lid from resting close to the coffin formed apertures which freely admitted all the air that was necessary.

He was borne on thus from the house toward the grave, and heard the voice of the priest from time to time, and rightly supposed that the remarks of the priest were addressed not so much to the brigands as to himself, so as to let him know that he was not deserted. The journey to the grave was accomplished without any inconvenience, and the coffin was at length put upon the ground.

Then it was lowered into the grave.

There was something in this which was so horrible to Hawbury that an involuntary shudder passed through every nerve, and all the terror of the grave and the bitterness of death in that one moment seemed to descend upon him. He had not thought of this, and consequently was not prepared for it. He had expected that he would be put down somewhere on the ground, and that the priest would be able to get rid of the men, and effect his liberation before it had gone so far.

It required an effort to prevent himself from crying out; and longer efforts were needed and more time before he could regain any portion of his self-control. He now heard the priest performing the burial rites; these seemed to him to be protracted to an amazing length; and so, indeed, they were; but to the inmate of that grave the time seemed longer far than it did to those who were outside. A thousand thoughts swept through his mind, and a thousand fears swelled within his heart. At last the suspicion came to him that the priest himself was unable to do any better, and this suspicion was confirmed as he detected the efforts which he made to get the men to leave the grave. This was particularly evident when he pretended to hear an alarm, by which he hoped to get rid of the brigands. It failed, however, and with this failure the hopes of Hawbury sank lower than ever.

But the climax of his horror was attained as the first clod fell upon his narrow abode. It seemed like a death-blow. He felt it as if it had struck himself, and for a moment it was as though he had been stunned. The dull, heavy sound which those heard who stood above, to his ears became transformed and enlarged, and extended to something like a thunder-peal, with long reverberations through his now fevered and distempered brain. Other clods fell, and still others, and the work went on till his brain reeled, and under the mighty emotions of the hour his reason began to give way. Then all his fortitude and courage sank. All thought left him save the consciousness of the one horror that had now fixed itself upon his soul. It was intolerable. In another moment his despair would have overmastered him, and under its impulse he would have burst through all restraint, and turned all his energies toward forcing himself from his awful prison house.

He turned himself over. He gathered himself up as well as he could. Already he was bracing himself for a mighty effort to burst up the lid, when suddenly the voice of Girasole struck upon his ear, and a wild fear for Ethel came to his heart, and the anguish of that fear checked at once all further thought of himself.

He lay still and listened. He did this the more patiently as the men also stopped from their work, and as the hideous earth-clods no longer fell down. He listened. From the conversation he gathered pretty accurately the state of affairs. He knew that Ethel was there; that she had been discovered and dragged forth; that she was in danger. He listened in the anguish of a new suspense. He heard the words of the priest, his calm denial of treachery, his quiet appeal to Girasole's good sense. Then he heard the decision of Girasole, and the party walked away with their prisoners, and he was left alone.

Alone!

At any other time it would have been a terrible thing thus to be left alone in such a place, but now to him who was thus imprisoned it afforded a great relief. The work of burial, with all its hideous accompaniments, was stayed. He could collect his senses and make up his mind as to what he should do.

Now, first of all, he determined to gain more air if possible. The earth that had fallen had covered up many of the chinks, so that his breathing had become sensibly more difficult. His confinement, with this oppression of his breathing, was intolerable. He therefore braced himself once more to make an effort. The coffin was large and rudely constructed, being merely an oblong box. He had more play to his limbs than he could have had in one of a more regular construction, and thus he was able to bring a great effort to bear upon the lid. He pressed. The screws gave way. He lifted it up to some distance. He drew in a long draught of fresh air, and felt in that one draught that he received new life and strength and hope.

He now lay still and thought about what he should do next. If it had only been himself, he would, of course, have escaped in that first instant, and fled to the woods. But the thought of Ethel detained him.

What was her position; and what could he do to save her? This was his thought.

He knew that she, together with the priest, was in the hands of four of the brigands, who were commanded to keep their prisoners safe at the peril of their lives. Where they were he did not know, nor could he tell whether she was near or at a distance. Girasole had led them away.

"IN AN INSTANT THE OCCUPANT OF THE GRAVE SPRANG FORTH."

He determined to look out and watch. He perceived that this grave, in the heart of the brigands' camp, afforded the very safest place in which he could be for the purpose of watching. Girasole's words had indicated that the work of burial would not be resumed that night, and if any passers-by should come they would avoid such a place as this. Here, then, he could stay until dawn at least, and watch unobserved. Perhaps he could find where Ethel was guarded; perhaps he could do something to distract the attention of the brigands, and afford her an opportunity for flight.

He now arose, and, kneeling in the coffin, he raised the lid. The earth that was upon it fell down inside. He tilted the lid up, and holding it up thus with one hand, he put his head carefully out of the grave, and looked out in the direction where Girasole had gone with his prisoners. The knoll to which he had led them was a very conspicuous place, and had probably been selected for that reason, since it could be under his own observation, from time to time, even at a distance. It was about half-way between the grave and the nearest fire, which fire, though low, still gave forth some light, and the light was in a line with the knoll to Hawbury's eyes. The party on the knoll, therefore, appeared thrown out into relief by the faint fire-light behind them, especially the priest and Ethel.

And now Hawbury kept his watch, and looked and listened and waited, ever mindful of his own immediate neighborhood, and guarding carefully against any approach. But his own place was in gloom, and no one would have thought of looking there, so that he was unobserved.

But all his watching gave him no assistance toward finding out any way of rescuing Ethel. He saw the vigilant guard around the prisoners. Once or twice he saw a movement among them, but it was soon over, and resulted in nothing. Now he began to despond, and to speculate in his mind as to whether Ethel was in any danger or not. He began to calculate the time that might be required to go for help with which to attack the brigands. He wondered what reason Girasole might have to injure Ethel. But whatever hope he had that mercy might be shown her was counterbalanced by his own experience of Girasole's cruelty, and his knowledge of his merciless character.

Suddenly he was roused by the rifle-shot and the confusion that followed. He saw the party on the mound start to their feet. He heard the shots that succeeded the first one. He saw shadows darting to and fro. Then the confusion grew worse, and all the sounds of battle arose—the cries, the shrieks, and the stern words of command.

All this filled him with hope. An attack was being made. They might all be saved. He could see that the brigands were being driven back, and that the assailants were pressing on.

Then he saw the party moving from the knoll. It was already much lighter. They advanced toward him. He sank down and waited. He had no fear now that this party would complete his burial. He thought they were flying with the prisoners. If so, the assailants would soon be here; he could join them, and lead them on to the rescue of Ethel.

He lay low with the lid over him. He heard them close beside him. Then there was the noise of rushing men, and Girasole's voice arose.

He heard all that followed.

Then Ethel's shriek sounded out, as she sprang toward the grave.

In an instant the occupant of the grave, seizing the lid, raised it up, and with a wild yell sprang forth.

The effect was tremendous.

The brigands thought the dead Antonio had come to life. They did not stop to look, but with a howl of awful terror, and in an anguish of fright, they turned and ran for their lives!

Girasole saw him too, with equal horror, if not greater. He saw Hawbury. It was the man whom he had killed stone-dead with his own hand. He was there before him—or was it his ghost? For an instant horror paralyzed him; and then, with a yell like a madman's, he leaped back and fled after the others.

CHAPTER XXXVI.

FLY! FLY!

IN the midst of that wild uproar which had roused Dacres and Mrs. Willoughby there was nothing that startled him so much as her declaration that she was not Arethusa. He stood bewildered. While she was listening to the sounds, he was listening to the echo of her words; while she was wondering at the cause of such a tumult, he was wondering at this disclosure. In a moment a thousand little things suggested themselves as he stood there in his confusion, which little things all went to throw a flood of light upon her statement, and prove that she was another person than that "demon wife" who had been the cause of all his woes. Her soft glance, her gentle manner, her sweet and tender expression—above all, the tone of her voice; all these at once opened his eyes. In the course of their conversation she had spoken in a low tone, often in a whisper, so that this fact with regard to the difference of voice had not been perceptible; but her last words were spoken louder, and he observed the difference.

Now the tumult grew greater, and the reports of the rifles more frequent. The noise was communicated to the house, and in the rooms and the hall below there were tramplings of feet, and hurryings to and fro, and the rattle of arms, and the voices of men, in the midst of which rose the stern command of Girasole.

"Forward! Follow me!"

Then the distant reports grew nearer and yet nearer, and all the men rushed from the house, and their tramp was heard outside as they hurried away to the scene of conflict.

"It's an attack! The brigands are attacked!" cried Mrs. Willoughby.

Dacres said nothing. He was collecting his scattered thoughts.

"Oh, may Heaven grant that we may be saved! Oh, it is the troops—it must be! Oh, Sir, come, come; help us to escape! My darling sister is here. Save her!"

"Your sister?" cried Dacres.

"Oh yes; come, save her! My sister—my darling Minnie!"

With these words Mrs. Willoughby rushed from the room.

"Her sister! her sister!" repeated Dacres—"Minnie Fay! *Her* sister! Good Lord! What a most infernal ass I've been making of myself this last month!"

He stood still for a few moments, overwhelmed by this thought, and apparently endeavoring to realize the full extent and enormous size and immense proportions, together with the infinite extent of ear, appertaining to the ass to which he had transformed himself; but finally he shook his head despondingly, as though he gave it up altogether. Then he hurried after Mrs. Willoughby.

Mrs. Willoughby rushed into Minnie's room, and clasped her sister in her arms with frantic tears and kisses.

"Oh, my precious darling!" she exclaimed.

"Oh dear!" said Minnie, "isn't this really too bad? I was *so* tired, you know, and I was just beginning to go to sleep, when those horrid men began firing their guns. I really do think that every body is banded together to tease me. I do *wish* they'd all go away and let me have a little peace. I am so tired and sleepy!"

While Minnie was saying this her sister was embracing her and kissing her and crying over her.

"Oh, come, Minnie, come!" she cried; "make haste. We must fly!"

"Where to?" said Minnie, wonderingly.

"Any where—any where out of this awful place: into the woods."

"Why, I don't see the use of going into the woods. It's all wet, you know. Can't we get a carriage?"

"Oh no, no; we must not wait. They'll all be back soon and kill us."

"Kill us! What for?" cried Minnie. "What do you mean? How silly you are, Kitty darling!"

At this moment Dacres entered. The image of the immeasurable ass was still very prominent in his mind, and he had lost all his fever and delirium. One thought only remained (besides that of the ass, of course), and that was—escape.

"Are you ready?" he asked, hurriedly.

"Oh yes, yes; let us make haste," said Mrs. Willoughby.

"I think no one is below," said he; "but I will go first. There is a good place close by. We will run there. If I fall, you must run on and try to get there. It is the bank just opposite. Once there, you are in the woods. Do you understand?"

"Oh yes, yes!" cried Mrs. Willoughby. "Haste! Oh, haste!"

Dacres turned, and Mrs. Willoughby had just grasped Minnie's hand to follow, when suddenly they heard footsteps below.

They stopped, appalled.

The robbers had not all gone, then. Some of them must have remained on guard. But how many?

Dacres listened and the ladies listened, and in their suspense the beating of each heart was audible. The footsteps below could be heard going from room to room, and pausing in each.

"There seems to be only one man," said Dacres, in a whisper. "If there is only one, I'll engage to manage him. While I grapple, you run for your lives. Remember the bank."

"Oh yes; but oh, Sir, there may be more," said Mrs. Willoughby.

"I'll see," said Dacres, softly.

He went cautiously to the front window and looked out. By the increased light he could see quite plainly. No men were visible. From afar the noise of the strife came to his ears louder than ever, and he could see the flashes of the rifles.

Dacres stole back again from the window and went to the door. He stood and listened.

And now the footsteps came across the hall to the foot of the stairs. Dacres could see the figure of a solitary man, but it was dark in the hall, and he could not make him out.

He began to think that there was only one enemy to encounter.

The man below put his foot on the lowest stair.

Then he hesitated.

Dacres stood in the shadow of the other doorway, which was nearer to the head of the stairs, and prepared to spring as soon as the stranger should come within reach. But the stranger delayed still.

At length he spoke:

"Hallo, up there!"

The sound of those simple words produced an amazing effect upon the hearers. Dacres sprang down with a cry of joy. "Come, come!" he shouted to the ladies; "friends are here!" And running down the stairs, he reached the bottom and grasped the stranger by both arms.

In the dim light he could detect a tall, slim, sinewy form, with long, black, ragged hair and white neck-tie.

"You'd best get out of this, and quick, too," said the Rev. Saul Tozer. "They're all off now, but they'll be back here in less than no time. I jest thought I'd look in to see if any of you folks was around."

By this time the ladies were both at the bottom of the stairs.

"Come!" said Tozer; "hurry up, folks. I'll take one lady and you take t'other."

"Do you know the woods?"

"Like a book."

"So do I," said Dacres.

He grasped Mrs. Willoughby's hand and started.

"But Minnie!" said Mrs. Willoughby.

"You had better let him take her; it's safer for all of us," said Dacres.

Mrs. Willoughby looked back as she was dragged on after Dacres, and saw Tozer following them, holding Minnie's hand. This reassured her.

Dacres dragged her on to the foot of the bank. Here she tried to keep up with him, but it was steep, and she could not.

Whereupon Dacres stopped, and, without a word, raised her in his arms as though she were a little child, and ran up the bank. He plunged into the woods. Then he ran on farther. Then he turned and doubled.

Mrs. Willoughby begged him to put her down.

"No," said he; "they are behind us. You can not go fast enough. I should have to wait and defend you, and then we would both be lost."

"But, oh! we are losing Minnie."

"No, we are not," cried Dacres; "that man is ten times stronger than I am. He is a perfect elephant in strength. He dashed past me up the hill."

"I didn't see him."

"Your face was turned the other way. He is ahead of us now somewhere."

"Oh, I wish we *could* catch up to him."

"AT THIS DACRES RUSHED ON FASTER."

At this Dacres rushed on faster. The effort was tremendous. He leaped over fallen timbers, he burst through the underbrush.

"Oh, I'm sure you'll *kill* yourself if you go so fast," said Mrs. Willoughby. "We can't catch up to them."

At this Dacres slackened his pace, and went on more carefully. She again begged him to put her down. He again refused. Upon this she felt perfectly helpless, and recalled, in a vague way, Minnie's ridiculous question of "How would you like to be run away with by a great, big, horrid man, Kitty darling?"

Then she began to think he was insane, and felt very anxious.

At last Dacres stopped. He was utterly exhausted. He was panting terribly. It had been a fearful journey. He had run along the bank up to that narrow valley which he had traversed the day before, and when he stopped it was on the top of that precipice where he had formerly rested, and where he had nurtured such dark purposes against Mrs. Willoughby.

Mrs. Willoughby looked at him, full of pity. He was utterly broken down by this last effort.

"Oh dear!" she thought. "Is he sane or insane? What *am* I to do? It is dreadful to have to go on and humor his queer fancies."

CHAPTER XXXVII.

MINNIE'S LAST LIFE-PRESERVER.

WHEN Tozer started after Dacres he led Minnie by the hand for only a little distance. On reaching the acclivity he seized her in his arms, thus imitating Dacres's example, and rushed up, reaching the top before the other. Then he plunged into the woods, and soon became separated from his companion.

Once in the woods, he went along quite leisurely, carrying Minnie without any difficulty, and occasionally addressing to her a soothing remark, assuring her that she was safe. Minnie, however, made no remark of any kind, good or bad, but remained quite silent, occupied with her own thoughts. At length Tozer stopped and put her down. It was a place upon the edge of a cliff on the shore of the lake, and as much as a mile from the house. The cliff was almost fifty feet high, and was perpendicular. All around was the thick forest, and it was unlikely that such a place could be discovered.

"'WORSE AND WORSE,' SAID TOZER."

"Here," said he; "we've got to stop here, and it's about the right place. We couldn't get any where nigh to the soldiers without the brigands seeing us; so we'll wait here till the fight's over, and the brigands all chased off."

"The soldiers! what soldiers?" asked Minnie.

"Why, they're having a fight over there—the soldiers are attacking the brigands."

"Well, I didn't know. Nobody told me. And did you come with the soldiers?"

"Well, not exactly. I came with the priest and the young lady."

"But you were not at the house?"

"No. They wouldn't take me all the way. The priest said I couldn't be disguised—but I don't see why not—so he left me in the woods till he came back. And then the soldiers came, and we crept on till we came nigh the lake. Well, then I stole away; and when they made an attack the brigands all ran there to fight, and I watched till I saw the coast clear; and so I came, and here we are."

Minnie now was quite silent and preoccupied, and occasionally she glanced sadly at Tozer with her large, pathetic, child-like eyes. It was a very piteous look, full of the most tender entreaty. Tozer occasionally glanced at her, and then, like her, he sat silent, involved in his own thoughts.

"And so," said Minnie at last, "you're not the priest himself?"

"The priest?"

"Yes."

"Well, no; I don't call myself a priest. I'm a minister of the Gospel."

"Well, you're not a *real* priest, then."

"All men of my calling are real priests—yes, priests and kings. I yield to no man in the estimate which I set upon my high and holy calling."

"Oh, but I mean a Roman Catholic priest," said Minnie.

"A Roman Catholic priest! Me! Why, what a question! Me! a Roman Catholic! Why, in our parts folks call me the Protestant Champion."

"Oh, and so you're only a Protestant, after all," said Minnie, in a disappointed tone.

"Only a Protestant!" repeated Tozer, severely—"*only* a Protestant. Why, ain't you one yourself?"

"Oh yes; but I hoped you were the other priest, you know. I did *so* want to have a Roman Catholic priest this time."

Tozer was silent. It struck him that this young lady was in danger. Her wish for a Roman Catholic priest boded no good. She had just come from Rome. No doubt she had been tampered with. Some Jesuits had caught her, and had tried to proselytize her. His soul swelled with indignation at the thought.

"Oh dear!" said Minnie again.

"What's the matter?" asked Tozer, in a sympathizing voice.

"I'm so sorry."

"What for?"

"Why, that you saved my life, you know."

"Sorry? sorry? that I saved your life?" repeated Tozer, in amazement.

"Oh, well, you know, I did so want to be saved by a Roman Catholic priest, you know."

"To be saved by a Roman Catholic priest!" repeated Tozer, pondering these words in his mind as he slowly pronounced them. He could make nothing of them at first, but finally concluded that they concealed some half-suggested tendency to Rome.

"I don't like this—I don't like this," he said, solemnly.

"What don't you like?"

"It's dangerous. It looks bad," said Tozer, with increased solemnity.

"What's dangerous? You look so solemn that you really make me feel quite nervous. What's dangerous?"

"Why, your words. I see in you, I think, a kind of leaning toward Rome."

"It isn't Rome," said Minnie. "I don't lean to Rome. I only lean a little toward a Roman Catholic priest."

"Worse and worse," said Tozer. "Dear! dear! dear! worse *and* worse. This beats all. Young woman, beware! But perhaps I don't understand you. You surely don't mean that your affections are engaged to any Roman Catholic priest. You can't mean *that*. Why, they can't marry."

"But that's just what I like them so for," said Minnie. "I like people that don't marry; I hate people that want to marry."

Tozer turned this over in his mind, but could make nothing of it. At length he thought he saw in this an additional proof that she had been tampered with by Jesuits at Rome. He thought he saw in this a statement of her belief in the Roman Catholic doctrine of celibacy.

He shook his head more solemnly than ever. "It's not Gospel," said he. "It's mere human tradition. Why, for centuries there was a married priesthood even in the Latin Church. Dunstan's chief measures consisted in a fierce war on the married clergy. So did Hildebrand's—Gregory the Seventh, you know. The Church at Milan, sustained by the doctrines of the great Ambrose, always preferred a married clergy. The worst measures of Hildebrand were against these good pastors and their wives. And in the Eastern Church they have always had it."

Of course all this was quite beyond Minnie; so she gave a little sigh, and said nothing.

"Now as to Rome," resumed Tozer. "Have you ever given a careful study to the Apocalypse—not a hasty reading, as people generally do, but a serious, earnest, and careful examination?"

"I'm sure I haven't any idea what in the world you're talking about," said Minnie. "I *wish* you wouldn't talk so. I don't understand one single word of what you say."

Tozer started and stared at this. It was a depth of ignorance that transcended that of the other young lady with whom he had conversed. But he attributed it all to "Roman" influences. They dreaded the Apocalypse, and had not allowed either of these young ladies to become acquainted with its tremendous pages. Moreover, there was something else. There was a certain light and trifling tone which she used in referring to these things, and it pained him. He sat involved in a long and very serious consideration of her case, and once or twice looked at her with so very peculiar an expression that Minnie began to feel very uneasy indeed.

Tozer at length cleared his throat, and fixed upon Minnie a very affectionate and tender look.

"My dear young friend," said he, "have you ever reflected upon the way you are living?"

At this Minnie gave him a frightened little look, and her head fell.

"You are young now, but you can't be young always; youth and beauty and loveliness all are yours, but they can't last; and now is the time for you to make your choice—now in life's gay morn. It ain't easy when you get old. Remember that, my dear. Make your choice now—now."

"Oh dear!" said Minnie; "I knew it. But I can't—and I don't want to—and I think it's *very* unkind in you. I don't want to make *any* choice. I don't want any of you. It's *so* horrid."

This was a dreadful shock to Tozer; but he could not turn aside from this beautiful yet erring creature.

"Oh, I entreat you—I implore you, my dear, *dear*—"

"I do *wish* you wouldn't talk to me that way, and call me your *dear*. I don't like it; no, not even if you *did* save my life, though really I didn't know there was any danger. But I'm not *your* dear."

And Minnie tossed her head with a little air of determination, as though she had quite made up her mind on that point.

"Oh, well now, really now," said Tozer, "it was only a natural expression. I *do* take a deep interest in you, my—that is—miss; I feel a sincere regard and affection and—"

"But it's no use," said Minnie. "You really *can't*, you know; and so, why, you *mustn't*, you know."

Tozer did not clearly understand this, so after a brief pause he resumed:

"But what I was saying is of far more importance. I referred to your life. Now you're not happy as you are."

"Oh yes, but I am," said Minnie, briskly.

Tozer sighed.

"I'm *very* happy," continued Minnie, "very, very happy—that is, when I'm with dear, darling Kitty, and dear, dear Ethel, and my darling old Dowdy, and dear, kind papa."

Tozer sighed again.

"You can't be *truly* happy thus," he said, mournfully. "You may think you are, but you *ain't*. My heart fairly yearns over you when I see you, so young, so lovely, and so innocent; and I know you can't be happy as you are. You must live otherwise. And oh, I pray you—I entreat you to set your affections elsewhere!"

"Well, then, I think it's very, very horrid in you to press me so," said, Minnie, with something actually like asperity in her tone; "but it's *quite* impossible."

"But oh, why?"

"Why, because I don't want to have things any different. But if I have to be worried and teased so, and if people insist on it so, why, there's only one that I'll *ever* consent to."

"And what is that?" asked Tozer, looking at her with the most affectionate solicitude.

"Why, it's—it's—" Minnie paused, and looked a little confused.

"It's what?" asked Tozer, with still deeper and more anxious interest.

"Why, it's—it's—Rufus K. Gunn."

"THE DISCOVERY OF A BODY ON THE SHORE OF THE LAKE."

CHAPTER XXXVIII.

THE IMPATIENT BARON.

THE brigands had resisted stubbornly, but finally found themselves without a leader. Girasole had disappeared; and as his voice no longer directed their movements, they began to fall into confusion. The attacking party, on the other hand, was well led, and made a steady advance, driving the enemy before them. At length the brigands lost heart, and took to flight. With a wild cheer the assailants followed in pursuit. But the fugitives took to the forest, and were soon beyond the reach of their pursuers in its familiar intricacies, and the victors were summoned back by the sound of the trumpet.

It was now daylight, and as the conquering party emerged from the forest they showed the uniform of the Papal Zouaves; while their leader, who had shown himself so skillful in forest warfare, proved to be no less a personage than our friend the Baron. Led by him, the party advanced to the old stone house, and here, drawing up his men in front, their leader rushed in, and searched every room. To his amazement, he found the house deserted, its only inmate being that dead brigand whom Girasole had mistaken for Hawbury. This discovery filled the Baron with consternation. He had expected to find the prisoners here, and his dismay and grief were excessive. At first he could not believe in his ill luck; but another search convinced him of it, and reduced him to a state of perfect bewilderment.

But he was not one who could long remain inactive. Feeling confident that the brigands were scattered every where in headlong flight, he sent his men out in different directions, into the woods and along the shore, to see if they could find any traces of the lost ones. He himself remained near the house, so as to direct the search most efficiently. After about an hour they came back, one by one, without being able to find many traces. One had found an empty coffin in a grave, another a woman's hood, a third had found a scarf. All of these had endeavored to follow up these traces, but without result. Finally a man approached who announced the discovery of a body on the shore of the lake. After him came a party who was carrying the corpse for the inspection of their captain.

The Baron went to look at it. The body showed a great gap in the skull. On questioning the men, he learned that they had found it on the shore, at the bottom of a steep rock, about half-way between the house and the place where they had first emerged from the woods. His head was lying pressed against a sharp rock in such a way that it was evident that he had fallen over the cliff, and had been instantly killed. The Baron looked at the face, and recognized the features of Girasole. He ordered it to be taken away and laid in the empty grave for future burial.

The Baron now became impatient. This was not what he had bargained for at all. At length he thought that they might have fled, and might now be concealed in the woods around; and together with this thought there came to his mind an idea of an effective way to reach them. The trumpeter could send forth a blast which could be heard far and wide. But what might, could, would, or should the trumpeter sound forth which should give the concealed listeners a certainty that the summons came from friends and not from foes? This the Baron puzzled over for some time. At length he solved this problem also, and triumphantly.

There was one strain which the trumpeter might sound that could not be mistaken. It would at once convey to the concealed hearers all the truth, and gently woo them home. It would be at once a note of victory, a song of joy, a call of love, a sound of peace, and an invitation—"Wanderer, come home!"

Of course there was only one tune that, to the mind of the Baron, was capable of doing this.

And of course that tune was "Yankee Doodle."

Did the trumpeter know it?

Of course he did.

Who does not know it?

All men know that tune. Man is born with an innate knowledge of the strain of "Yankee Doodle." No one can remember when he first learned it. The reason is because he never learned it at all. It was born in him.

So the trumpeter sounded it forth, and wild and high and clear and far the sounds arose; and it was "Blow, bugle, blow, set the wild echoes flying; and answer, echoes, answer, Yankee Doodle dying."

And while the trumpet sounded the Baron listened and listened, and walked up and down, and fretted and fumed and chafed, and I'm afraid he swore a little too; and at last he was going to tell the trumpeter to stop his infernal noise, when, just at that moment, what should he see all of a sudden emerging from the woods but three figures!

And I'll leave you to imagine, if you can, the joy and delight which agitated the bosom of our good Baron as he recognized among these three figures the well-known face and form of his friend Hawbury. With Hawbury was a lady whom the Baron remembered having seen once in the upper hall of a certain house in Rome, on a memorable occasion, when he stood on the stairs calling *Min*. The lady was very austere then, but she was very gracious now, and very wonderfully sweet in the expression of her face. And with them was a stranger in the garb of a priest.

Now as soon as the party met the Baron, who rushed to meet them, Hawbury wrung his hand, and stared at him in unbounded astonishment.

"You!" he cried; "yourself, old boy! By Jove!"

"Yes," said the Baron. "You see, the moment we got into that ambush I kept my eye open, and got a chance to spring into the woods. There I was all right, and ran for it. I got into the road again a couple of miles back, got a horse, rode to Civita Castellana, and there I was lucky enough to find a company of Zouaves. Well, Sir, we came here flying, mind, I tell you, and got hold of a chap that we made guide us to the lake. Then we opened on them; and here we are, by thunder! But where's Min?"

"Who?" asked Hawbury.

"Min," said the Baron, in the most natural tone in the world.

"Oh! Why, isn't she here?"

"No. We've hunted every where. No one's here at all." And the Baron went on to tell about their search and its results. Hawbury was chiefly struck by the news of Girasole.

"He must have gone mad with terror," said Hawbury, as he told the Baron about his adventure at the grave. "If that's so," he added, "I don't see how the ladies could be harmed. I dare say they've run off. Why, we started to run, and got so far off that we couldn't find our way back, even after the trumpet began to sound. You must keep blowing at it, you know. Play all the national tunes you can—no end. They'll find their way back if you give them time."

And now they all went back to the house, and the Baron in his anxiety could not talk any more, but began his former occupation of walking up and down, and fuming and fretting and chafing, and, I'm again afraid, swearing—when all of a sudden, on the bank in front of him, on the very top, just emerging from the thick underbrush which had concealed them till that moment, to their utter amazement and indescribable delight, they beheld Scone Dacres and Mrs. Willoughby. Scone Dacres appeared to Hawbury to be in a totally different frame of mind from that in which he had been when he last saw him; and what perplexed him most, yea, and absolutely confounded him, was the sight of Scone Dacres with his demon wife, whom he had been pursuing for the sake of vengeance, and whose frenzy had been so violent that he himself had been drawn with him on purpose to try and restrain him. And now what was the injured husband doing with his demon wife? Doing! why, doing the impassioned lover most vigorously; sustaining her steps most tenderly; grasping her hand; pushing aside the bushes; assisting her down the slope; overwhelming her, in short; hovering round her, apparently unconscious that there was in all the wide world any other being than Mrs. Willoughby. And as Hawbury looked upon all this his eyes dilated and his lips parted involuntarily in utter wonder; and finally, as Dacres reached the spot, the only greeting which he could give his friend was,

"By Jove!"

And now, while Mrs. Willoughby and Ethel were embracing with tears of joy, and overwhelming one another with questions, the Baron sought information from Dacres.

Dacres then informed him all about Tozer's advent and departure.

"Tozer!" cried the Baron, in intense delight. "Good on his darned old head! Hurrah for the parson! He shall marry us for this—he, and no other, by thunder!"

Upon which Mrs. Willoughby and Ethel exchanged glances, but said not a word. Not they.

But in about five minutes, when Mrs. Willoughby had Ethel apart a little by herself, she said,

"Oh, Ethel dear, isn't it dreadful?"

"What?" asked Ethel.

"Why, poor Minnie."

"Poor Minnie?"

"Yes. Another horrid man. And he'll be claiming her too. And, oh dear! what shall I do?"

"Why, you'll have to let her decide for herself. I think it will be—this person."

Mrs. Willoughby clasped her hands, and looked up with a pretty little expression of horror.

"And do you know, dear," added Ethel, "I'm beginning to think that it wouldn't be so *very* bad. He's Lord Hawbury's friend, you know, and then he's very, very brave; and, above all, think what we all owe him."

Mrs. Willoughby gave a resigned sigh.

And now the Baron was wilder with impatience than ever. He had questioned Dacres, and found that he could give him no information whatever as to

Tozer's route, and consequently had no idea where to search. But he still had boundless confidence in "Yankee Doodle."

"That's the way," said Dacres; "we heard it ever so far, and it was the first thing that told us it was safe to return. We didn't dare to venture before."

Meanwhile Hawbury had got Dacres by himself, and poured a torrent of questions over him. Dacres told him in general terms how he was captured. Then he informed him how Mrs. Willoughby was put in the same room, and his discovery that it was Minnie that the Italian wanted.

"Well, do you know, old chap," continued Dacres, "I couldn't stand it; so I offered to make it all up with her."

"Oh, I see you've done that, old boy. Congrat—"

"Pooh! wait a minute," said Dacres, interrupting him. "Well, you know, she wasn't my wife at all."

At this Hawbury stood utterly aghast.

"What's that?"

"She wasn't my wife at all. She looks confoundedly like what my wife was at her best, but she's another person. It's a most extraordinary likeness; and yet she's isn't any relation, but a great deal prettier woman. What made me so sure, you know, was the infernally odd coincidence of the name; and then I only saw her off and on, you know, and I never heard her voice. Then, you know, I was mad with jealousy; and so I made myself worse and worse, till I was ripe for murder, arson, assasination, and all that sort of thing, you know."

To all this Hawbury listened in amazement, and could not utter a word, until at last, as Dacres paused, he said,

"By Jove!"

"Well, old man, I was the most infernal ass that ever lived. And how I must have bored you!"

"By Jove!" exclaimed Hawbury again. "But drive on, old boy."

"Well, you know, the row occurred just then, and away went the scoundrels to the fight, and in came that parson fellow, and away we went. I took Mrs. Willoughby to a safe place, where I kept her till I heard the trumpet, you know. And I've got another thing to tell you. It's deuced odd, but she knew all about me."

"The deuce she did!"

"Yes, the whole story. Lived somewhere in the county. But I don't remember the Fays. At any rate, she lived there; and do you know, old fellow, the county people used to think I beat my wife!"

"By Jove!"

"Yes; and afterward they raised a report that my cruelty had driven her mad. But I had a few friends that stood up for me; and among others these Fays, you know, had heard the truth of it, and, as it happened, Kitty—"

"Kitty?"

"Well, Mrs. Willoughby, I mean—her name's Kitty—has always known the truth about it; and when she saw me at Naples she felt interested in me."

"Oho!" and Hawbury opened his eyes.

"Well, she knew all about it; and, among other things, she gave me one piece of intelligence that has eased my mind."

"Ah! what's that?"

"Why, my wife *is* dead."

"Oh, then there's no doubt about it?"

"Not a bit. She died eight years ago, and in an insane asylum."

"By Jove! Then she was mad all the time."

"Yes; that accounts for it, and turns all my curses into pity."

Dacres was silent now for a few moments. At length he looked at Hawbury with a very singular expression.

"Hawbury, old boy."

"Well, Sconey?"

"I think we'll keep it up."

"Who?"

"Why, Kitty and I—that is, Mrs. Willoughby and I—her name's Kitty, you know."

"Keep what up?"

"Why, the—the—the fond illusion, and all that sort of thing. You see I've got into such an infernal habit of regarding her as my wife that I can't look on her in any other light. I claimed her, you know, and all that sort of thing, and she thought I was delirious, and felt sorry, and humored me, and gave me a very favorable answer."

"HE GAVE A LOUD CRY OF JOY, AND THEN SPRANG UP THE BANK."

"Humored you?"

"Yes; that's what she says now, you know. But I'm holding her to it, and I've every reason to believe, you know—in fact, I may as well say that it is an understood thing, you know, that she'll let it go, you know, and at some early day, you know, we'll have it all formally settled, and all that sort of thing, you know."

Hawbury wrung his friend's hand.

"See here, old boy; you see Ethel there?"

"Yes."

"Who do you think she is?"

"Who?"

"*Ethel Orne!*"

"Ethel *Orne*!" cried Dacres, as the whole truth flashed on his mind. "What a devil of a jumble every thing has been getting into!—By Heaven, dear boy, I congratulate you from the bottom of my soul!"

And he wrung Hawbury's hand as though all his soul was in that grasp.

But all this could not satisfy the impatience of the Baron. This was all very well in its way, merely as an episode; but he was waiting for the chief incident of the piece, and the chief incident was delaying very unaccountably.

So he strode up and down, and he fretted and he fumed and he chafed, and the trumpeter kept blowing away.

Until at last—

Just before his eyes—

Up there on the top of the bank, not far from where Dacres and Mrs. Willoughby had made their appearance, the Baron caught sight of a tall, lank, slim figure, clothed in rusty black, whose thin and leathery face, rising above a white neck-tie, peered solemnly yet interrogatively through the bushes; while just behind him the Baron caught a glimpse of the flutter of a woman's dress.

He gave a loud cry of joy, and then sprang up the bank.

******

But over that meeting I think we had better draw a veil.

CHAPTER XXXIX.

ASTONISHING WAY OF CONCLUDING AN ADVENTURE.

THE meeting between the Baron and Minnie gave a new shock to poor Mrs. Willoughby, who looked with a helpless expression, and walked away for a little distance. Dacres and Hawbury were still eagerly conversing and questioning one another about their adventures. Tozer also had descended and joined himself to the priest; and each of these groups had leisure for a prolonged conversation before they were interrupted. At length Minnie made her appearance, and flung herself into her sister's arms, while at the same time the Baron grasped Tozer by both hands, and called out, in a voice loud enough to be heard by all,

"You shall marry us, parson—and this very day, by thunder!"

These words came to Mrs. Willoughby's ears in the midst of her first joy at meeting her sister, and shocked her inexpressibly.

"What's that, Minnie darling?" she asked, anxiously. "What is it? Did you hear what that dreadful—what the—the Baron said?"

Minnie looked sweetly conscious, but said nothing.

"What *does* he mean?" asked her sister again.

"I suppose he means what he says," replied Minnie, with a timid air, stealing a shy look at the Baron.

"Oh dear!" said Mrs. Willoughby; "there's another dreadful trouble, I know. It's very, very hard—"

"Well, I'm sure," said Minnie, "I can't help it. They all do so. That clergyman came and saved me, and he wasn't a Roman Catholic clergyman at all, and he proposed—"

"Proposed!" cried Mrs. Willoughby, aghast.

"Oh yes," said Minnie, solemnly; "and I had hard work preventing him. But, really, it was *too* absurd, and I would not let him be too explicit. But I didn't hurt his feelings. Well, you know, then all of a sudden, as we were sitting there, the bugle sounded, and we came back. Well, then, Rufus K. Gunn came—and you know how very violent he is in his way—and he said he saved my life again, and so he proposed."

"*He* proposed! Why, he had proposed before."

"Oh yes; but that was for an engagement, and this was for our marriage."

"Marriage!"

"Oh yes; and, you see, he had actually saved my life twice, and he was very urgent, and he is so awfully affectionate, and so—"

"Well, what?" cried Mrs. Willoughby, seeing Minnie hesitate.

"Why, he—"

"Well?"

"I mean, I—"

"You what? Really, Minnie dearest, you might tell me, and not keep me in such dreadful suspense."

"Why, what could I say?"

"But what *did* you say?"

"Why, I think I—said—yes," said Minnie, casting down her eyes with indescribable sweetness, shyness, meekness, and resignation. Mrs. Willoughby actually shuddered.

"Now, Kitty," exclaimed Minnie, who at once noticed it, "you needn't be so horrid. I'm sure you can't say any thing against him *now*. You needn't look so. You *always* hated him. You *never* would treat him kindly."

"But this—this marriage. It's too shocking."

"Well, he saved my life."

"And to-day! How utterly preposterous! It's shameful!"

"Well, I'm sure I can't help it."

"It's too horrid!" continued Mrs. Willoughby, in an excited tone. "It will break poor papa's heart. And it will break poor darling aunty's heart. And it will break my heart."

"Now, Kitty dearest, this is too silly in you. If it hadn't been for him, I would now be married to that wretched Count, who hadn't sufficient affection for me to get me a chair to sit on, and who was very, very rude to you. You didn't care, though, whether I was married to him or not; and now when I am saved from him you have nothing but very unpleasant things to say about Rufus K. Gunn."

"Oh dear, what *would* I give if you were only safe home!"

"Well, I'm sure I don't see what *I* can do. People are always saving my life. And there is Captain Kirby hunting all over Italy for me. And I *know* I will be saved by somebody—if—if—I—I—if—I—if—you know—that is—I'm sure—"

"Nonsense!" said Mrs. Willoughby, as Minnie broke down in confusion. "It is *too* absurd. I won't talk about it. You are a silly child. Oh, how I *do* wish you were home!"

At this juncture the conversation was interrupted by the Baron.

"It is not my fashion, ma'am," said he, gravely, "to remind another of any obligation under which he may be to me; but my claims on Minnie have been so opposed by you and the rest of her friends that I have to ask you to think of them. Your father knows what my first claims are. You yourself, ma'am, know perfectly well what the last claims are which I have won to-day."

The Baron spoke calmly, firmly, and with dignity. Mrs. Willoughby answered not a word.

"If you think on your position last night, and Minnie's, ma'am," resumed the Baron, "you'll acknowledge, I expect, that it was pretty hard lines. What would you have given a few hours ago for a sight of my uniform in that old house yonder? If I had come then to save Minnie from the clutches of that *I*talian, wouldn't you have given her to me with all your heart, and your prayers too? You would, by thunder! Think, ma'am, on your sufferings last night, and then answer me."

Mrs. Willoughby involuntarily thought of that night of horror, and shuddered, and said nothing.

"Now, ma'am, just listen to this. I find on coming here that this Italian had a priest here all ready to marry him and Minnie. If I'd been delayed or defeated, Minnie would have been that rascal's wife by this time. The priest was here. They would have been married as sure as you're born. You, ma'am, would have had to see this poor, trembling, broken-hearted, despairing girl torn from your arms, and bound by the marriage tie to a ruffian and a scoundrel whom she loathed. And now, ma'am, I save her from this. I have my priest too, ma'am. He ain't a Roman Catholic, it is true—he's an orthodox parson—but, at the same time, I ain't particular. Now I propose to avail myself this day of his invaluable services at the earliest hour possible; but, at the same time, if Min prefers it, I don't object to the priest, for I have a kind of Roman Catholic leaning myself.

"Now you may ask, ma'am," continued the Baron, as Mrs. Willoughby continued silent—"you may ask why I'm in such a thundering hurry. My answer is, because you fit me off so. You tried to keep me from Min. You locked me out of your house. You threatened to hand me over to the police (and I'd like to see one of them try it on with me). You said I was mad or drunk; and finally you tried to run away. Then you rejected my advice, and plunged head-foremost into this fix. Now, in view of all this, my position is this—that I can't trust you. I've got Min now, and I mean to keep her. If you got hold of her again, I feel it would be the last of her. Consequently I ain't going to let her go. Not me. Not by a long chalk.

"Finally, ma'am, if you'll allow me, I'll touch upon another point. I've thought over your objections to me. It ain't my rank—I'm a noble; it ain't money—I'm worth a hundred thousand dollars; it ain't my name—for I call myself Atramonte. It must be something in me. I've come to the conclusion that it's my general style—my manners and customs. Very well. Perhaps they don't come up to your standard. They mayn't square with your ideas. Yet, let me inform you, ma'am, there are other standards of action and manner and speech than those to which you are accustomed, and mine is one of them. Minnie doesn't object to that. She knows my heart is all right, and is willing to trust herself to me. Consequently I take her, and I mean to make her mine this day."

As the Baron paused Mrs. Willoughby began, first of all, to express her gratitude, and then to beg him to postpone the marriage. She declared that it was an unheard-of thing, that it was shameful, that it was shocking, that it was dreadful. She grew very much excited; she protested, she entreated. Finally she burst into tears, and appealed to Lord Hawbury in the most moving terms. Hawbury listened very gravely, with his eyes wandering over to where Ethel was; and Ethel caught the expression of his face, and looked quite confused.

"Oh, think, only think," said Mrs. Willoughby, after an eloquent and pathetic appeal—"think how the poor child will be talked about!"

"Well, really—ah—'pon my life," said Hawbury, with his eyes still wandering over toward Ethel, "I'm sure I don't—ah—share your views altogether, Mrs. Willoughby; for—ah—there *are* times, you know, when a fellow finds it very uncommonly desirable—runaway matches, you know, and all that sort of thing. And, by Jove! to tell the truth, I really admire the idea, by Jove! And really—ah—I'm sure—I wish most confoundedly it was the universal fashion, by Jove!"

"But she'll be so talked about. She'll make herself so shockingly *conspicuous*."

"Conspicuous? By Jove!" said Hawbury, who seemed struck by the idea. At that moment Minnie began talking to her sister, and Hawbury went off to Ethel, to whom he began talking in the most earnest manner. The two wandered off for some distance, and did not return for a full half hour. When they did return Ethel looked somewhat embarrassed, and Hawbury was radiant. With this radiance on his face he went up to Mrs. Willoughby, leaving Ethel in the background.

"Oh, by-the-way," said he, "you were remarking that your sister would be too conspicuous by such a hasty marriage."

"Yes," said Mrs. Willoughby, anxiously.

"Well, I thought I would tell you that she needn't be so *very* conspicuous; for, in fact—that is, you know, Ethel and I—she told you, I suppose, about our mistake?"

"Oh yes."

"And I think I've persuaded her to save Minnie from being too conspicuous."

Mrs. Willoughby gave Hawbury a look of astonishment and reproach.

"You!" she cried; "and Ethel!"

"Why, I'm sure, we're the very ones you might expect it from. Think how infernally we've been humbugged by fate."

"Fate!" said Mrs. Willoughby. "It was all your own fault. She was chosen for you."

"Chosen for me? What do you mean?"

"By your mother."

"My mother?"

"Yes."

"She said one of Biggs's nieces."

"Ethel is that niece."

"The devil!" cried Hawbury. "I beg pardon. By Jove!"

Hawbury, overwhelmed by this, went back to Ethel, and they wandered off once more. The Baron had already wandered off with Minnie in another direction. Tozer and the priest had gone to survey the house.

Seeing Mrs. Willoughby thus left alone, Dacres drifted up to her. He came up silently.

"Kitty," said he, in a low voice, "you seem sad."

By which familiar address it will be seen that Dacres had made some progress toward intimacy with her.

Mrs. Willoughby did not seem at all offended at this, but looked up with one of her frankest smiles, and the clouds of perplexity passed away. She was an exceedingly pretty woman, and she was certainly not over twenty-four.

"I'm so worried," she said, plaintively.

"What's the matter?" asked Dacres, in a tone of the deepest and tenderest sympathy.

"Why, these horrid men; and, what's worse, Lord Hawbury is actually encouraging Mr.—the—the Baron; and I'm *so* worried. Oh dear!"

"But why should you be worried?"

"It's so horrid. It's shocking. It's not to be thought of."

"But why not?" asked Dacres.

"Why, it's—it's so horrid," said Mrs. Willoughby.

Dacres stood looking at her for a long time.

"Kitty," said he at last.

Mrs. Willoughby looked up.

Dacres looked all around. He then took her hand.

"Isn't it too bad," he said, "to let Minnie—"

"What?"

"To let her go through this ordeal alone?"

"Alone!" exclaimed Mrs. Willoughby, looking in wonder at him.

"Yes."

"What *do* you mean?"

"Couldn't *we* accompany her?"

Mrs. Willoughby snatched away her hand.

"Are you mad?" she cried. "I do believe the whole world's mad to-day."

"Mad!" cried Dacres. "Yes, I'm mad—insane—raving! Won't you be merciful again? Won't you, Kitty? Won't you 'humor' my ravings? Oh, do. Oh, Kitty! dear Kitty—!"

"It's positive insanity!"

"Oh, Kitty!"

"You're raving!"

"Won't you 'humor' me—just this once! only this once."

"Hush! there they come," said Mrs. Willoughby, suddenly snatching away her hand, which Dacres had somehow got hold of again, and moving a little further away from him.

It was the Baron and Minnie who were coming back again, while Hawbury and Ethel were seen a little further away.

There they all stood—there, on the spot where they had found the crisis of their fortunes; and as they stood there the two clergymen, Catholic and Protestant, slowly came out of the house.

www.ingramcontent.com/pod-product-compliance
Ingram Content Group UK Ltd.
Pitfield, Milton Keynes, MK11 3LW, UK
UKHW031346260325
456749UK00003B/617